D1537300

World Geography

McDougal Littell

Evanston, Illinois • Boston • Dallas

Contents

UNIT 6 Africa *cont.*

CHAPTER 20 Today's Issues in Africa

UNIT 7 Southwest Asia

CHAPTER 21 Harsh and Arid Lands

CHAPTER 22 Religion, Politics, and Oil

CHAPTER 23 Today's Issues in Southwest Asia

UNIT 8 South Asia

CHAPTER 24 The Land Where Continents Collided

CHAPTER 25 A Region of Contrasts

UNIT ◄9► East Asia

CHAPTER 27 A Rugged Terrain

CHAPTER 28 Shared Cultural Traditions

CHAPTER 29 Today's Issues in East Asia

UNIT ◄10► Southeast Asia, Oceania, and Antarctica

CHAPTER 30 A Region of Extremes

CHAPTER 31 Migration and Conquest

CHAPTER 32 Today's Issues in Southeast Asia, Oceania, and Antarctica

Being a Strategic Reader

How To Use This
Reading Study Guide

The purpose of this *Reading Study Guide* is to help you read and understand your geography textbook, *World Geography.* You can use this *Reading Study Guide* in two ways.

1. Use the *Reading Study Guide* side-by-side with your geography book.
- Turn to the section that you are going to read in the textbook. Then, next to the book, put the pages from the *Reading Study Guide* that accompany that section. All of the heads in the *Reading Study Guide* match the heads in the textbook.
- Use the *Reading Study Guide* to help you read and organize the information in the textbook.

2. Use the *Reading Study Guide* to study for tests on the textbook.
- Reread the summary of every chapter.
- Review the definitions of the Places & Terms in the *Reading Study Guide*.
- Review the diagram of information that you filled out as you read the summaries.
- Review your answers to questions.

Strategy: Read the Places & Terms and the definition of each. The Places & Terms are in dark type in the section.

Try This: What are the definition of "geography" and "absolute location"?

Name _____

The Five Themes of Geography

BEFORE YOU READ
In this section, you will learn what geography is and about methods geographers use.
   In the next section, you will read about the geographer's tools.

AS YOU READ
Use this chart to take notes about the five themes of geography.

5 Themes

PLACES & TERMS

geography study of the distribution and interaction of physical and human features on Earth

absolute location the exact place where a geographic feature is found

relative location a place in relation to other places around it

hemisphere each half of the globe

equator the imaginary line that divides the north and south halves of the earth

prime meridian imaginary line that divides the east and west halves of Earth

latitude imaginary lines that run parallel to the equator

longitude imaginary lines that go around the earth over the poles

The Geographer's Perspective (page 5)

What *is geography?*

The word "geography" comes from a Greek word that means, "to describe the earth." Geographers look at the use of space on the earth and the *interactions* that take place there. They look for patterns and connections between people and the land on which they live. So **geography** is the study of the *distribution* and interaction of physical and human features on earth.

   Geographers use many methods to study the use of space on earth. The most common one is a map. Maps are representations of portions of the earth.

   Geographers also use photographs to gain visual evidence about a place. They organize information into charts, graphs, or tables. This helps them to learn about geographic patterns and to understand changes over time.

   Another basic tool used by geographers is the five themes of geography. These themes organize information about geography into five categories.

1. What are some of the tools and methods used by geographers?

_____

Theme: Location (page 6)

How *is location described?*

Geographers describe location in two ways. <u>Absolute location</u> is the exact place where a geographic feature is found. <u>Relative location</u> describes a place in relation to other places around it.

   To describe absolute location, geographers use a grid system of imaginary lines. Earth is divided into two equal halves, and each half is called a <u>hemisphere</u>.

   The <u>equator</u> is the imaginary line that divides the north and south halves. The <u>prime meridian</u> is the imaginary line that divides the earth east and west.

   To locate places north and south, geographers use <u>latitude</u> lines, imaginary lines that run parallel to the equator. <u>Longitude</u> lines are imaginary lines that go around the earth over the poles. Each site on earth can have only one absolute location.

Looking at the Earth **5**

Strategy: Fill in the diagram as you read. The diagram will help you organize information in the section.

Try This: What is the purpose of this diagram?

Strategy: Read the summary. It contains the main ideas and the key information under the head.

Try This: What do you think this section will be about?

Strategy: Underline main ideas and key information as you read.

Try This: Read the summary under the head "Theme: Place." Underline information that you think is important.

The Five Themes of Geography *continued*

2.What are longitude and latitude?

_____

Theme: Place (page 7)

What *defines place?*

Place includes the physical features and cultural landscape of a location. All locations on earth have physical features that set them apart. Some examples are climate, landforms, and vegetation.

Other features are products of humans interacting with the environment. Building roads or houses are interactions with the environment. Other interactions are the result of human contact. Because a location's culture and its use of space may change over time, the description of place may also change.

3. Why might a description of place change?

_____

Theme: Region (pages 7–8)

What *characteristics define a region?*

A region is an area of the earth's surface that is defined by shared characteristics. Regions usually have more than one element that unifies them. These elements may include physical, political, economic, or cultural characteristics.

A formal region is defined by a limited number of related characteristics. In this textbook, the regions are generally defined by continental area and similar cultural styles. Africa, the United States and Canada, and Latin America are examples of formal regions.

A functional region is organized around a set of interactions and connections between places. Usually a functional region is characterized by a hub. A hub is central place with many links to outlying areas. For example, a city and its suburbs would form a functional region.

A perceptual region is a region in which people *perceive* the characteristics of a region in the same way. A set of characteristics may not be precisely the same for all people.

4. How is a formal region different from a functional region?

_____

Theme: Human-Environment Interaction (page 8)

How *do people relate to their environments?*

People learn to use what the environment offers them. They may change that environment to meet their needs. They also learn to live with parts of the environment that they cannot control.

People living in similar environments do not respond to them in the same way. A place with lots of sunshine may mean vacation to one person, and good farming to another.

Human beings actively work to change their environments to make them a better place. They may want changes to provide needed goods. People may drain swamps or dig irrigation ditches to improve their lives. Sometimes the changes can cause problems, such as pollution.

5. Why do people alter their environments?

_____

Theme: Movement (page 9)

How *do geographers analyze movement?*

Geographers study movement by looking at three types of distance: *linear*, time, and psychological.

Linear distance means how far across the earth an idea, a person, or a product travels. Physical geography can change linear distance by forcing a route to shift because of land or water barriers. Time distance is how long it takes a person, product, or idea to travel. Now it often takes less time to travel the same linear distance because of inventions like airplanes or automobiles.

Psychological distance is a term used to describe the way people view distance. Studies show that as we become familiar with a place, we think it is closer than it actually is.

6. What are the three types of distance that geographers use?

_____

Strategy: When you see a word in italic type, read the definition in the Glossary at the end of the chapter.

Try This: What does *linear* mean? Look at the Glossary at the end of the chapter to find the definition.

Strategy: Answer the question at the end of each part.

Try This: Write an answer to Question 6.

At the end of every chapter in the *Reading Study Guide,* you will find a Glossary and a section called After You Read. The Glossary gives definitions of all the words in italic type in the chapter summaries. After You Read is a two-page chapter review. Use After You Read to identify those parts of the chapter that you need to study more for the test on the chapter.

Strategy: Review all of the Places & Terms before completing Parts A and B of After You Read.

Try This: Use the *Reading Study Guide* for Chapter 1 to complete the exercise under Part A.

Name _____ Date _____

Glossary/After You Read

distortion a deforming of normal shapes in an image

distribution position, arrangement, or frequency of occurrence (for example, of people or resources) over an area

interaction when people or things act upon or influence each other

linear related to or like a line

navigational related to determining position, course of travel, and distance

perceive become aware of through the senses; see, observe

portable capable of being carried

Places & Terms

A. Write the name or term in each blank that bests completes the meaning of the paragraph.

absolute location   compass rose

longitude   cartographer

latitude

When a (1)_____ creates a map, he or she will add a number

of elements that help in the reading of the map. On a map you will find

(2)_____ lines, running parallel to the

(3)_____ lines, circling the earth and g

necessary for describing the (4)_____

addition, he or she will add a (5)_____

map will be able to tell which way is north.

B. Write the letter of the name or term next to the descriptio

a. equator   d. globe

b. prime meridian   e. topographic map

c. map projection   f. hemisphere

_____ 1. A three-dimensional representation of the e

_____ 2. Imaginary line that divides the north and sou

_____ 3. A way of drawing the earth's surface that re

_____ 4. A representation of natural and man-made f

_____ 5. Half of the earth, when it is divided north an

Strategy: Review the chapter summaries before completing the Main Ideas questions. Write a complete sentence for every answer.

Try This: In your own words, what is Question 1 asking for?

Main Ideas

1. What are some of the tasks of the geographer?

_____

_____

2. What are at least three of the five themes of geography?

_____

_____

3. With psychological distance, what makes some locations seem closer? What makes some seem farther away?

_____

_____

4. Geographers once used only land-based methods for doing surveys for mapmaking. What methods do they use more often today?

_____

_____

5. Which theme map would be best to illustrate the geographic theme of movement?

_____

_____

Thinking Critically

Answer the following questions on a separate sheet of paper.

1. Why do you think that it is important to be able to identify a place's absolute location?

2. In this chapter, you read that the Geographic Information System may help geographers make predictions about the impact of human activities on the environment. Why might this be useful?

Strategy: Write one or two paragraphs for every Thinking Critically question.

Try This: In your own words, what is Question 1 asking for?

The Five Themes of Geography

BEFORE YOU READ

In this section, you will learn what geography is and about methods geographers use.

In the next section, you will read about the geographer's tools.

AS YOU READ

Use this graphic to take notes about the five themes of geography.

5 Themes

PLACES & TERMS

geography study of the distribution and interaction of physical and human features on Earth

absolute location the exact place where a geographic feature is found

relative location a place in relation to other places around it

hemisphere each half of the globe

equator the imaginary line that divides the north and south halves of the earth

prime meridian imaginary line that divides the east and west halves of Earth

latitude imaginary lines that run parallel to the equator

longitude imaginary lines that go around the earth over the poles

The Geographer's Perspective (page 5)

***What** is geography?*

The word "geography" comes from a Greek word that means, "to describe the earth." Geographers look at the use of space on the earth and the *interactions* that take place there. They look for patterns and connections between people and the land on which they live. So <u>geography</u> is the study of the *distribution* and interaction of physical and human features on earth.

Geographers use many methods to study the use of space on earth. The most common one is a map. Maps are representations of portions of the earth.

Geographers also use photographs to gain visual evidence about a place. They organize information into charts, graphs, or tables. This helps them to learn about geographic patterns and to understand changes over time.

Another basic tool used by geographers is the five themes of geography. These themes organize information about geography into five categories.

1. What are some of the tools and methods used by geographers?

_____

_____

Theme: Location (page 6)

***How** is location described?*

Geographers describe location in two ways. <u>Absolute location</u> is the exact place where a geographic feature is found. <u>Relative location</u> describes a place in relation to other places around it.

To describe absolute location, geographers use a grid system of imaginary lines. Earth is divided into two equal halves, and each half is called a <u>hemisphere</u>.

The <u>equator</u> is the imaginary line that divides the north and south halves. The <u>prime meridian</u> is the imaginary line that divides the earth east and west.

To locate places north and south, geographers use <u>latitude</u> lines, imaginary lines that run parallel to the equator. <u>Longitude</u> lines are imaginary lines that go around the earth over the poles. Each site on earth can have only one absolute location.

Looking at the Earth **5**

2. What are longitude and latitude?

_____

Theme: Place (page 7)

What *defines place?*

Place includes the physical features and cultural landscape of a location. All locations on earth have physical features that set them apart. Some examples are climate, landforms, and vegetation.

Other features are products of humans interacting with the environment. Building roads or houses are interactions with the environment. Other interactions are the result of human contact. Because a location's culture and its use of space may change over time, the description of place may also change.

3. Why might a description of place change?

_____

Theme: Region (pages 7–8)

What *characteristics define a region?*

A region is an area of the earth's surface that is defined by shared characteristics. Regions usually have more than one element that unifies them. These elements may include physical, political, economic, or cultural characteristics.

A formal region is defined by a limited number of related characteristics. In this textbook, the regions are generally defined by continental area and similar cultural styles. Africa, the United States and Canada, and Latin America are examples of formal regions.

A functional region is organized around a set of interactions and connections between places. Usually a functional region is characterized by a hub. A hub is central place with many links to outlying areas. For example, a city and its suburbs would form a functional region.

A perceptual region is a region in which people *perceive* the characteristics of a region in the same way. A set of characteristics may not be precisely the same for all people.

4. How is a formal region different from a functional region?

_____

Theme: Human-Environment Interaction (page 8)

How *do people relate to their environments?*

People learn to use what the environment offers them. They may change that environment to meet their needs. They also learn to live with parts of the environment that they cannot control.

People living in similar environments do not respond to them in the same way. A place with lots of sunshine may mean vacation to one person, and good farming to another.

Human beings actively work to change their environments to make them a better place. They may want changes to provide needed goods. People may drain swamps or dig irrigation ditches to improve their lives. Sometimes the changes can cause problems, such as pollution.

5. Why do people alter their environments?

_____

Theme: Movement (page 9)

How *do geographers analyze movement?*

Geographers study movement by looking at three types of distance: *linear,* time, and psychological.

Linear distance means how far across the earth an idea, a person, or a product travels. Physical geography can change linear distance by forcing a route to shift because of land or water barriers. Time distance is how long it takes a person, product, or idea to travel. Now it often takes less time to travel the same linear distance because of inventions like airplanes or automobiles.

Psychological distance is a term used to describe the way people view distance. Studies show that as we become familiar with a place, we think it is closer than it actually is.

6. What are the three types of distance that geographers use?

_____

The Geographer's Tools

BEFORE YOU READ

In the last section, you read about the methods geographers use.
In this section, you will read about the geographer's tools.

AS YOU READ

Use this graphic to take notes about geographer's tools.

Tools

PLACES & TERMS

globe a three-dimensional representation of the earth

map two-dimensional graphic representations of selected parts of the earth's surface

cartographer a mapmaker

map projection a way of drawing the earth's surface that reduces the distortion caused by converting three dimensions to two dimensions

topographic map a representation of natural and man-made features on earth

Landsat a series of satellites that can photograph the entire earth in 16 days

Geographic Information Systems (GIS) a system that uses digital map information to create a databank to produce specialized maps

Maps and Globes
TWO OR THREE DIMENSIONS (page 10)

What tools do cartographers use?

A geographer's tools include maps, globes, and data. A map's purpose is to show locations of places on the earth. Maps also show where places are in relation to other places around them.

A **globe** is a three-dimensional representation of the earth. It provides a way to view the earth as it sits in space. Because the earth is round, we can see only one-half of it at a time. Globes are not always practical because they are not easily *portable*.

People often prefer to use **maps**, which are two-dimensional representations of selected parts of the earth's surface. Maps are portable and can be drawn to any scale needed.

The disadvantage of a map is that *distortion* occurs when a three-dimensional image is converted to two dimensions. A **cartographer**, or mapmaker, solves this problem by using different

types of map projections. A **map projection** is a way of drawing the earth's surface that reduces distortion.

1. Why do cartographers need to use projections when drawing maps?

_____

_____

TYPES OF MAPS (page 11)
What kinds of maps are available?

The three types of maps are general reference, thematic, and navigational. A general reference map is sometimes called a **topographical map**. It shows natural and man-made features on the earth. Thematic maps focus on specific kinds of information, such as climate or population density. *Navigational* maps are used by sailors and pilots to plot a course to sail or fly.

2. What are thematic maps used for?

_____

_____

The Science of Mapmaking
SURVEYING/SATELLITES (pages 11–12)

How *do satellites help geographers?*

The first step in making a map is to complete a field survey. Surveyors observe, measure, and record what they see in a specific area. Today, the observing, measuring, and recording are done by aerial photography or by satellites. Cartographers then use this information and computers to construct maps.

The best known satellites that provide geographic data, are Landsat and GOES. **Landsat** is actually a series of satellites that can photograph the entire earth in 16 days. GOES—Geostationary Operational Environment Satellite—is a weather satellite. It maintains a constant view of the same area of the earth. GOES gathers images that are useful in forecasting the weather.

3. What kind of information does GOES collect?

_____

_____

GIS/GPS (page 13)

How *is a Geographic Information System used?*

The geographer's newest tool is the **Geographic Information System (GIS)**. This system uses digital map information to produce a specialized map. GIS provides specialized information to solve problems. For example, it may help builders find a suitable site to build an airport.

Another tool of geographers is the Global Positioning System (GPS). The system uses a series of 24 satellites called Navstars. They send the exact latitude, longitude, altitude, and time to a hand-held receiver.

4. What would you use a GPS for?

_____

_____

Geography Skills Handbook

BEFORE YOU READ

In the last section, you read about the geographer's tools.

This handbook covers the basic map skills and information that geographers rely on as they investigate the world—the skills you will need as you study geography.

AS YOU READ

Use this graphic to take notes about the geography tools you read about.

Tools of Geography

PLACES & TERMS

legend a list that explains the symbols and use of color on the map

compass rose starlike symbol that shows you the directions on the map

scale the ratio between a unit of length on the map and a unit of distance on the earth

Reading a Map (page 15)

How can you interpret what a map shows?

All maps have the following elements.

The title explains the subject. Symbols represent such items as capital cities, economic activities, or natural resources. Labels are words or phrases that explain features on the map. Colors show a variety of information on a map, depending on the map's purpose. The <u>legend</u>, which is also called a map key, lists and explains the symbols and colors on the map.

Lines of latitude are the imaginary lines that measure distance north or south of the equator. Lines of longitude are the imaginary lines that measure the distance east and west of the prime meridian. Though these lines are imaginary, they are drawn on maps to make it possible to determine location.

The <u>compass rose</u> is a starlike symbol that shows directions—north (N), south (S), east (E), and west (W)—on the map. Sometimes only north is indicated. A <u>scale</u> is included to show the ratio

between a unit of length on the map and a unit of distance on the earth.

1. Which element explains symbols and a map's use of color?

_____

_____

Scale (page 16)

How is scale shown?

A geographer decides what scale to use by determining how much detail needs to be shown.

A ratio scale shows the ratio of distance on the map compared to real earth measurements. For example this may be written as 1:30,000,000. This means a ratio of one inch on the map is equal to 30,000,000 inches on Earth.

A bar scale also shows the relationship of map distance to earth distance. For example, if the bar scale is 1 inch to 500 miles, then there would be an inch-long bar labeled 500 miles.

2. Why would a geographer use large scale?

Using the Geographic Grid (page 17)

How does the grid work?

Geographers use a grid system to identify absolute location. This system uses two kinds of imaginary lines. These are latitude lines which are often called parallels, and longitude lines called meridians. Lines also mark the hours of the day as the earth rotates. Every 15° east or west is equal to 1 hour.

Absolute location can be learned by noting where latitude and longitude lines cross. For more precision, each degree can be divided into 60 minutes ('). The absolute location of Dakar, Senegal, for example, is written 14° 40' N (latitude) and 17° 26' W (longitude).

3. Why are latitude lines often called parallels?

Projections (pages 18–19)

What causes distortion?

A projection is a way of showing the curved surface of the earth on a flat map. Because the earth is round, a flat map will distort some aspect of the earth's surface. Distance, shape, direction, or area may be distorted by a projection.

A planar projection is a projection on a flat surface. It shows the earth so that a line from the central point to any other point on the map gives the shortest distance between two points.

A conical projection is a projection onto a cone. This projection shows shape fairly well, but it distorts landmasses at the edges of the map.

A cylindrical projection is a projection onto a cylinder. The projection shows the entire earth on one map.

4. What elements might be distorted by a projection?

Using Different Types of Maps
(pages 20–21)

What do a physical map or a political map show?

Physical maps help you see the types of landforms and bodies of water found in a specific area. They show the relative location and characteristics of a place or region. On a physical map, color, shading, or contour lines are used to indicate elevation or altitude, also called relief.

Political maps show features on the earth's surface that humans created. A political map might include cities, states, provinces, territories, or countries.

5. What information might appear on a political map?

Thematic Maps (pages 22–23)

What other information can maps show?

Geographers also use theme maps, which focus on a specific idea. With all theme maps, look first at the title to determine the theme. Then look at the legend to determine what information is being presented.

Theme maps can be presented in a variety of ways. Qualitative maps use color, symbols, dots, or lines.

Cartograms present information about a country based on a set of data other than land area. The size of each country is drawn in proportion to that data rather than to its land size.

Flow line maps illustrate movement of people, goods, or ideas. The information is usually shown in a series of arrows. Location, direction, and scope of movement can be seen. Time may be indicated.

6. What are the different types of themes maps?

Chapter **1** Looking at the Earth **Reading Study Guide**

Glossary/After You Read

distortion a deforming of normal shapes in an image

distribution position, arrangement, or frequency of occurrence (for example, of people or resources) over an area

interaction when people or things act upon or influence each other

linear related to or like a line

navigational related to determining position, course of travel, and distance

perceive become aware of through the senses; see, observe

portable capable of being carried

Places & Terms

A. Write the name or term in each blank that bests completes the meaning of the paragraph.

absolute location   compass rose

longitude   cartographer

latitude

When a (1)_____ creates a map, he or she will add a number

of elements that help in the reading of the map. On a map you will find

(2)_____ lines, running parallel to the equator, and

(3)_____ lines, circling the earth and going over the poles. These are

necessary for describing the (4)_____ of any place the on the earth. In

addition, he or she will add a (5)_____, so that anyone reading the

map will be able to tell which way is north.

B. Write the letter of the name or term next to the description that explains it best.

a. equator   d. globe

b. prime meridian   e. topographic map

c. map projection   f. hemisphere

_____ 1. a three-dimensional representation of the earth

_____ 2. imaginary line that divides the north and south halves of the earth

_____ 3. a way of drawing the earth's surface that reduces distortion

_____ 4. a representation of natural and man-made features on earth

_____ 5. half of the earth, when it is divided north and south or east and west

Main Ideas

1. What are some of the tasks of the geographer?

_____

_____

2. What are at least three of the five themes of geography?

_____

_____

3. With psychological distance, what makes some locations seem closer? What makes some seem farther away?

_____

_____

4. Geographers once used only land-based methods for doing surveys for mapmaking. What methods do they use more often today?

_____

_____

5. Which theme map would be best to illustrate the geographic theme of movement?

_____

_____

Thinking Critically

Answer the following questions on a separate sheet of paper.

1. Why do you think that it is important to be able to identify a place's absolute location?

2. In this chapter, you read that the Geographic Information System may help geographers make predictions about the impact of human activities on the environment. Why might this be useful?

The Earth Inside and Out

BEFORE YOU READ
In the last chapter, you read about some of the skills geographers use.

In this section, you will learn where the earth is in the solar system and the materials that make up the earth.

AS YOU READ
Use this graphic organizer to take notes on details of the earth's location and structure.

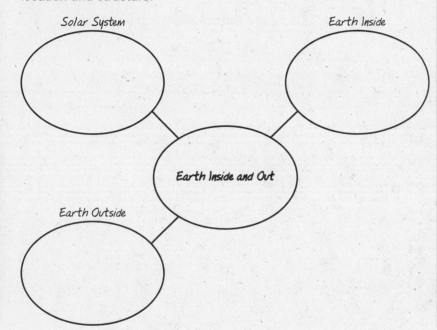

PLACES & TERMS

continent landmasses above water on earth

solar system the sun plus the nine known planets and other celestial bodies orbiting the sun

core the solid metallic center of the earth

mantle a soft layer of molten rock that floats on top of the core

crust the thin layer of rock at the surface of the earth

magma molten rock that is the result of the magma melting the underside of the earth's crust

atmosphere layer of gases, including oxygen, that surrounds the earth

lithosphere the solid rock portion of the earth's surface

hydrosphere the water elements of the earth, including oceans, seas, rivers, lakes, and water in the atmosphere

biosphere the part of the earth where plants and animals live

continental drift theory that a supercontinent divided and drifted apart over time

The Solar System (page 27)

How far are we from the sun?

Our sun is a medium-sized star on the edge of a *galaxy* called the Milky Way. The earth is the third planet out from the sun. Its distance from the sun is 93 million miles.

The solar system consists of the sun and the nine known planets, as well as other *celestial* bodies that orbit the sun. The **solar system** also contains comets, spheres covered with ice and dust that leave trails of vapor as they race through space. Asteroids—large chunks of rocky material—are also found in our solar system.

1. Of what does the solar system consist?

_____

_____

The Structure of the Earth
INSIDE THE EARTH (page 28)

What is the lithosphere?

The earth is about 24,900 miles in *circumference* and about 7,900 miles in *diameter*. Although the earth seems like a solid ball, it is really more like a series of shells that float on each other.

The <u>core</u> is the solid metallic center of the earth and is made up of iron and nickel. Floating on the core is the <u>mantle</u>, a soft layer of molten rock that is about 1,800 miles thick. The <u>crust</u> is the thin layer of rock at the surface of the earth. <u>Magma</u> is created when the mantle melts the underside of the crust.

Surrounding the earth is a layer of gases called the <u>atmosphere</u>. It contains the oxygen we breathe. It also protects the earth from radiation and space debris. It is where weather and climate take place.

The solid rock portion of the earth's surface is the <u>lithosphere</u>. Some of the lithosphere is below water and forms the floor of the ocean. The huge landmasses above water on the earth are called <u>continents</u>. There are seven continents: North America, South America, Europe, Asia, Africa, Australia, and Antarctica.

The <u>hydrosphere</u> is made up of the water elements on the earth. This includes oceans, seas, rivers, lakes, and water in the atmosphere. The atmosphere, the lithosphere, and the hydrosphere form the <u>biosphere</u>. It is the part of the earth where plants and animals live.

2. What are the layers inside the earth?

_____

_____

CONTINENTAL DRIFT (page 29)

How do continents move?

Alfred Wegener of Germany presented a theory called <u>continental drift</u>. He said the earth once had a single supercontinent. It split into many pieces called plates. These plates moved around the earth, crashed into each other, and split again. Finally, they became the continents that are located in their current positions.

In the 1960s, scientists discovered the youngest rocks were near cracks in the seafloor. This seemed to suggest that the sea floor was spreading and pushing the continents apart. The continents continue to move today.

3. How did the continents take shape?

_____

_____

Bodies of Water and Landforms

BEFORE YOU READ

In the last section, you learned where the earth is in the solar system and how it is constructed.

In this section, you will read about the features on the earth's surface.

AS YOU READ

Use this graphic organizer to take notes on details of the earth's landforms and bodies of water.

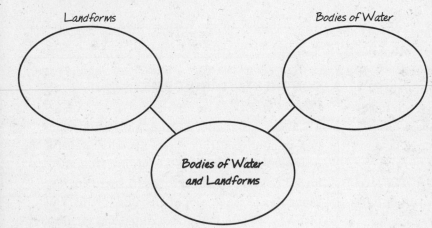

Landforms

Bodies of Water

Bodies of Water and Landforms

PLACES & TERMS

hydrologic cycle the continuous circulation of water between the atmosphere, oceans, and earth

drainage basin an area drained by a major river and its tributaries

ground water water held in rock pores beneath the soil

water table the level at which the rock is saturated

landform naturally formed features on the earth's surface

continental shelf the earth's surface from the edge of a continent to the edge of the deep part of the ocean

relief the difference in elevation of a landform from the lowest point to the highest point

topography the combination of characteristics of the landforms and their distribution in a region

Bodies of Water

OCEANS AND SEAS (page 32)

How *does ocean water circulate?*

Water supports plants and animals, and it helps distribute heat on the earth.

The ocean is an interconnected body of salt water that covers about 71 percent of our planet. Even though it is one ocean, geographers have divided it into four main parts. The oceans are the Atlantic Ocean, the Pacific Ocean, the Indian Ocean, and the Arctic Ocean.

The salty water of the ocean circulates through three basic motions: currents, waves, and tides. Currents act like rivers flowing through the ocean. Waves are swells or ridges produced by winds. Tides are the regular rise and fall of the ocean. They are caused by the *gravitational* pull of the moon or the sun.

The motion of the ocean helps distribute the heat on the planet. Winds blow over the ocean and are either heated or cooled by the water. When the winds blow across the land, they change the temperature of the air over the land.

1. How does the motion of the ocean distribute heat?

_____

_____

HYDROLOGIC CYCLE (page 32–33)

What *is the hydrologic cycle?*

The <u>hydrologic cycle</u> is the continuous circulation of water between the atmosphere, the oceans, and the earth. Water from the surface of the oceans, other bodies of water, and from plants evaporates into the atmosphere. The water then exists in the atmosphere as vapor. When the vapor cools it condenses. Then precipitation, either rain or snow, falls to the earth. The rain or snow soaks into the ground, evaporates into the atmosphere, or flows into rivers to be recycled.

2. How does water get into the atmosphere?

_____

_____

LAKES, RIVERS, AND STREAMS (page 33)
What *is a drainage basin?*

Lakes hold more than 95 percent of all the earth's fresh water. There are freshwater lakes and some saltwater lakes.

Rivers and streams move water to or from larger bodies of water. Smaller streams are called tributaries. They pour water into larger rivers. Rivers and streams connect into drainage systems that look like trees and branches. Geographers call an area drained by a major river and its tributaries a **drainage basin.**

Some water on the surface of the earth is held by the soil. Some water is held in the pores of rock below the soil. This is called **ground water**. The level at which the rock is *saturated* marks the rim of the **water table**. The water table may rise or fall depending on the amount of precipitation in the region. It might also change based on the amount of water pumped out of the ground. Underground rock layers that store water are called aquifers.

3. Where is water under the ground found?

_____

_____

Landforms
OCEANIC LANDFORMS (pages 33–36)

What *is the continental shelf ?*

<u>Landforms</u> are naturally formed features on the surface of the earth. The earth's surface shows a wide range of different landforms. These include mountains, valleys, plateaus, mesas, plains, bays, peninsulas, islands, and volcanoes.

The sea floor has landforms similar to those above water. The earth's surface from the edge of a continent to the edge of the deep part of the ocean is called the **continental shelf**. The floor of the ocean has ridges, valleys, canyons, and plains. Ridges mark places where new crust is being formed on the edges of the continental plate.

Mountain chains similar to those on the continents cover parts of the ocean floor. The longest continuous range is the Mid-Atlantic Range. It extends thousands of miles north to south through the middle of the Atlantic Ocean.

Islands dot the ocean surface. Islands may be formed by volcanic action, deposits of sand, or by deposits of coral skeletons.

4. What landforms are found in oceans?

_____

_____

CONTINENTAL LANDFORMS (page 36)
What *is relief?*

The major geographic feature that separates one type of landform from another is relief. **Relief** is the difference in elevation of a landform from the lowest point to the highest point. There are four categories of relief: mountains, hills, plains, and plateaus. A mountain, for example, has great relief compared to a plain. A plain has very little relief, or difference between the high and low points.

Topography is the combination of the characteristics of landforms and their distribution in a region. A topographic map shows the landforms with their vertical dimensions and in relationship to other landforms.

5. What does a topographic map show?

_____

_____

Internal Forces Shaping the Earth

BEFORE YOU READ

In the last section, you read about the features of the earth's surface.
   In this section, you will learn about the forces that move and shape the earth from the inside.

AS YOU READ

Use this graphic organizer to take notes on details of internal forces that shape the earth.

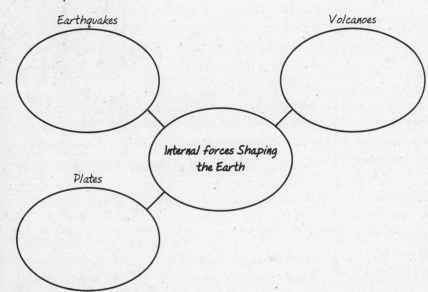

Earthquakes

Volcanoes

Internal forces Shaping the Earth

Plates

PLACES & TERMS

tectonic plate an enormous moving piece that forms the earth's crust

fault a fracture in the earth's crust

earthquake violent movement of the earth caused by the movement of tectonic plates

seismograph a device that measures the size of an earthquake

epicenter point on the earth's surface directly above an earthquake

Richter scale a scale that measures the energy released during an earthquake

tsunami a giant wave in the ocean caused by an earthquake

volcano an opening in the earth's crust where magma and gases escape

lava what magma is called when it reaches the earth's surface

Ring of Fire a zone around the rim of the Pacific Ocean where most active volcanoes are found

Plate Tectonics (pages 37–38)

What *are tectonic plates?*

The internal forces that shape the earth's surface begin immediately beneath the crust. The magma beneath the crust circulates like a conveyer belt. The heated magma moves up toward the crust, cools, and circulates downward. Above this circulation system are the <u>tectonic plates</u>, enormous moving pieces that form the earth's crust.

1. How does magma move under the earth's crust?

_____

_____

PLATE MOVEMENT (pages 38–39)

How *do plates move?*

The tectonic plates move in one of four ways:
1) sliding past each other in a shearing motion;
2) subduction, or diving under another plate;
3) convergence, or crashing into one another;
4) spreading, or moving apart.

   Three types of boundaries mark plate movements:
   • **Divergent boundary** Plates move apart.
   • **Convergent boundary** Plates collide with each other.
   • **Transform boundary** Plates slide past one another.

When two plates meet each other, they may cause folding and cracking of the rock. Because the rocks are under great pressure, they become more flexible and will bend or fold, creating changes in the crust. However, sometimes the rock is not flexible and will crack under the pressures exerted by the plate movement. This *fracture* in the earth's crust is called a <u>fault</u>. It is at the fault line that the plates move past each other.

2. What happens when plates meet each other ?

_____

_____

Earthquakes
EARTHQUAKE LOCATIONS (pages 39–40)
Where *do earthquakes occur?*

As the plates grind or slip past one another at a fault, the earth shakes or trembles. This movement of the earth is an <u>earthquake</u>. A special device called a <u>seismograph</u> can detect them.

The location in the earth where an earthquake begins is called the focus. The point directly above the focus on the earth's surface is the <u>epicenter</u>. Nearly 95 percent of all recorded earthquakes occur around the boundaries of the major tectonic plates.

3. What is a seismograph?

_____

_____

EARTHQUAKE DAMAGE (page 40)
What *is a tsunami?*

Earthquakes cause squeezing, stretching, and shearing motions in the earth's crust that damage land and structures. Ground motion can cause landslides, displacement of land, fires, and collapsed buildings. *Aftershocks* are smaller-scale quakes that occur after the initial shock. The <u>Richter scale</u> uses information collected by seismographs to determine the relative strength of an earthquake.

Sometimes an earthquake can cause a tsunami, a giant wave in the ocean. A tsunami travels at speeds of up to 450 miles per hour. It produces waves of 50

to 100 feet or higher. Tsunamis may travel across wide stretches of the ocean.

4. How is earthquake damage caused?

_____

_____

Volcanoes (pages 40–41)
What *is a volcano?*

A <u>volcano</u> occurs when magma, gases, and water from the lower part of the crust or mantle collect in underground chambers and eventually pour out of cracks in the earth's surface. Most volcanoes are found along the tectonic plate boundaries.

Magma that has reached the earth's surface is called <u>lava</u>. The most dramatic volcanic action is an eruption. This occurs when which hot lava, gases, ash, dust, and rocks explode out of vents in the earth's crust. Volcanoes do not erupt on a predictable schedule.

5. What happens during a volcanic eruption?

_____

_____

RING OF FIRE (page 41)
What *is the Ring of Fire?*

The <u>Ring of Fire</u> is a zone around the rim of the Pacific Ocean. It is the location of the vast majority of active volcanoes and earthquakes. Other volcanoes appear over "hot spots" where the crust is very thin and occasionally magma melts through.

Hot springs and geysers also are indicators of "hot spots" in the earth's crust. Hot springs occur when ground water circulates near a magma chamber.

Not all volcanic action is bad. Volcanic ash produces fertile soil. In some places, the hot springs, steam, and heat generated by the magma is tapped for energy.

6. What are hot springs and geysers ?

_____

_____

External Forces Shaping the Earth

BEFORE YOU READ

In the last section, you read about the forces that move and shape the earth from the inside.

In this section, you will learn about external forces that can alter landscapes and create the soil needed for plant life.

AS YOU READ

Use this graphic organizer to take notes on details of the external forces that shape the earth.

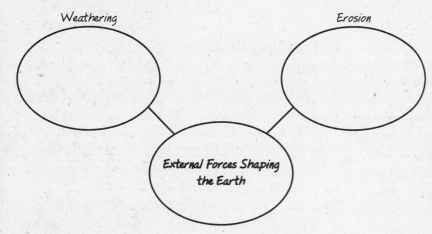

Weathering

Erosion

External Forces Shaping the Earth

PLACES & TERMS

weathering physical or chemical processes that change the characteristics of rock on or near the earth's surface

sediment small pieces of rock

mechanical weathering process that breaks down rock

chemical weathering process that changes rock into a new substance

erosion weathered material moved by wind, water, ice, or gravity

delta landform created when sediment is deposited as a river enters the ocean

loess wind-blown silt and clay sediment that produces very fertile soil

glacier a large, long-lasting mass of ice

glaciation the changing of landforms by the movement of glaciers

moraine a ridge of rocks left behind by a glacier

humus organic matter in the soil

Weathering
MECHANICAL WEATHERING (page 42)

***What** is weathering?*

<u>Weathering</u> refers to physical and chemical processes that change the characteristics of rock on or near the earth's surface. Weathering creates smaller and smaller pieces of rock called <u>sediment</u>. Examples of sediment are mud, sand, or silt, which is very fine particles of rock.

Processes that break rock into smaller pieces are called <u>mechanical weathering</u>. All sorts of agents can break apart rocks. Some examples are ice or frost and plant growth. Human activities such as drilling and blasting in a mine are also mechanical weathering processes.

1. What is sediment?

_____

_____

CHEMICAL WEATHERING (page 43)

***How** do rocks decompose?*

<u>Chemical weathering</u> occurs when rock is changed into a new substance. This happens because of elements in the air or water and the minerals in the rock interact.

Decomposition, or breakdown, can happen in several ways. Some minerals react to oxygen in the air and begin to crumble. Sometimes minerals are combined with water or carbon dioxide to form weak acids. The acids break down the rock.

Climate has a great affect on rocks. Climates that are warm and moist will produce more chemical weathering than cool, dry areas will. Rocks in cold and dry or hot and dry areas generally experience greater mechanical weathering.

2. How does climate affect rock decomposition?

_____

Erosion

WATER EROSION (pages 43–44)

What *is erosion?*

Erosion occurs when weathered material is moved by wind, water, ice, or gravity. Glaciers, waves, stream flow, or blowing winds are erosion agents. Erosion reshapes landforms, coastal regions, and riverbeds and banks.

There are three kinds of water erosion. One happens when water flows in a stream or river. Another form of water erosion is abrasion. This is the grinding away of rock by transported particles in the water. A third eroding action of water occurs when the water dissolves chemical elements in the rock.

Land cut by a stream gets deeper and wider. As the water slows, it drops the sediment it is carrying. When a river enters the ocean, the sediment is deposited into a fan-like landform called a **delta**.

Wave action along coastlines also changes the land. Sediment deposited by waves may build up sandbars or islands.

3. What are three kinds of water erosion?

_____

WIND EROSION (page 44)

How *does wind erosion change the land?*

In many ways, wind erosion is similar to water erosion. Wind transports sediment and deposits it in other locations. Depending on the type of wind-born sediment, new landforms may be produced. Deposits of **loess**, wind-blown silt and clay sediment that produce very fertile soil, are found many feet deep in some areas of the world.

4. What is loess?

_____

GLACIAL EROSION (page 44)

What *is glaciation?*

A **glacier** is a large, long-lasting mass of ice. Glaciers form in mountainous areas and in regions that are regularly covered with heavy snowfall and ice.

Glaciation is the changing of landforms by slowly moving glaciers. Massive glaciers cut U-shaped valleys in the land.

On top or within the ice are other rocks carried by the glacier. When the glacier melts, these rocks are left behind. Rocks left behind by a glacier may form a ridge or a hill called a **moraine**.

5. Where do glaciers form?

_____

Building Soil (page 45)

What *is soil?*

Soil is the loose mixture of weathered rock, organic matter, air, and water that supports plant growth. Organic matter in the soil helps to support the growth of plants by providing needed plant food. Water and air share space in the soil. When it rains, pore-like spaces fill with water.

Soil's fertility—its ability to nurture plants—is affected by several things. They include the texture of the soil, the amount of organic material (called **humus**), and the amount of air and water in the soil.

Five factors affect soil:

- **Parent material** The chemical composition affects fertility.
- **Relief** Steeper slopes erode easily and produce soil slowly.
- **Organisms** Small animals such as worms and ants help loosen soil. Bacteria helps material decompose; this supplies food for plants.
- **Climate** Hot and cold climates produce different soils. The same is true for wet and dry climates.
- **Time** The amount of time to produce soil varies.

6. What are the five soil factors geographers study?

_____

Name _____   Date _____

Glossary/After You Read

aftershocks are smaller-scale earthquakes that occur after the initial earthquake

celestial of or relating to the sky or heavens

circumference the distance around the outside of a circle or sphere

decomposition breakdown of materials

diameter the length of a straight line through the center of an object

fracture to break

gravitational having to do with gravity

moderate to make less severe, to cause to avoid extremes

saturated soaked, filled with as much water as can be held

Places & Terms

A. Write the letter of the name or term next to the description that explains it best.

a. continental drift   d. mechanical weathering

b. seismograph   e. hydrologic cycle

c. topography

_____ 1. A special device that measures and records the vibrations created by an earthquake.

_____ 2. The continuous circulation of water between the atmosphere, the oceans, and the earth.

_____ 3. A theory that states that the earth once had a single supercontinent that divided, with the pieces moving slowly apart.

_____ 4. The combination of characteristics of the landforms and their distribution in a region.

_____ 5. The breaking down of rocks into smaller pieces, without changing their composition.

B. Circle the place or term that best completes each sentence.

1. The layer that floats above the earth's core is the _____.

   magma   mantle   crust

2. The _____ is a layer of gases immediately surrounding the earth.

   atmosphere   lithosphere   hydrosphere

3. An area drained by a major river and its tributaries is called a _____.

   water table   aquifer   drainage basin

4. A[n] _____ is a giant wave caused by an earthquake.

   epicenter   tsunami   fault

5. _____ happens when landforms are changed by a slowly moving mass of ice.

glaciation   precipitation   subduction

Main Ideas

1. What is the name given to the part of the earth where plants and animals live, and what are its three parts?

_____

_____

2. What are the differences between currents, waves, and tides?

_____

_____

3. In what ways can the earth's internal forces affect the lives of people?

_____

_____

4. Why might erosion make it important for people to be careful where they build?

_____

_____

5. Why is soil important?

_____

_____

Thinking Critically

Answer the following questions on a separate sheet of paper.

1. How do the theories of continental drift and plate tectonics fit together?

2. Thinking over all that you learned in this chapter, why do you think the earth displays such a wide variety of landforms? Give examples.

Seasons and Weather

BEFORE YOU READ

In the last section, you read about the external forces that shaped the earth.

In this section, you will learn about how the earth's rotation creates weather and seasons.

AS YOU READ

Use this graphic to take notes on the earth's seasons and weather.

Seasons and Weather

PLACES & TERMS

solstice the day on which the sun is at its farthest north or farthest south latitude

equinox when the day and night are the same length; happens twice a year

weather the atmosphere at a particular location and time

climate weather at a particular location over a long period of time

precipitation water droplets falling in the form of rain, sleet, snow, or hail

rain shadow the land on the leeward side of hills or mountains

hurricane storms that form over warm, tropical ocean

typhoon hurricane in Asia

tornado powerful, funnel-shaped column of spiraling air

blizzard a heavy snowstorm with winds of more than 32 miles per hour

drought a long period without rain or with very minimal rainfall

Seasons (page 49)

Why *do we have seasons?*

The earth tilts at a 23.5° angle in relation to the sun. As the earth revolves around the sun, different parts of the earth receive the direct rays of the sun for more hours of the day. This causes the changing seasons. For example, the northern half of the earth tilts toward the sun in summer. In the winter, this half is tilted away from the sun.

Two lines of latitude, the Tropic of Cancer and the Tropic of Capricorn, mark the farthest points north and south that the sun's rays shine directly overhead at noon. The day that this happens is called a <u>solstice</u>.

Another signal of seasonal change is the equinox. Twice a year the sun is directly over the equator. This is called the <u>equinox</u>. At this time the days and nights

all over the world are equal in length. The equinoxes mark the beginning of spring and autumn.

1. How is a solstice different from an equinox?

_____

Weather

WHAT CAUSES THE WEATHER (page 50)

How *do climate and weather differ?*

Weather and climate are often confused. <u>Weather</u> is the condition of the atmosphere at a particular location and time. <u>Climate</u> is the term for weather conditions at a particular location over a long period of time.

Daily weather is the result of several factors. One factor is the amount of solar energy received by a location. Large masses of air absorb and distribute this solar energy.

A second factor is landforms and bodies of water at a location. Water heats and cools slowly, while land heats and cools rapidly. So the presence of bodies of water will affect the temperature. A third factor is *elevation* above sea level. The higher you are the cooler it will be.

2. What are three factors that affect weather?

_____

PRECIPITATION (pages 50–51)
What causes precipitation?

Another factor that affects the weather is the amount of water vapor in the atmosphere. This helps determine whether there will be **precipitation**. Precipitation is water droplets falling in the form of rain, sleet, snow, or hail. Warm air rises, and as it does it cools, losing its ability to hold water vapor. The water vapor *condenses,* and the water droplets form into clouds. When the amount of water in a cloud is too heavy for the air to hold, it generally rains or snows.

Geographers classify precipitation as convectional, orographic, or frontal. Convectional precipitation occurs in hot moist climates where the sun quickly heats the air.

Orographic precipitation falls on the windward side of hills or mountains. The mountains block moist air and force it upward. The land on the *leeward* side is called a **rain shadow**, because it gets little rain from the descending dry air.

Frontal movement causes precipitation. A front is the boundary between two air masses that have different temperature or humidity.

3. What are the three basic types of precipitation?

_____

Weather Extremes
HURRICANES (page 51)

What is a hurricane?

Hurricanes are storms that form over warm, tropical ocean waters. In Asia, these storms are called as **typhoons** or tropical cyclones. The storm begins when air flows over ocean water with a temperature of 80° or more. It picks up huge amounts of moisture and heat energy. Winds moving in a hurricane may be as strong as 200 miles per hour.

4. What causes hurricanes?

_____

TORNADOES (pages 51–52)
How does a tornado form?

A **tornado**, or twister, is a powerful funnel-shaped column of spiraling air. They are born from thunderstorms. Unlike hurricanes, tornadoes form quickly and sometimes without warning.

In a tornado, winds swirl counter-clockwise around a low-pressure center. These winds reach 300 miles per hour. Most tornadoes have small diameters, travel about a mile, and last a few minutes.

5. How do hurricanes and tornadoes differ?

_____

BLIZZARDS/DROUGHTS/FLOODS (pages 52–53)
Where are snowbelts found?

A **blizzard** is a heavy snowstorm with winds of more than 32 miles per hour and reduced visibility. Because of their location, some areas of the country are especially susceptible to snowstorms that produce huge amounts of snow.

A **drought** is a long period without rain or with very minimal rainfall. The lack of water results in crop failures, reduced levels in water storage facilities, and the deaths of animals.

In a flood, water fills streams and rivers until they reach *flood stage.* This is the point where the banks of a river or stream can no longer hold the water.

6. What is flood stage?

_____

Climate

BEFORE YOU READ

In the last section, you learned how the earth's rotation creates weather and seasons.

In this section, you will read about the factors that create and change climate.

AS YOU READ

Use this graphic to take notes on the factors that affect climate.

Climate

PLACES & TERMS

convection the transfer of heat in the atmosphere by upward motion of the air

El Niño the warming of waters off the west coast of South America

greenhouse effect the theory that gases released by burning coal and petroleum traps of solar energy, causing higher temperatures

Factors Affecting Climate
WIND CURRENTS/OCEAN CURRENTS

(pages 54–55)

What *is convection?*

Wind and ocean currents help distribute the sun's heat from one part of the world to another. This is done through <u>convection</u>. Convection is the transfer of heat in the atmosphere by upward motion of the air.

Convection occurs when the sunlight heats the atmosphere. The heated air expands. A region of low air pressure is created by this expansion. Cooler denser air in a nearby high-pressure region rushes into the low-pressure area.

Ocean currents are like rivers flowing in the ocean. Warm water flows away from the equator toward the poles, and cold water flows back toward the equator. Winds blowing over the ocean currents are heated or cooled by the currents. The winds then affect the lands that the winds blow across.

Currents also affect the precipitation in an area.

Cold ocean currents flowing along a coastal region chill the air. Sometimes they prevent warm air and the moisture it holds from falling to earth.

1. How do wind and ocean currents affect the climate?

_____

_____

ZONES OF LATITUDE (pages 55–56)
How *does latitude location affect climate?*

Geographers divide the earth into three general regions of latitude: low or tropical, middle or temperate, and high or polar. Tropical regions are found on either side of the equator.

Lands in tropical regions are hot all year long. In some areas, a shift in wind patterns causes variations in climate. The high latitude or polar regions circle the North Pole and South Pole. They are cold all year. During summer in the polar regions, the temperature reaches a high of only 50° F.

The earth's two temperate regions lie at the

Climate and Vegetation **25**

middle latitudes. They are between the tropics and the polar regions. Within the temperate regions, climates can vary greatly. The variations range from relatively hot to relatively cold. These variations occur because solar heating is greater in the summer than in the winter.

2. What are the three general regions of latitude?

_____

ELEVATION/TOPOGRAPHY (page 56)

How *does elevation affect climate?*

Another factor in determining a region's climate is elevation, or distance above sea level. The air temperature drops as elevation increases. Climates above 12,000 feet become like those in Arctic areas.

Landforms also affect climate. This is especially true of mountain areas. Remember that as winds move up the side of a mountain they cool. They also lose their ability to hold moisture and release rain or snow. By the time the winds reach the other side of the mountain, they are dry and become warmer as they flow down the mountain.

3. What happens to winds as they move up the side of a mountain?

_____

Changes in Climate

EL NIÑO (pages 56–57)

How *does El Niño affect the weather?*

Climates change over time. Changes in climate are natural and the result of human activities.

An example of a natural change is El Niño. This is warming of the waters off the west coast of South America. About every two to seven years, the eastern winds that blow over the central Pacific Ocean slow or reverse direction. This changes the ocean temperature and affects the weather worldwide.

Usually, these easterly winds bring seasonal rains and push warm ocean water toward Asia and Australia. In El Niño years, however, the winds push warm water and heavy rains toward the Americas. This can cause floods and mudslides

there. At the same time Australia and Asia experience drought conditions.

When the winds blow in the opposite direction, to the west, the warmer waters are pushed to the lands on the western Pacific rim. This is called La Niña. La Niña causes increased precipitation in places such as India and increased dryness on the eastern side of the Pacific.

4. What happens in the Americas during El Niño?

_____

GLOBAL WARMING (page 58)

What *is global warming?*

Scientists agree that air temperatures on the earth are increasing. Over the last 100 years, the temperature of the earth increased by one degree. But in the last 25 years, the rate has increased to 3.5 degrees.

Some scientists believe that this warming is part of the earth's natural warming and cooling cycles.

Other scientists argue that global temperature increases are caused by the **greenhouse effect**. The greenhouse effect occurs when the layer of gases released by the burning of coal and petroleum traps solar energy. This causes higher temperatures in the same way that a greenhouse traps solar energy.

As more nations become industrialized, the amount of greenhouse gases will also increase. Some scientists predict that, if global warming continues, ice caps will melt, flooding coastal areas, covering islands, and changing the global climate.

5. What are some of the predicted results of the greenhouse effect?

_____

Name _____   Date _____

World Climate Regions

BEFORE YOU READ

In the last section, you read about the factors that create and change climate.

   In this section, you will learn about the different climates that exist around the world.

AS YOU READ

Use this graphic to take notes on world climate regions.

World Climates

PLACES & TERMS

tundra flat, treeless lands forming a ring around the Arctic Ocean; also, the climate region there

permafrost constantly frozen subsoil

Defining a Climate Region (page 59)

How *are climate regions defined?*

Geographers use information about the weather over many years to describe a climate region. The two most important factors in defining different climates are temperature and precipitation. They also use the location on a continent, topography, and elevation to help describe the climate.

   The most common characteristic used to define climate is latitude. There are five general climate regions based on latitude. They are Tropical, Dry, Mid-Latitude, High Latitude, and Highland. Within the regions there are variations.

1. What are the five general climate regions?

_____

_____

Types of Climates

TROPICAL WET/TROPICAL WET AND DRY (pages 60–61)

What *are tropical climates like?*

The tropical wet region has little variation in temperature over the year. It is always hot, with an average temperature of 79° F. The days begin sunny, but rain falls almost daily. The average amount of rain in a year is about 100 inches.

   A tropical wet and dry climate has a rainy season in summer and a dry season in winter. Temperatures are cooler in the dry season and warmer in the wet season. Rainfall is less than in the tropical wet climate region. It falls mostly in the wet season.

2. Which climate has two seasons? What are they?

_____

_____

SEMIARID/DESERT (pages 61–62)
How do dry climates differ?

A semiarid climate region does receive precipitation, just not very much. Generally areas receive about 18 inches per year. Summers are hot. Winters are mild to cold. Some semiarid locations can have snow. This climate region is found in the interior of continents or in the zone around deserts. Even though it is dry, the region contains some of the most productive agricultural lands in the world.

Deserts receive less than ten inches of rain per year. They can also be hot or cool/cold. Hot deserts have low humidity and high temperatures during the day. At night, temperatures drop because the dry air cannot hold heat well. Cool/cold deserts are found in the mid-latitudes in the Northern Hemisphere.

3. Where are cool /cold deserts found?

_____

_____

MEDITERRANEAN/ MARINE WEST COAST/HUMID SUBTROPICAL (page 62)
What are climates like near large bodies of water?

The Mediterranean climate zone is named for the land around the Mediterranean Sea. Its summers are dry and hot, and its winters are cool and rainy. This climate region supports a dense population and rich agricultural activity.

The marine west coast climate region is frequently cloudy, foggy, and damp. The winds that blow over the warm ocean water keep the temperatures warm. Precipitation in this climate region is evenly distributed throughout the year.

Long periods of summer heat and humidity are found in humid subtropical climate regions. These areas are found on the east coast of continents. They often have hurricanes in late summer or autumn. Winters are mild to cool, depending on latitude.

4. How is a Mediterranean climate different from a marine west coast climate ?

_____

_____

HUMID CONTINENTAL /SUBARCTIC (pages 62–63)
What climate has four seasons?

A great variety in temperature and precipitation characterizes the humid continental climate region. It is found in the mid-latitude interiors of Northern Hemisphere continents. Air masses chilled by Arctic ice and snow flow south over these areas. They collide with tropical air masses coming from the south. This causes changing weather conditions. These areas experience four seasons.

Evergreen forests called taiga cover the lands in the subarctic region. Huge temperature variations occur in this region between summer and winter. Summers are short and cool, and winters are always very cold. Temperatures at or below freezing last five to eight months of the year.

5. Why does the humid continental region experience changing weather ?

_____

_____

TUNDRA/ICE CAP/HIGHLANDS (page 63)
What is permafrost?

The tundra region is located in the Northern Hemisphere. Very little precipitation falls here, usually less than 15 inches per year. The land has **permafrost**. This means the subsoil is constantly frozen. The summer lasts for only a few weeks. Then the temperature may reach about 40° F.

Snow, ice, and permanently freezing temperatures are typical of the ice cap climate region. It is so cold that it rarely snows. These regions are sometimes called polar deserts. This is because they receive less than ten inches of precipitation a year.

The highland climate varies with latitude, elevation, other topography, and continental location.

6. Why are ice caps called polar deserts?

_____

_____

Name _____ Date _____

Soils and Vegetation

BEFORE YOU READ

In the last section, you read about the world's different climates.

In this section, you will learn about the earth's soil and vegetation regions.

AS YOU READ

Use this graphic to take notes on soil and vegetation.

Soils and Vegetation

PLACES & TERMS

ecosystem an interdependent community of plants and animals

biome a regional ecosystem

deciduous broadleaf trees, such as maple, oak, birch, and cottonwood

rain forest a forest located in the tropical zone; covered with a heavy concentration of deciduous trees

coniferous another name for needleleaf trees

savanna grassy, mostly treeless plains in the tropical region

steppe temperate grassland region in some part of the Northern Hemisphere

Soil Regions (page 65)

Why *is soil important?*

Soil is a thin layer of weathered rock, organic material, air, and water. The world's food supply depends greatly on the top six inches of soil (sometimes called topsoil).

Such factors as depth, texture, and humus content of the soil help determine the type of vegetation that can be supported in a region. The type of vegetation helps to set up what human activities may take place. Soil characteristics and climate are major influences on vegetation regions.

1. What soil factors help determine the type of vegetation that can be supported in a region?

_____

_____

Vegetation Regions (page 65)

What *is an ecosystem?*

Vegetation regions are natural environments. They provide the stage for human activities such as farming, raising livestock, and producing timber. Soil, temperature, and moisture influence the type of vegetation that thrives naturally in a region.

Vegetation patterns are based on large-scale ecosystems and the environment. An **ecosystem** is an interdependent community of plants and animals. A regional ecosystem is referred to as a **biome**. Biomes are further divided into forest, grassland, desert, and tundra.

2. What are four types of biomes?

_____

_____

FORESTLANDS (page 66)
How are forestlands classified?

Forest regions are classified by the types of trees they support, broadleaf or needleleaf. Broadleaf trees, are also called <u>deciduous</u> trees. Examples of deciduous trees are maple, oak, birch, and cottonwood. The <u>rain forest</u> is located in the tropical zone. It is heavily covered with broadleaf trees. In the tropical rain forest region, some broadleaf trees remain green all year.

In other parts of the deciduous region, leaves fall at least once a year. This region is located in the Northern Hemisphere. Sometimes deciduous trees are mixed with needleleaf trees. These are trees such as pine, fir, and cedar. Needleleaf trees are also called <u>coniferous</u> trees because they have cones. They are found in forests in northern regions of North America, Asia, and Europe.

Trees and shrubs adapted to dry land areas make up the Mediterranean shrub and desert and dry shrub regions. In some locations, the drought-resistant trees and shrubs are called chaparral.

3. What is the difference between deciduous and coniferous trees?

_____

_____

GRASSLANDS/DESERT AND TUNDRA (page 66)
Where are grasslands found?

Grasslands are mostly flat regions dotted with a few trees. They are called by different names. In the tropical grassland region, they are called <u>savannas</u>. In the Northern Hemisphere's temperate grassland region, the terms <u>steppe</u> or prairie are used. Vast areas of Russia are covered with steppe. In the Southern Hemisphere, the temperate grasslands may be called as pampas.

The plants that live in the desert and tundra climate regions are specially adapted to tolerate the dry or cold conditions. In the tundra, plants that hug the ground, are best adapted to survive the cold, dry climate. Examples are mosses and lichens. In the desert, plants that can conserve water and withstand heat can be found. Plants such as cactus, sagebrush, or other shrubs dot the landscape.

4. What kinds of plants are found in tundra and desert areas?

_____

_____

Human Impact on the Environment
(page 67)

How do humans affect their world?

As you can imagine, the impact of humans on soil and vegetation is immense. Throughout this book, you will read about the ways that human beings have adapted to the land. People change their lifestyles or change the land by altering it to meet their needs. Changes can include building dams or *irrigation* systems, planting food crops, or slashing and burning the vegetation.

Unfortunately, humans can cause damage to soil and vegetation. Fragile biomes such as the tundra are easily damaged. Desert land is easily eroded. Building new houses destroys vegetation.

In some regions of the world, the careless use of land often leaves it in a condition that will not support life.

5. Why do humans sometimes alter the environment?

_____

_____

Name _____   Date _____

Glossary/After You Read

condense to go from a less dense to a more dense form, as with steam to water

elevation distance above a reference point usually sea level

flood stage the point where the banks of a river or stream can no longer hold the water.

irrigation a system for supplying water, especially where land would not naturally have an adequate water supply

leeward situated away from the wind

Places & Terms

A. Write the name or term in each blank that best completes the meaning of the paragraph.

equinox   solstice

precipitation   weather

rain shadow

The beginning of summer is the longest day of the year and is known as the summer

(1)_____. Twice a year on the (2)_____, the days

and nights all over the world are equal in length. (3)_____ is the

condition of the atmosphere at a particular location and time. When air gets colder or

thinner, water vapor may turn to (4)_____. When the windward side of

a mountain range gets all the moisture, the leeward side of the mountain is called a

(5)_____.

B. Circle the place or term that best completes each sentence.

1. The transfer of heat in the atmosphere by the upward motion of the air is
   _____.

   greenhouse effect   convection   climate

2. Some places are so cold that the subsoil is constantly frozen. This is called
   _____.

   tundra   biome   permafrost

3. Broadleaf trees are also known as _____ trees.

   deciduous   coniferous   chaparral

4. An interdependent community of plants and animals is a[n] _____.

   savanna   steppe   ecosystem

5. A _____ is a storm that forms over warm, tropical waters and circles
   around a calm eye.

   hurricane   blizzard   tornado

Main Ideas

1. What is a drought?

_____

_____

2. What are three or more major factors that influence climate?

_____

_____

3. What is the greenhouse effect?

_____

_____

4. How are deserts defined?

_____

_____

5. What types of trees are most common in the rain forest?

_____

_____

Thinking Critically

Answer the following questions on a separate sheet of paper.

1. How do elevation and latitude affect the type of climate found in a region?

2. In what ways do people adapt to climate and vegetation in a region?

The Elements of Culture

BEFORE YOU READ

In the last section, you read about the impact of human land use on the vegetation.

In this section, you will learn about how humans relate to each other and express themselves.

AS YOU READ

Use this graphic organizer to take notes on the elements of culture.

> Human Geography
>
> Cultural

PLACES & TERMS

culture the total knowledge, attitudes, and behaviors shared by and passed on by the members of a specific group

society shares a common language, a sense of identity, and its culture

ethnic group shares language, customs, and heritage but has an identity as a separate group within their region

innovation taking existing elements and creating something new from them

diffusion the spread of ideas, inventions, or patterns of behavior

cultural hearth a place from where ideas, materials, and technology spread out to other cultures

acculturation the acceptance or adoption of an innovation by a society

dialect speech patterns related to class, region, or other cultural changes

religion the belief in a supernatural power or powers that are regarded as creators and maintainers of the universe

Defining Culture (page 71)

What *is culture?*

<u>Culture</u> is the total knowledge, attitudes, and behaviors shared by and passed on by the members of a specific group. It helps people know how they should behave. It ties us to one group and separates us from others. It helps us solve the problems that all humans face.

A group that shares a common language, a sense of identity, and its culture is called a <u>society</u>. The term <u>ethnic group</u> refers to a specific group that shares language, customs, a common heritage, and an identity. They see themselves as a separate group and distinct from other groups in the region where they live.

1. How is an ethnic group defined?

_____

_____

Culture Change and Exchange (page 72)

Why *do changes occur?*

Cultures and societies are always in the process of changing. Taking existing elements of society and creating something new to meet a need is called <u>innovation</u>. Innovation and invention may happen on purpose or by accident.

Good ideas or inventions spread when people from different societies come into contact with one another. This spread of ideas, inventions, or patterns of behavior is called <u>diffusion</u>. A <u>cultural hearth</u> is a place from where ideas, materials, and technology spread out to other cultures.

Just being exposed to an innovation does not guarantee that people in a society will accept it. Before accepting an innovation, individuals must decide if an innovation is useful. **Acculturation** occurs when individuals in a society accept an innovation.

2. Why is innovation sometimes necessary?

_____

Language (page 73)

How *many languages are there?*

Language is one of the most important elements of culture. It allows people within a culture to communicate. Language helps establish cultural identity and a sense of unity.

But language can also divide people. Sometimes more than one **dialect**, or version, of a language is spoken in an area. A dialect refers to changes in speech patterns related to class, region, or other cultural changes.

Geographers estimate that between 3,000 and 6,500 languages are spoken across the world today. Languages with the same origin are called language families.

Language can be diffused in many ways. It may follow trade routes. Sometimes a blend of languages develops. The blended language aids communication among groups speaking several languages. Diffusion can also be the result of *migration*.

3. How does language both unite and divide?

_____

Religion (page 75)

How *are religions categorized?*

Religion is the belief in a *supernatural* power or powers that are regarded as creators and maintainers of the universe. Religions establish beliefs and values of a group. It defines how people worship the *divine* being or forces. It also tells them how to behave toward each other.

Traditionally, religions have been categorized in three ways. Monotheistic is a belief in one god. Polytheistic is a belief in many gods. Animistic is a belief in divine forces in nature.

Religions spread across the world through diffusion and converts. Converts are people who are take up a new religion and give up their former beliefs.

4. How have religions spread?

_____

Major Religions (pages 75–77)

What *are the world's major religions?*

Judaism is the oldest monotheistic religion. It is concentrated in Israel. Followers are called Jews. It has a long tradition of faith and culture tied tightly together.

Christianity evolved from the teachings of Judaism. It, too, is monotheistic. Christianity is based on the teachings of Jesus Christ.

Islam is based on the teachings of the Prophet Muhammad. Islam is a monotheistic religion. Its followers worship God, who in Arabic is called Allah.

Hinduism is an ethnic religion concentrated in India. It is usually considered to be polytheistic. Hinduism's rigid caste system shapes Hindus' lives.

An offshoot of Hinduism is Buddhism. It developed about 563 B.C. in India. Its founder, Siddhartha Gautama, is called the Buddha, or Enlightened One.

5. Which religions are monotheistic?

_____

Creative Cultural Expressions (page 77)

How *do different cultures express themselves?*

Cultures produce performing arts, visual arts, and written arts. Music is a cultural aspect found in all societies. However, the instruments and styles differ. Visual arts include architecture, painting, sculpture, and textiles.

Oral and written literature includes poems, folk tales, and stories. They often portray aspects of the attitudes and behaviors of the culture.

6. What forms do creative expressions take?

_____

Population Geography

BEFORE YOU READ
In the last section, you learned about how humans relate to each other and express themselves.

In this section, you will read about how geographers study the number and distribution of people.

AS YOU READ
Use this graphic organizer to take notes on population geography.

> Human Geography
>
> Population

PLACES & TERMS
birthrate the number of live births per thousand population

fertility rate the average number of children a woman would have in her lifetime

mortality rate also called the death rate, the number of deaths per thousand

infant mortality rate the number of deaths among infants under age one per thousand live births

rate of natural increase the rate at which the population is growing

population pyramid graphic device that shows gender and age distribution of population

push-pull factors reasons why people migrate

population density average number of people who live in a measurable area

carrying capacity the number of organisms a piece of land can support

Worldwide Population Growth
(pages 78–79)

What is mortality rate?

To understand population growth, geographers use several different statistics. One is the **birthrate**. It is the number of live births per thousand people in the population. Another way to study population is to look at the fertility rate. The **fertility rate** shows the average number of children an average woman might have in her lifetime.

The **mortality rate** is also called the death rate. It is the number of deaths per thousand people in the population. Geographers also look at **infant mortality rates**. The infant mortality rate shows the number of deaths among infants under age one per thousand live births.

To find the rate at which population is growing, subtract the mortality rate from the birthrate. The

result is the <u>rate of natural increase</u> or population growth.

1. How is population growth figured?

_____

_____

POPULATION PYRAMID (page 79)
What are population pyramids?

Another way to analyze population is to use a **population pyramid**. This is a type of graph that shows sex and age distribution of a population. A population pyramid allows geographers to see how such events as wars, famines, and epidemics affect the population of a country or region.

2. Why do geographers use population pyramids?

_____

_____

Population Distribution

HABITABLE LANDS (page 80)

Where *on the earth do most people live?*

The billions of people in the world are not spread equally across the earth. Almost 90 percent of the world's population lives in the Northern Hemisphere. One out of every two people lives in either East Asia or South Asia.

Factors such as climate, altitude, and access to water influence where people choose to live. Almost two-thirds of the world's population lives in the zone between 20° N and 60° N. The lands in this zone have the most suitable climate and vegetation for human settlement. The lands are warm enough and wet enough to make agriculture possible. Large populations are also found along seacoasts and river valleys.

3. What factors affect where people live?

_____

_____

URBAN–RURAL MIX/MIGRATION (pages 80–81)

Why *do people move?*

More than half of the world's population lives in rural areas. More people are moving into cities. Cities with populations of more than one million people are growing fastest. Twenty-six giant cities are home to a total of more than 250 million people.

The movement of people from one location to another also changes the distribution of population. Reasons for migrating are sometimes called <u>push-pull factors</u>. Push factors are when people feel pushed out of a region. Push factors might include a natural disaster. Pull factors encourage people to go to another land. Countries with lots of jobs and high salaries attract people.

4. How do push-pull factors affect migration?

_____

_____

Population Density (pages 81–82)

What *is population density?*

To understand how heavily populated an area is, geographers use a figure called <u>population density</u>. This figure is the average number of people who live in a measurable area such as a square mile. The number is found by dividing the number of people in an area by the amount of land they occupy. New Jersey has a density of 1,098 people per square mile. The United States averages out to 70.3 persons per square mile.

Population density numbers maybe misleading. The population is not distributed evenly across the land. Certain areas may be densely populated, while others are thinly populated.

5. How is population density figured?

_____

_____

CARRYING CAPACITY (page 82)

How *many people can the land support?*

<u>Carrying capacity</u> is the number of animals or humans a piece of land can support. An area with fertile land may be able to support many people. A land of poor quality or with little land available for cultivation can only support a few people.

The level of technology available to a group living on the land may affect carrying capacity. Improved farming practices may increase the carrying capacity of land.

6. What is carrying capacity?

_____

_____

Political Geography

BEFORE YOU READ

In the last section, you learned how geographers study population growth and density.

In this section, you will read about how the world's population forms into political units.

AS YOU READ

Use this graphic organizer to take notes on political geography.

```
┌─────────────────────────────────────────┐
│          Human Geography                 │
│                                          │
│                                          │
└─────────────────────────────────────────┘
              │
┌─────────────────────────────────────────┐
│            Political                     │
│                                          │
│                                          │
│                                          │
└─────────────────────────────────────────┘
```

PLACES & TERMS

state an independent unit that occupies a specific territory and has control of its internal and external affairs

nation a group of people with a common culture living in a territory and having a strong sense of unity

nation-state when a nation and a state occupy the same territory

democracy government in which citizens hold political power either directly or through elected representatives

monarchy government in which a ruling family holds political power and may or may not share the power with citizens

dictatorship government in which an individual or group holds complete power

communism government in which nearly all political power and means of production are held by the government

landlocked having no outlet to the sea

Nations of the World (page 83)

What is a country?

A country can be described in several ways. The political term <u>state</u> is used describe an independent unit that occupies a specific territory and has control of its internal and external affairs. Often, the term country is used to mean state.

<u>Nation</u> refers to a group of people with a common culture living in a territory and having a strong sense of unity. When a nation and a state occupy the same territory, that territory is called a <u>nation-state</u>. Many countries of the world are nation-states. However, it is possible for a nation not to have a territory. A group like this is called a stateless nation.

1. What is a nation-state?

_____

_____

TYPES OF GOVERNMENT (page 83)

How do types of government differ?

Generally, a type of government falls into one of four categories. In a <u>democracy</u>, citizens hold political power either directly or through elected representatives. In a <u>monarchy</u>, a ruling family, king, or queen holds political power and may or may not share the power with citizens.

In a <u>dictatorship</u>, an individual or group holds complete political power. <u>Communism</u> is a system in which nearly all political power and means of production are held by the government.

2. What are the four types of governments?

_____

_____

Geographic Characteristics of Nations (pages 84–85)

What *is a landlocked country?*

Three geographic characteristics are important in describing a country: size, shape, and relative location.

A larger nation may be more powerful because it has more resources. It may also have more people to build military or economic power.

The shape of a country can have an impact on how easily it can be governed. A long narrow country may be difficult to rule because contact with people in a distant part of the country may be difficult. Shape may affect how goods are moved to all areas of the country or how the country relates to neighboring countries.

The relative location of a country can be very important. For example, a nation surrounded by hostile neighbors must deal with issues of protection and security. A **landlocked** country is one with no outlet to the sea. Access to water means easy access to shipping. A landlocked nation must find ways to get goods into and from its land.

3. What geographic characteristics describe a country?

_____

_____

National Boundaries (pages 85–86)

Why *do states set boundaries?*

Boundaries or borders set the limits of the area controlled by the state. Inside the borders, the state can do such things as collect taxes, set up a legal code, or have an official language. A state may claim all of the resources found inside its boundaries. The two basic types of international boundaries are natural and artificial.

A natural boundary is based on physical features of the land. For example, rivers, lakes, or chains of mountains are natural boundaries. Traditionally, a boundary that uses a river or a lake divides the body of water in the middle.

Usually, an artificial boundary is a straight line following latitude or longitude lines. The 49°N latitude line that separates the United States and Canada is an example. These lines are often established in boundary treaties between countries. Sometimes a conquering country puts boundary lines on lands it has taken over.

4. What are some examples of natural and artificial boundaries?

_____

_____

Regional Political Systems (page 86)

What *other political units exist?*

Countries often are divided into smaller political units. This is done to make governing more efficient. The most common local units of government are cities, towns, and villages.

Smaller political units often combine to form larger regional units. They may do this to promote *mutual* goals. Countries, provinces, and states are examples.

Countries may join with each other to form international political, military, or economic units. The largest political unit is the United Nations. This group has nearly 200 members who work to improve political, cultural, and economic conditions across the globe.

5. Why do countries sometimes join together?

_____

_____

Urban Geography

BEFORE YOU READ

In the last section, you read about how the world's population forms into political units.

In this section, you will learn that almost half of the world's population lives in cities.

AS YOU READ

Use this graphic organizer to take notes on urban geography.

```
┌──────────────────────────────────────────────┐
│              Human Geography                   │
│                                                │
│                                                │
└──────────────────────┬───────────────────────┘
              ┌─────────┴──────────────────────┐
              │            Urban                 │
              │                                  │
              │                                  │
              └──────────────────────────────────┘
```

PLACES & TERMS

city area with large populations, center of business and culture

urban geography the study of how people use space in cities

suburb political unit touching the central city or touching other suburbs that touch the city

metropolitan area a functional area made up of the city, its suburbs, and its exurbs

urbanization rise in the number of cities and the changes in lifestyle that result

central business district (CBD) the commercial core of the city

Growth of Urban Areas (pages 87–88)

What *makes up an urban area??*

Today, almost half of the world's population lives in cities. **Cities** are not just areas with large populations. They are also centers of business and culture. Geographers have developed the field of **urban geography** to study of how people use space in cities.

An urban area develops around a main city called the central city. The built-up area around the central city may include **suburbs**. Suburbs are political units touching the central city or touching other suburbs that touch the city. Some suburbs are mostly homes with a few businesses. Other suburbs have a whole range of urban activities.

Exurbs are smaller cities or towns with open land between them and the central city. The city, its suburbs, and its exurbs are linked together economically. They form a functional area called a **metropolitan area**. When several metropolitan areas grow together a *megalopolis* is formed

The rise in the number of cities and the changes in lifestyles because people are living in cities are called **urbanization**.

1. What are suburbs?

_____

_____

City Locations (page 88)

What *is a good location for a city?*

Many cities are found on a river, lake, or coast. These locations have access to good transportation. Other cities are found in places with easy access to natural resources.

Cities are places where goods are moved from one type of transportation to another. In the city of Chicago, Illinois, for example, goods may arrive by truck or train. Then, the goods are moved to ships on the Great Lakes.

Cities attract businesses and people to work in those businesses. Cities may specialize in certain economic activities because of their location. For example, the city of Pittsburgh, Pennsylvania, is located close to iron ore and coal sources. It became a steel-producing center.

Urban areas may grow because of economic or governmental activities. In 1960, Brasilia, a new capital of Brazil, was constructed. Its population has grown to 1.8 million people. Cultural, educational, or military activities may also attract people to a specific location.

2. Why would location be important to a city?

_____

_____

Land Use Patterns (page 89)

How *is urban land used?*

Urban geographers also study land use in cities and the activities that take place in cities. Basic land use patterns found in all cities are:
- **residential,** including single-family homes and apartment buildings,
- **industrial,** areas for manufacturing of goods,
- **commercial,** private businesses and retail businesses.

The core of a city is almost always based on commercial activity. This area of the city is called the **central business district (CBD)**. Business offices and stores are found in this part of the city. In some cities, expensive housing may also be found here. The value of land in the CBD is high. In fact, the land is so expensive that tall buildings must be built to get the most value from the land.

As you move away from the CBD, other activities become more important. Residential housing begins to be the main type of land use.

The farther you get from the CBD, the lower the value of the land. Lower land values may lead to less expensive housing. In these less expensive areas are industrial activities and retail areas, such as shopping centers, markets, or bazaars.

3. What is the CBD?

_____

_____

The Functions of Cities (page 90)

Why *do cities need so much space?*

The city is the center of many types of functions. For example, within a few city blocks of the CBD, you might find retail shops, entertainment, and public transportation. Business, education, and government services are also provided in the CBD.

Cities need a great deal of space to serve all these functions. This makes good transportation important. Geographers often study a city's transportation system to understand how well the city is fulfilling its functions.

Major cities have several forms of *mass transit*. Mass transit includes bus systems, subways, or commuter trains. They move people to and from the areas of the city where the various functions take place. In some areas, freeway systems link people in the suburbs to the city.

4. Why is transportation essential in cities?

_____

_____

Chapter **4** Section 5 (pages 91–95)   *Reading Study Guide*

Economic Geography

BEFORE YOU READ

In the last section, you learned that almost half of the world's population lives in cities.

In this section, you'll read about the systems and resources that drive the world's economies.

AS YOU READ

Use this graphic organizer to take notes on economic geography.

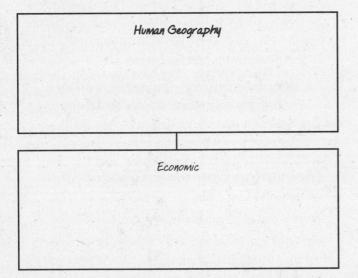

Human Geography

Economic

PLACES & TERMS

economy the production and exchange of goods and services

economic system the way people produce and exchange goods

command economy production of goods and services is determined by a central government

market economy production of goods and services is determined by the demand from consumers

natural resources materials on or in the earth that have economic value

infrastructure the basic support system needed to keep an economy going

per capita income amount of money earned by each person in a political unit

GNP the total value of all goods and services produced by a country in a time period

GDP the value of only goods and services produced within a country in a time period

Economic Systems (page 91)

What *are some ways people produce and exchange goods?*

An **economy** consists of the production and exchange of goods and services among a group of people. Geographers study economic geography by looking at the economic activities in a region.

The way people produce and exchange goods is called an **economic system**. Today, there are four basic types of economic systems.

- **Traditional Economy** Goods and services are traded. Money is not exchanged.
- **Command Economy** Production of goods and services is decided by a central government. The government usually owns the means of production.
- **Market Economy** Production of goods and

services is decided by the demand from consumers.

- **Mixed Economy** A combination of command and market economies. It is set up to provide goods and services to benefit all people.

1. How do command and market economies differ?

_____

Economic Activities (page 92)

What is subsistence agriculture ?

People meet their needs in a variety of ways. Some groups raise just enough food or animals to meet their own needs. This is called *subsistence* agriculture. In other areas people produce crops or animals to meet a demand in a larger market.

Industries are an important economic activity. Commercial industries meet the needs of people in a very large area. Small family-run industries may make goods to be sold locally. No matter how small or large a business is, it operates at one of four economic levels.

- **Primary Activities** involve gathering raw materials.
- **Secondary Activities** involve adding value to materials by changing their form.
- **Tertiary Activities** furnish personal or professional services.
- **Quaternary Activities** provide information, management, and research services.

2. What are the levels of economic activity?

The Economics of Natural Resources
(page 93)

What *are nonrenewable resources?*

An important part of economic geography is knowing which resources a nation has. <u>Natural resources</u> are materials on or in the earth that have economic value.

Natural resources are not distributed equally around the world. When geographers study a country's economy, they look closely at the location of the resources. They also look at the quality and quantity of the natural resources. They also divide natural resources into three basic types:

- **Renewable** These resources, such as trees, can be replaced through natural processes. Examples are trees.
- **Nonrenewable** These resources cannot be replaced once they have been removed from the ground—metals and *fossil fuels.*
- **Inexhaustible energy sources** These power-producing resources are the result of solar or Earth processes. They include sunlight, *geothermal* heat, winds, and tides.

3. What do geographers look for when studying a country's natural resources?

Economic Support Systems (page 94)

What *is infrastructure?*

A nation's <u>infrastructure</u> consists of the basic support system needed to keep an economy going. This would include such things as power systems, water, and sewer systems.

One of the most important parts of the infrastructure is transportation. Geographers look at the patterns of roads and highways, ports, and airports. This helps them to get an idea of how *accessible* an area is.

Communications systems give geographers an idea of how a country is linked internally. It also shows how the country is tied to the outside world.

One sign of the development of a country is how much technology is available. The education system is also a part of the infrastructure.

4. Why do economic geographers study a country's communications systems?

Measuring Economic Development
(pages 94–95)

How *do geographers compare economies?*

Geographers use a variety of standards to make comparisons among economies. One is <u>per capita income</u>. This is the average amount of money earned by each person in a political unit. Another way to compare is based on country's economic activities. A third method might be a comparison of a society's standard of living, health, or education.

A statistic commonly used to measure the economy of a country is the <u>Gross National Product (GNP)</u>. The GNP is the total value of all goods and services produced by a country over a specified period of time. The <u>GDP</u>, or <u>Gross Domestic Product</u>, is the value of only the goods and services produced within a country in a period of time.

5. What is the difference between GNP and GDP statistics?

Name _____   Date _____

Glossary/After You Read

accessible easy to reach, communicate with, or make use of

divine of or relating to a god, godlike

fossil fuels resources such as coal, petroleum, and natural gas

geothermal of or relating to the heat of the earth's interior

mass transit public transportation such as buses, subways or commuter trains

megalopolis a very large city formed by the merging of two or more metropolitan areas

migration moving from one place to another

mutual common, joint, equally shared

subsistence barely able to support life

supernatural of or relating to that which exists beyond the visible universe, usually used in relation to God, gods, or other spiritual beings

Places & Terms

A. If the statement is true, write "true" on the line. If it is false, write the word or words that would replace the underlined words to make it true.

_____ 1. A religion that worships many gods is said to be monotheistic.

_____ 2. An ethnic group is a specific group that shares language, customs, and a common heritage, but lives as a separate group within a region.

_____ 3. The infant mortality rate is the number of live births per thousand population.

_____ 4. In a democracy, citizens hold political power either directly or through elected representatives.

_____ 5. The materials on or in the earth that have economic value are called an infrastructure.

B. Write the name or term in each blank that best completes the meaning of the paragraph.

urbanization   diffusion

acculturation   innovation

infrastructure

Change is a common element of any culture or society. But change comes in a number of ways. With (1)_____, needs are met by creating something new out of existing elements of the society. Through (2)_____, these ideas, inventions, or patterns of behavior spread to other areas. If the ideas or inventions are useful, then (3)_____ occurs, and the new idea or invention is accepted or adopted by the society. (4)_____ is one change that has dramatically affected lives, as more and more people have moved from rural areas to cities. Today, technology has become part of the (5)_____ that supports an economy.

Main Ideas

1. Why is it that people are not distributed equally across the earth?

   _____

   _____

2. How is carrying capacity related to population density?

   _____

   _____

3. Why might it be a disadvantage for a country to be landlocked?

   _____

   _____

4. What are two geographic factors that might make a good location for a city?

   _____

   _____

5. What are some networks that are part of the infrastructure a country?

   _____

   _____

Thinking Critically

Answer the following questions on a separate sheet of paper.

1. Why are language and religion such important aspects of culture?

2. What are some advantages and disadvantages of trying to use more inexhaustible energy sources?

THE UNITED STATES AND CANADA

Landforms and Resources

BEFORE YOU READ

In the last chapter, you read about human geography—the way humans in general relate to their environment.

In this section, you will learn about the physical features and resources of the United States and Canada.

AS YOU READ

Use this chart to take notes about the landforms and resources of the United States and Canada.

Landforms	
Resources	

PLACES & TERMS

Appalachian Mountains major mountain chain in the eastern United States and Canada

Great Plains largely treeless area in the interior lowlands

Canadian Shield rocky, flat area that surrounds Hudson Bay

Rocky Mountains mountain chain in the western United States and Canada

Continental Divide line of the highest points in the Rockies that marks the separation between rivers flowing to the east and to the west

Great Lakes five large lakes found in the central United States and Canada

Mississippi River North America's longest river

Mackenzie River Canada's longest river

Landscape Influenced Development
(page 117)

How vast are these countries?

The United States and Canada occupy the central and northern four-fifths of the continent of North America. Culturally, the region is known as Anglo-America. This is because both countries were colonies of Great Britain at one time and because most of the people speak English. In addition to their physical geography and cultural heritage, the two countries are also bound together by strong economic and political ties.

The United States and Canada stretch across North America. In total area, they are the second (Canada) and third (the United States) largest countries in the world, behind Russia.

The United States and Canada are rich in natural resources. They have much fertile soil and water and many forests and minerals. This geographic richness has attracted immigrants from around the world for centuries.

1. What binds Canada and the United States together?

_____

_____

Many and Varied Landforms
(pages 119–121)

What features do these countries share?

All the major types of landforms are found in the United States and Canada.

A flat, coastal plain runs along the Atlantic Ocean and the Gulf of Mexico. One section is called the Atlantic Coastal Plain. It begins as a narrow lowland in the northeastern United States and widens as it extends into Florida. The broader section is called the Gulf Coastal Plain. It stretches from Florida to Texas along the Gulf of Mexico.

West of the coastal plain are the Appalachian Highlands. The **Appalachian Mountains** are part of the region. They stretch some 1,600 miles from Newfoundland to Alabama.

A huge area of mainly level land covers the interior of North America. Huge glaciers flattened the land thousands of years ago. The area has some of the most *productive* soil in the world.

The interior lowlands are divided into three subregions—the Interior Plains, the Great Plains, and the Canadian Shield. The Interior Plains spread out from the Appalachians to about 300 miles west of the Mississippi River. To the west are the **Great Plains**. These plains are a largely treeless area that rise to about 4,000 feet. North of the plains is the **Canadian Shield**. It is a rocky, flat region that covers nearly two million square miles around Hudson Bay.

West of the plains are the *massive*, rugged **Rocky Mountains**, the other major mountain system of the United States and Canada. The Rockies are a series of ranges that extend about 3,000 miles from Alaska south to New Mexico. Many peaks are more than 12,000 feet high. The **Continental Divide** is the line of the highest points in the Rockies. It marks the division between rivers flowing eastward and westward.

Between the Rockies and the Pacific Ocean is an area of mixed landforms. A series of ranges, including the Sierra Nevada and the Cascade Range, run parallel to the Pacific coastline from California to Alaska. Major earthquakes occur in the vicinity of the Pacific ranges. Between these ranges and the Rockies are steep cliffs, deep canyons, and lowland desert areas called basins.

Canada's northernmost lands are islands near the Arctic Circle. Two chains of volcanic islands are part of the westernmost United States. The Aleutian Islands extend in an arc off the coast of Alaska. The Hawaiian Islands lie in the central Pacific, about 2,400 miles southwest of the mainland.

2. What is the Continental Divide?

_____

_____

Resources Shape Ways of Life
(pages 121–122)

Which minerals are abundant?

Canada and the United States are bordered by three oceans—Atlantic, Pacific, and Arctic. The Gulf of Mexico is the southern boundary of the United States. As a result, both countries have important shipping and fishing industries.

Inland, there are large rivers and lakes that serve as sources of transportation, irrigation, hydroelectric power, fresh water, and fisheries. Eight of the world's fifteen largest lakes are found in the United States and Canada. Among these are the **Great Lakes**—Huron, Ontario, Michigan, Erie, and Superior.

The **Mississippi River** runs almost the length of the United States. It is part of the continent's longest and busiest river system. Canada's largest river is the **Mackenzie River**.

The United States and Canada contain some of the most fertile soils in the world. Because of this fact, North America is the world's leading food exporter.

The United States and Canada also have huge forests. About one-half of Canada is covered by woodlands. About one-third of the United States is. Both countries are major producers of lumber and forest products.

Huge quantities of minerals and fossil fuels gave both countries the means to industrialize rapidly. Deposits of iron ore, nickel, copper, gold, and uranium are located in the Canadian Shield. Gold, silver, copper, and uranium are found in the western mountains.

Both countries have large deposits of coal, natural gas, and oil. Both countries also are leading mineral producers.

3. What do significant water resources provide?

_____

_____

Name _____   Date _____

THE UNITED STATES AND CANADA
Climate and Vegetation

BEFORE YOU READ

In the last section, you read about the landforms and resources of the United States and Canada.

In this section, you will learn how climate and vegetation affect life in the United States and Canada.

AS YOU READ

Use this chart to take notes about the climate and vegetation of the United States and Canada.

Climate	
Vegetation	

PLACES & TERMS

permafrost permanently frozen ground

prevailing westerlies winds that blow from west to east

Everglades huge swampland in southern Florida

Shared Climates and Vegetation

(pages 123–124)

***Where** is the mildest shared climate found?*

The Arctic coastlines of Alaska and Canada have tundra climate and vegetation. Winters here are long and bitterly cold. Summers are brief and chilly. The land is a huge, treeless plain.

Much of the rest of Canada and Alaska have a subarctic climate. This climate has very cold winters and short, mild summers. A vast forest of needle-leafed evergreens covers the region. In some areas, there is **permafrost**, or permanently frozen ground.

The Rocky Mountains and the Pacific ranges have highland climate and vegetation. Temperature and vegetation vary with *elevation* and latitude. Generally, the temperature is colder and the vegetation is less in the higher, more northerly mountains. The mountains also affect the temperature and the amount of precipitation in nearby lower areas.

The north central and northeastern United States and much of southern Canada have a humid continental climate. Winters are cold and summers are warm. Climate and soil make this one of the world's most productive agricultural areas. It *yields* an *abundance* of dairy products, grain, and livestock.

In the upper part of this zone, summers are short. There are mixed forests of deciduous and needle-leafed evergreen trees. Most of the population of Canada is located here. The lower part of the zone is in the United States. Here, summers are longer. Generally, deciduous forests are found east of the Mississippi River. Temperate grasslands are found to the west.

The Pacific coast from northern California to southern Alaska has a climate described as marine west coast. Here, climate is affected by three factors. They are Pacific Ocean currents, the coastal mountains, and the **prevailing westerlies**. These are winds that blow from west to east. Summers are warm. Winters are long and mild but rainy and foggy. Vegetation includes dense forests of broad-leaved deciduous trees, needle-leafed evergreens, and giant California redwoods. The Washington coast even has a rain forest.

1. What climate do the prevailing westerlies create?

_____

_____

2. Which climates provide the longest growing seasons?

_____

_____

Differences in Climate and Vegetation (pages 124–126)

***What** are the Everglades?*

The milder, dry, and tropical climates of North America are found south of 40°N latitude. Much of the United States is located in these climate zones.

The southern states have a humid subtropical climate. This means that summers are hot and *muggy*. Winters are usually mild and cool. Moist air from the Gulf of Mexico brings rain during the winter. The combination of mild temperatures and enough rain provides a long growing season. A variety of crops are grown. Broad-leafed deciduous trees and needle-leafed evergreen trees are found here.

The central and southern coasts of California have a Mediterranean climate. Summers are dry, sunny, and warm. Winters are mild and somewhat rainy. A long growing season and irrigation make this a rich farming areas for fruits and vegetables.

The Great Plains and the dry northern parts of the Great Basin have a semiarid climate. The weather is dry. There are only about 15 inches of rain annually. Vegetation is mainly short grasses and shrubs.

The southwestern states have a desert climate. Here the weather is usually hot and dry. Less than ten inches of rain falls each year. Some cactus plants *thrive,* but much of the area is *barren* rock or sand.

In the United States, only Hawaii and southern Florida have tropical climates. The islands of Hawaii have a tropical wet climate that produces lush rain forests.

Southern Florida has a tropical wet and dry climate. It is always warm, but there are wet and dry seasons. Vegetation is mainly tall grasses and scattered trees, such as in the <u>Everglades</u>. The Everglades a huge swampland that covers some 4,000 square miles.

Effects of Extreme Weather (page 126)

***How** does weather hurt some areas?*

Weather can be harsh and sometimes deadly. In both cold and mild climates, severe storms can trigger widespread devastation.

Warm air from the Gulf of Mexico and cold Canadian air masses sometimes clash over the plains region. The result are violent thunderstorms, tornadoes, and blizzards. Tornadoes strike so often in one area of the Great Plains that it is called "Tornado Alley." In summer and fall, hurricanes sweep along the Atlantic and Gulf coasts. They can cause great damage. Winter snowstorms may bring normal life to a temporary halt in many cities.

Disasters can also result from too much water or not enough. Heavy rainfall can touch off flooding. Lands along major rivers, such as the Mississippi, are especially at risk. Too little rain or too much heat may bring on droughts and dust storms or cause forest fires.

3. What creates storms over the Great Plains?

_____

_____

THE UNITED STATES AND CANADA
Human-Environment Interaction

BEFORE YOU READ

In the last section you read about the climate and vegetation of the United States and Canada.

In this section, you will learn about the impact humans have had on the environment in the United States and Canada.

AS YOU READ

Use this graphic to take notes about the human-environment interaction in the United States and Canada.

Human-Environment Interaction

PLACES & TERMS

nomad person who moves from place to place

Beringia land bridge that once connected what are now Siberia and Alaska

St. Lawrence Seaway North America's most important deepwater ship route, connecting the Great Lakes to the Atlantic Ocean

lock section of a waterway with closed gates where water levels are raised or lowered

Settlement and Agriculture Alter the Land (page 127)

Where *did the first settlers come from?*

The first inhabitants of North America were nomads. **Nomads** are people who move from place to place. These people probably came from Asia over a land bridge that once connected what are now Siberia and Alaska. It was called **Beringia**.

These early migrants moved over the land. They hunted game and fish and gathered wild plants to eat. Water was necessary for survival. So, these first Americans made temporary settlements along coastlines and near rivers and streams. They were able to live in the extremes of temperature and climate in North America. They also adapted to the region's many environments. These included mountains, forests, plains, and deserts.

About 3,000 years ago, agriculture replaced hunting and gathering as the primary method of food production. Many early settlements became

permanent. As people began to grow crops, they changed the landscape to meet their needs. In wooded areas, early farmers cut down trees for houses and fuel. To plant crops, they plowed the rich soil of river valleys. They dug ditches for irrigation. Many of the plants that they were the first to grow are now *staples* throughout the world. These included corn, beans, and vegetables.

1. What led to settlements becoming permanent?

_____

_____

Building Cities (page 128)

How *did Montreal adapt to cold weather?*

Where a city is built and how it grows depends a great deal on physical setting. Landscape, climate, are important. So are the availability of water and natural resources.

Montreal, Quebec, is Canada's second largest city and a major port. Early French explorers liked Montreal's location. It is located on a large island where the St. Lawrence and Ottawa rivers meet. The French built a permanent settlement there in 1642. To make the city's severe winters more livable, people went inside and underground. In fact, large areas of Montreal of have been developed underground. These include a network of shops and restaurants.

Los Angeles has a mild climate year-round, unlike Montreal. It also has a good location on the Pacific Coast. Hundreds of thousands of people began pouring into this once small Spanish settlement by the early 1900s. During the 1980s, Los Angeles became the second most populous city in the United States.

Rapid growth brought problems. These included air pollution, inadequate water supplies, and construction on earthquake-threatened land. Los Angeles now covers about 469 square miles.

2. What do the locations of these two cities have in common?

_____

_____

Overcoming Distances (pages 128–130)

***What** connects the Great Lakes to the Atlantic Ocean?*

Some of the early people who came across the land bridge cut trails to the east. Others followed the Pacific Coast south toward warmer climates. Still others remained in the northwest, in what are now Alaska and northern Canada.

Later, the Europeans came. They set up colonies along the Atlantic Coast. Then, they moved inland. As they did, they carved overland trails, such as the National and Wilderness roads and the Oregon and Santa Fe trails. They also used inland waterways, such as the Mississippi and Ohio rivers. To connect bodies of water, they built canals. The Erie Canal across upstate New York opened in 1825. It was the first navigable water link between the Atlantic and the Great Lakes.

North America's most important deepwater ship route—the <u>St. Lawrence Seaway</u>—was completed in the 1950s. The seaway connects the Great Lakes to the Atlantic Ocean by way of the St. Lawrence River. Ships are raised and lowered some 600 feet by a series of <u>locks</u>. These are sections of the waterway with closed gates where water levels are raised or lowered.

Railroad building began in North America in the early 19th century. Many of the continent's physical features presented natural barriers. Railroad workers had to cut down forests, build bridges, and blast tunnels through mountains to make way.

The first *transcontinental* railroad across the United States was completed in 1869. A trans-Canada railroad was completed in 1885. These railroads promoted economic development and national unity as they went.

Before the railroads came, there were roads that connected towns and cities. Today, both the United States and Canada have extensive roadway systems.

The Trans-Canada Highway is Canada's primary roadway. It stretches about 4,860 miles. In the United States, the Interstate Highway System is a 46,000-mile network of highways that crisscross the country.

3. What spurred road building in the 20th century?

_____

_____

Name _____ Date _____

Glossary/After You Read

abundance an ample quantity

barren unproductive, producing hardly any vegetation

elevation height above the level of the sea, altitude

massive impressively large

muggy being warm, damp, and stuffy

productive having the quality of producing, especially abundantly

staple something having widespread and constant use or appeal

thrive to grow vigorously

transcontinental extending or going across a continent

yield to bear or bring forth

Places & Terms

A. Write the place or term in each blank that best complete the paragraph.

Mackenzie River   Canadian Shield

Mississippi River   Rocky Mountains

Continental Divide   Appalachian Mountains

North America has two major mountain chains that run north to south: the ancient

(1)_____ in the eastern half of the continent and the much younger,

much higher (2)_____ in the western half. Between these great ranges

there is an area of interior lowlands. The rocky northern part of this lowland region, the

(3)_____, encircles Hudson Bay. Water resources are abundant. Of the

region's many rivers, the (4)_____ is Canada's largest. The

(5)_____, part of the continent's longest and busiest river system, runs

almost the length of the United States.

B. Write the letter of the place or term next to the description that explains it best.

a. Everglades   d. Beringia

b. prevailing westerlies   e. lock

c. nomad

_____ 1. person who moves from place to place

_____ 2. huge tropical swampland in southern Florida

_____ 3. section of a waterway with closed gates where water levels are raised or lowered

_____ 4. winds that blow from west to east

_____ 5. land bridge that once connected what are now Siberia and Alaska

Main Ideas

1. What are four or more of the landforms shared by the United States and Canada?

_____

_____

2. Why is the land considered one of the continent's great resources?

_____

_____

3. Why are so many climate regions found in the United States?

_____

_____

4. What five climate regions do Canada and the United States share?

_____

_____

5. Why did the United States and Canada build the St. Lawrence Seaway?

_____

_____

Thinking Critically

Answer the following questions on a separate sheet of paper.

1. How have the natural resources of Canada and the United States affected how people live?

2. What are the similarities and differences between the activities of early settlers and those of later settlers?

History and Government of the United States

BEFORE YOU READ

In the last section, you read about the impact of human settlement on this region.

In this section, you will learn how one part of this region, the United States, developed and governs itself.

AS YOU READ

Use this graphic organizer to take notes on the history and government of the United States.

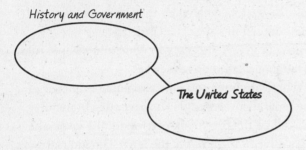

History and Government

The United States

PLACES & TERMS

migration movement of people from one place to another

Columbian Exchange movement of plants, animals, and diseases between the Eastern and Western hemispheres

Louisiana Purchase territory between the Mississippi River and the Rocky Mountains purchased by the United States from France

frontier free, open land that had been available for settlement in the West

suburb community on the outskirts of a city

representative democracy government where the people rule through elected representatives

Creating a Nation (pages 135–136)

***What** is the Columbian Exchange?*

The United States occupies about two-fifths of the North American continent. It is rich in natural resources. It has a moderate climate, fertile soil, and abundant water supplies. This natural wealth has attracted waves of immigrants seeking a better life. So is the constant **migration**, or movement, of people within the country.

The first inhabitants of North America were nomads who came from Asia at least 14,000 years ago. These Native American peoples developed separate cultures over the centuries. They alone occupied the land until Europeans began to explore in the 15th century.

In the early 1600s, the French settled along the northern Atlantic Coast and the St. Lawrence River in what is now Canada. During the 1600s and 1700s, the English colonized the Atlantic coast from present-day Maine south to Georgia.

European colonies often *displaced* Native Americans. The coming of Europeans also began the **Columbian Exchange**. This was the movement

of plants, animals, and diseases between the Eastern and Western hemispheres.

In 1763, Great Britain gained control of all of North America east of the Mississippi. But its control did not last long. Britain's 13 American colonies began to resent policies forced on them by a distant government. Their protests led to the American Revolution (1775–1783) and the founding of the United States.

In 1803, the United States nearly doubled in size. The government purchased the vast plains region between the Mississippi River and the Rocky Mountains from France. This territory became known as the **Louisiana Purchase**.

Immigrants from western Europe arrived in great numbers in the early 1800s. Meanwhile, people were placing loyalty to their region, or section, above loyalty to the nation. In 1861, these tensions led to a bloody, four-year civil war.

1. What nearly doubled the size of the United Stataes in 1803?

_____

An Industrial and Urban Society
(page 137)

When *was the frontier filled?*

Millions of Americans were on the move in the second half of the 19th century. Pioneers *blazed* trails across prairie, plains, and mountains.

To make way for white settlers, the U.S. government removed Native Americans. In 1869, a transcontinental railway was completed. Railroads then brought people to the West. They also took western cattle and products to markets in the East. By 1890, the free, open land that had been available for settlement—**the frontier**—was now filled.

As the West was being settled, immigrants mainly from western and eastern Europe poured into the United States. Both the recent immigrants and large numbers of Americans from rural areas went to the cities to work in the growing industries. The United States was being transformed from a rural, agricultural nation to an urban, industrialized one.

2. How did the United States change in the 19th century?

_____

World Power and Domestic Change
(pages 137–138)

What *was the Cold War?*

The United States had tried to avoid foreign involvement as it grew. Its many natural and human resources had made it almost self-sufficient. Also, it was protected from foreign conflicts by two oceans. But a global economic depression and two world wars brought changes.

The last half of the 20th century was a time of social change. Large numbers of people began moving from cities to surrounding **suburbs**. These are communities on the outskirts of cities. These years also saw much social unrest. During the 1960s and 1970s, the civil rights and women's rights movements worked for equality for all.

The U.S. economy boomed despite some periods of economic downturn. Providing services and information technology soon passed industrial production in importance.

American political influence was also spreading around the world. During the Cold War (1945–1990), the United States became the leader of the world's non-Communist nations. When communism in Europe collapsed in 1991, the United States became the world's only superpower.

3. How did the United States avoid foreign conflict at first?

_____

Governing the People (page 139)

What *is a federal republic?*

One of the strengths of the United States is the political system created by the U.S. Constitution. It was adopted in 1787. The United States is a **representative democracy** in which the people rule through elected representatives.

There are three separate and equal branches of the federal government. The executive branch, headed by the president, carries out the laws. The legislative branch makes the laws. The judicial branch interprets the laws.

4. What is the responsibility of the executive branch?

_____

Name _____ Date _____

Economy and Culture of the United States

BEFORE YOU READ

In the last section, you learned how the United States developed and governs itself.

In this section, you will read about the strength of the American economy and the diverse culture of the United States.

AS YOU READ

Use this graphic organizer to take notes on the economy and culture of the United States.

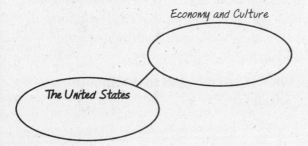

Economy and Culture

The United States

PLACES & TERMS

export goods sold to another country

free enterprise economic system in which private individuals own most of the resources, technology, and businesses and can operate them with little government control

service industry any kind of economic activity that provides a service rather than a product

postindustrial economy economic phase in which manufacturing no longer plays a dominant role

multinational corporation that engages in business worldwide

The World's Great Economic Power

(pages 140–142)

***What** is a postindustrial economy?*

The United States has the largest and most powerful economy in the world. It is also the most *diverse* and most technologically advanced economy. In global trade, it accounts for ten percent of the world's exports. <u>Exports</u> are goods sold to another country.

Three factors have contributed to the overall success of the American economy. The United States has an abundance of natural resources, a skilled labor force, and a stable political system that has allowed the economy to develop. The economy is run largely on <u>free enterprise</u>. In this economic system, private individuals own most of the resources, technology, and businesses. They can operate them with little control from the government.

The industrial output of the United States is larger than that of any other country in the world. The country's leading industries are petroleum,

steel, chemicals, electronics, transportation equipment, food processing, consumer goods, telecommunications, lumber, and mining.

The American economy today is driven by service industries. A <u>service industry</u> is any kind of economic activity that provides a service rather than a product. This economic phase is called a <u>postindustrial economy</u>. In this type of economy, manufacturing no longer plays a dominant role.

The United States is the world's major trading nation. It leads the world in the value of its exports and *imports*. Many American corporations engage in business worldwide and are called <u>multinationals</u>.

1. What three factors contributed to U.S. economic success?

_____

_____

A Diverse Society (pages 142–143)

How *many religions are practiced in the United States?*

The United States is a nation of different races and ethnic traditions. The majority of Americans—about 70 percent—trace their ancestry to Europe. Hispanic Americans, African Americans, Asian Americans, and Native Americans make up the rest of the population.

English has been the dominant language of the United States since its founding. Spanish is the second most commonly spoken language.

Religious freedom is a fundamental principal of American society. Today, more than 1,000 different religious groups practice their faiths in the United States. By far, the majority of the American people—85 percent—are Christians. Jews and Muslims each account for about 2 percent of the religious population.

The rich artistic heritage of the United States is a result of its diverse population. Native Americans were its first artists, making pottery, weavings, and carvings.

Truly American styles began to develop in painting, literature, music, and architecture in the 19th century. They showed the country's expansive landscape and the uniqueness of American life.

2. Why is there ethnic diversity in the United States?

_____

_____

American Life Today (pages 143–144)

Where *do Americans live?*

More than 280 million people live in the United States. About 80 percent of Americans live in cities or nearby suburbs. Americans moved first from rural areas to cities and then from cities to suburbs. The move to the suburbs was made possible by the widespread ownership of automobiles.

A highly developed transportation network aids mobility. Americans also move from state to state and region to region. They want to find better jobs, milder climates, and lifestyles that suit them.

Nearly 50 percent of Americans are employed. Many of these jobs are highly skilled positions that require advanced education. Americans have always valued education. They see it as a means to provide equality and opportunity. Nine out of ten students are in the public school system, where education is free through high school. There are also more than 2,300 four-year colleges and universities in the United States.

Americans have many choices for leisure-time activities. They can take part in a wide range of sports as either *spectators* or players. Americans also engage in hobbies, visit museums and libraries, and watch television and movies.

But not all Americans live well. Some are jobless or homeless. Both government and society are trying to bring these people into mainstream American life.

3. What made the shift to the suburbs possible?

_____

_____

Subregions of the United States

BEFORE YOU READ

In the last section, you read about the economy and culture of the United States.

In this section, you will learn about the four subregions of the United States.

AS YOU READ

Use this graphic organizer to take notes on the economy and culture of the United States.

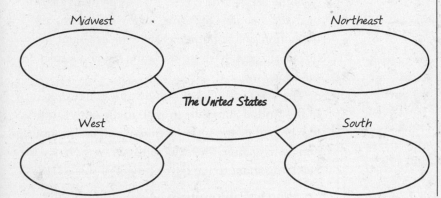

PLACES & TERMS

New England six northern states of the Northeast subregion

megalopolis area in which several large cities and surrounding areas grow together

the Midwest subregion that contains the 12 states of the north central United States

the South subregion of 16 states that covers about one-fourth of the land area of the United States

metropolitan area large city and its nearby suburbs and towns

the West subregion of 13 states that stretches from the Great Plains to the Pacific Ocean and includes Alaska and Hawaii

The Northeast (pages 145–147)

What *is a megalopolis?*

The Northeast includes Maine, Vermont, New Hampshire, Massachusetts, Rhode Island, and Connecticut. These states are called **New England**. The other three—Pennsylvania, New York, and New Jersey—are sometimes referred to as the Middle Atlantic States. Many of the places first settled by Europeans are located here, along the Atlantic coast.

Many people still fish and farm, as early settlers did. But the area's coastal and inland waters turned it into the heart of trade, commerce, and industry for the country.

Most Northeasterners are now employed in such manufacturing and service industries as electronics, communications, chemicals, medical research, finance, and tourism.

Traditional industries and cold winters earned the Northeast the title of "rust belt." In recent times, many "rust belt" industries have moved to warmer climates.

The nation's first **megalopolis** (a region in which several large cities and surroundings areas grow together) developed in the Northeast. The "Boswash" megalopolis, as it is called, covers a 500-mile area from Boston to Washington, D.C.

1. Which states make up New England?

_____

_____

The Midwest (page 147)

Why *is this region called the "heartland?"*

The subregion that contains the 12 states of the north central United States is called the **Midwest**. It is known as the American heartland because of its central location.

Vast, largely flat plains are a major feature of the region. So are many waterways. They include the Great Lakes and the Mississippi River and its many tributaries.

Shaping an Abundant Land **57**

The Midwest is the nation's "breadbasket." It has fertile soil, adequate rainfall, and a favorable climate. These factors enable Midwesterners to produce more food and feed more people than farmers in any similar area in the world.

Agriculture is also the basis of many of the region's industries. They include meatpacking, food processing, farm equipment, and *grainmilling.* Its central location and excellent waterways make the Midwest a trade, transportation, and distribution center.

2. What makes the Midwest a "breadbasket?"

_____

_____

The South (page 148)

How *is the South changing?*

The South is a subregion that covers about one-fourth of the area of the United States. Like the Northeast, the South was also the site of early European settlement. Virginia was England's first American colony.

The South's mix of cultures shows the diversity of its early settlers. There are people of British heritage, descendants of Africans brought as slave laborers, and Hispanics. Louisiana has Cajuns of French-Canadian origin and Creoles of French and Spanish descent. Also, many Hispanics from Cuba call Florida home.

The South is often referred to as the "sunbelt" because of its warm climate. Agriculture was the South's first economic activity. Cotton, tobacco, fruits, peanuts, and rice are still grown there.

The South's humid subtropical climate at first *hindered* industrialization. But industry was given a boost by the widespread use of air conditioning in the 1950s. The subregion also has vast stores of oil, coal, natural gas, and water.

In recent times, the South has attracted many industries moving away from the harsh weather of the "rust belt." The South's climate draws millions of tourists and retirees, too. There are also many rapidly growing **metropolitan areas**—large cities and their nearby suburbs and towns—in the South.

3. What helped industrialization in the South?

_____

_____

The West (pages 148–149)

What *economic activities are found here?*

The West is a subregion of 13 states that stretches from the Great Plains to the Pacific Ocean and includes Alaska and Hawaii. Its dramatic landscapes include high mountains, dense forests, sunny beaches, and icy tundra.

Some areas of the West, such as its many deserts, have few people. California, on the other hand, is the nation's most *populous* state. Its excellent farmland, good harbors, and mild climate attract millions.

The West is the most rapidly growing subregion in the United States. Its growth in the 20th century was helped by the introduction of air conditioning and by irrigation. The availability of water has also been important to the development of inland cities.

4. Why is California so heavily populated?

_____

_____

Chapter 6 Shaping an Abundant Land

Glossary/After You Read

blazing creating and marking a trail (a *blaze* is a trail marker)

displaced removed from the usual place; pushed out and replaced

diverse having many different forms or aspects

grainmilling grinding of grains at a mill to produce flour or meal

hindered made progress slow or difficult

imports things that are bought from other countries

populous crowded, densely populated

spectators onlookers, people who watch

Places & Terms

A. Write the letter of the place or term next to the description that explains it best.

a. the Midwest   d. Louisiana Purchase

b. New England   e. postindustrial economy

c. Columbian Exchange   f. free enterprise

_____ 1. economic phase when manufacturing no longer plays a dominant role

_____ 2. the movement of plants, animals, and diseases between the Eastern and Western hemispheres

_____ 3. economic system in which private individuals own most of the resources, technology, and businesses and can operate them with little government control

_____ 4. the six northern states of the Northeast region

_____ 5. the territory between the Mississippi River and the Rocky Mountains purchased by the United States from France

B. Circle the place or term that best completes each sentence.

1. A region in which several large cities and surrounding areas grow together is a

   _____.

   metropolitan area   megalopolis   multinational

2. A government in which people rule through elected representatives is a

   _____.

   federal republic   free enterprise   representative democracy

3. _____ is the movement of people from one place to another.

   sectionalism   export   migration

4. _____ is also sometimes called the heartland or the nation's breadbasket.

   the South   the Midwest   the West

5. The most populous state in the nation is found in _____.

    the West   New England   the South

Main Ideas

1. What has attracted immigrants to the United States over the centuries?

2. How was the economy changing in the second half of the 20th century?

3. How has the success of the American economy affected the lives of Americans?

4. What current trends do the four subregions of the United States have in common?

Thinking Critically

Answer the following questions on a separate sheet of paper.

1. English is the most commonly spoken language in the word today, even in countries where it is not the official language. What aspects of American economy and culture have contributed to this?

2. Why do you think that the United States has been such an economic power?

History and Government of Canada

BEFORE YOU READ

In the last section, you read about the four subregions of the United States.

In this section, you will learn how Canada developed and governs itself.

AS YOU READ

Use this graphic organizer to take notes on the history and government of Canada.

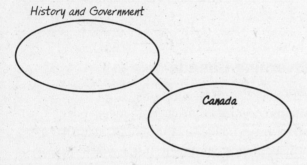

History and Government

Canada

PLACES & TERMS

province political unit of a country

Dominion of Canada confederation of Canadian provinces

confederation political union

parliamentary government system where legislative and executive functions are combined in a legislature called a parliament

parliament legislature

prime minister head of a parliamentary government

The First Settlers and Colonial Rivalry
(pages 155–156)

Who settled Canada?

Canada's vast size and its cold climate *significantly* affected its development. As you read in Chapter 5, people from Asia began moving into North America thousands of years ago.

Some early people remained in what are now the Canadian Arctic and Alaska. These people were ancestors of the Inuit (or Eskimos). Others gradually moved south, into present-day British Columbia and beyond.

Europeans first came in the 15th century. In 1497, explorer John Cabot landed in Newfoundland. He claimed the area for England. Then, during the 16th and 17th centuries, French explorers claimed much of North America. Their settlements in Canada were called New France. The British colonized North America along the Atlantic coast.

The coastal fisheries and the inland fur trade were important to both countries. Soon, there was conflict. The French and British challenged each

other's territorial claims. Britain defeated France in the French and Indian War, 1754–1763.

1. Why did France and Britain fight?

_____

_____

Steps Toward Unity (pages 156–157)

What was the British North America Act?

Canada had become a land of two distinct cultures by the end of the 18th century. There were the Roman Catholic French and the Protestant English. Conflicts erupted between the two groups. So, in 1791, the British government split Canada into two **provinces**, or political units. Upper Canada (later, Ontario) located near the Great Lakes had an English-speaking majority. Lower Canada (later, Quebec) located along the St. Lawrence River had a French-speaking population.

Over the next few decades, Montreal, Toronto, and Quebec City developed as major cities in the

Developing a Vast Wilderness **61**

region. Population grew, as large numbers of immigrants came from Great Britain. Railways and canals were built. Also, explorers moved across western lands to find better fur-trading areas.

Tension between English-speaking and French-speaking settlers continued. The British government decided that major reform was needed. In 1867, it passed the British North America Act. This law created the **Dominion of Canada**.

The Dominion was to be a loose **confederation**, or political union. It would consist of Ontario (Upper Canada), Quebec (Lower Canada), and the British colonies of Nova Scotia and New Brunswick on the Atlantic coast.

The Dominion grew rapidly. Manitoba, British Columbia, and Prince Edward Island were added. By 1871, Canada stretched to the Pacific Ocean. Soon, the Yukon Territory, Alberta, and Saskatchewan followed.

2. Why was the Dominion of Canada formed?

_____

_____

Continental Expansion and Development (pages 157–158)

What was the first step for growth?

Canada had much available land to settle. It tried to make it easier for pioneers to get to this land. In 1872, the government began to build a transcontinental railroad. In 1885, the main line of the railway, from Montreal to Vancouver, was completed.

A little more than a decade later, gold was discovered in the Yukon. Fortune hunters from around the world headed to Canada. Not long after, copper, zinc, and silver deposits were found. These discoveries led to the building of new railroads and towns. At the same time, immigrants from other parts of Europe besides Britain were coming to Canada's vast open lands.

Early settlers had lived in rural areas and engaged in farming. But Canada became increasingly urban and industrial as its population grew and natural resources were developed. Cities and towns first sprang up wherever farming was possible. Later, these same areas became manufacturing and service industry centers.

Most of this growth took place within 100 miles of the U.S. border. There, the climate was warmer and the land more productive. Also, transportation linking east and west was more readily available.

3. What brought immigrants to Canada in the late 1800s?

_____

_____

Governing Canada (page 158)

What is a parliament?

Britain recognized Canada as an independent nation in 1931. Like Great Britain, Canada has a **parliamentary government**. It is a system where legislative and executive functions are combined in a legislature called a **parliament**.

A central federal government and smaller provincial and territorial governments govern Canada. Canada is an independent country, but its symbolic head of state is still the British *monarch*. All legislative matters are the responsibility of the Parliament. The majority party's leader in Parliament becomes **prime minister**, or head of the government.

Each of Canada's ten provinces has its own legislature and premier (prime minister).

4. How is it determined who heads the government?

_____

_____

Chapter **7** Section 2 (pages 159–163)   *Reading Study Guide*

Economy and Culture of Canada

BEFORE YOU READ

In the last section, you learned how Canada developed and governs itself.

In this section, you will read about the strength of Canada's economy and the diversity of its people.

AS YOU READ

Use this graphic organizer to take notes on the economy and culture of Canada.

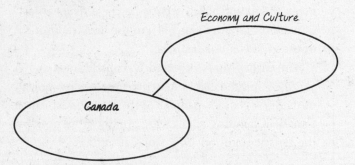

PLACES & TERMS

First Nations Canada's native peoples

métis people of mixed French and native heritage

reserve public land set aside by the government for Canada's native peoples

An Increasingly Diverse Economy
(pages 159–160)

What *industries contribute to Canada's wealth?*

Canada's early economy was based on the trade of its many natural resources. Canada's native peoples started trading with European fishermen in the 16th century. Its native peoples are called the <u>First Nations</u>.

Farming, logging, mining, and fishing were early economic activities and remain important to Canada's economy.

Canada produces large amounts of food for *domestic* use and for sale abroad. Canada's biggest export trade is in forest products. No other country exports more wood pulp and paper products than Canada. Mining is a major industry because of Canada's vast mineral deposits.

The coastlines of the Atlantic, Pacific and Arctic oceans provide Canadians with an abundance of fish. But Canadian fish *consumption* per person is low. So, much of the fish catch is exported.

About 15 percent of Canadians earn their living from manufacturing. However, it is Canada's service industries that are the country's real economic powerhouse. More than 60 percent of Canada's GDP comes from service industries. These industries employ more Canadians than all other industries combined. Service industries include finance, utilities, trade, transportation, real estate, communications, insurance, and tourism.

Canada's economy has always relied on trade. The United States is Canada's chief trading partner.

In 1994, Canada and the United States, along with Mexico, signed the North American Free Trade Agreement (NAFTA). This pact made trade between them even easier.

1. Where does Canada's greatest economic strength lie today?

_____

_____

_____

A Land of Many Cultures (pages 161–162)

Who *are the métis?*

Canada is a land of diverse cultures. Its first settlers came from Asia. Thousands of years later, Europeans arrived. English and French explorers began colonizing the land. Interaction between the French and native peoples gave rise to another culture, the métis. The **métis** are people of mixed French and native ancestry.

Later immigrants from Europe and Asia have also made their contributions to the cultural mix of Canada. As in the United States, Canada's cultural richness has come from all corners of the world.

Canada is officially a bilingual country. It has an English-speaking majority and a French-speaking minority.

Cultural differences caused conflict as the English and French settled Canada. The English were largely Protestant. The French were Roman Catholic. Religious and cultural conflicts between the two groups have continued over the years. Today, these two groups continue to *dominate* Canadian society.

Where people settled in Canada has always been influenced by the country's harsh environment and by the accessibility of transportation routes. Canada's port cities and its rich farmlands make up the country's most densely settled areas. Most Canadians live on a 100-mile-wide strip of land just north of the Canadian-U.S. border.

Canada's population has become more urban. At the beginning of the 20th century, about one-third of the people lived in urban areas. One hundred years later, nearly four-fifths were city dwellers. Many of Canada's native people are located on the country's 2,300 **reserves**. These reserves are public lands set aside for native peoples by the government.

2. What historic conflicts still exist in Canada?

_____

_____

Life in Canada Today (pages 162–163)

What *sports do Canadians enjoy?*

Most Canadians live active personal and professional lives. They enjoy a high standard of living. In 1998, Canada's labor force was nearly evenly split between men and women. Canada's population is well educated. Today, Canada boasts a 97 percent literacy rate.

Canadians value their leisure time. Sports such as skating, ice hockey, fishing, skiing, gold, and hunting are popular. The Canadian love of sport stretches back to its native peoples. They developed the game of lacrosse.

Canada's long history and cultural diversity have given the nation a rich artistic heritage. The earliest Canadian literature was born in the oral traditions of the First Nations peoples.

The early visual art included realistic Inuit carvings and the elaborately decorated totem poles of the First Nations peoples of the West Coast. Later, Canadian painting styles were greatly influenced by the artistic traditions of European settlers.

3. Where did Canada's love of sport have its roots?

_____

_____

Subregions of Canada

BEFORE YOU READ

In the last section, you read about the economy and culture of Canada.

In this section, you will learn how each of Canada's four subregions is unique.

AS YOU READ

Use this graphic organizer to take notes on the economy and culture of Canada.

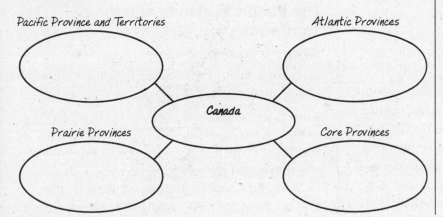

Pacific Province and Territories

Atlantic Provinces

Canada

Prairie Provinces

Core Provinces

PLACES & TERMS

Atlantic Provinces four provinces—Prince Edward Island, New Brunswick, Nova Scotia, and Newfoundland—located in eastern Canada

Ontario one of Canada's Core Provinces

Quebec one of Canada's Core Provinces

Prairie Provinces provinces of Manitoba, Saskatchewan, and Alberta

British Columbia Canada's westernmost province

Nunavut territory that is home to many of Canada's Inuit

The Atlantic Provinces (pages 166–167)

Why is this region's population so small?

Canada is divided into ten provinces and three territories. Eastern Canada is the location of the four <u>Atlantic Provinces</u>—Prince Edward Island, New Brunswick, Nova Scotia, and Newfoundland.

The Atlantic Provinces are home to just eight percent of Canada's population. Most people live in the region's coastal cities. The small population is due largely to the provinces' rugged *terrain* and *severe* weather.

About 85 percent of the land in Nova Scotia cannot be farmed because of rocky hills and poor soil. In New Brunswick, forests cover 90 percent of the land. Newfoundland is visited by fierce storms.

New Brunswick's dense forests provide the province with its largest industry—logging. The Gulf of St. Lawrence and coastal waters supply plentiful seafood for export. Also, there is mining for zinc, copper, lead, and silver.

Logging and fishing are *mainstays* of the economy of Nova Scotia, too. This province has one of the largest fish-processing plants in North America. Shipbuilding and trade provide more employment and revenue.

Fishing was the principal industry in Newfoundland until the 20th century. Today, the province also has major mining and logging industries. Its hydroelectric-power resources are important, too. They are a part of a system that supplies power to Quebec and parts of the northeastern United States.

1. What are the primary industries of this region?

_____

_____

The Core Provinces—Quebec and Ontario (pages 167–168)

Why *is this called Canada's heartland?*

Canada's most dynamic region are **Quebec** and **Ontario**, Canada's Core Provinces.

Quebec and Ontario are often referred to as Canada's heartland. Three out of five Canadians live here. Most of the settlement in these inland provinces is found along the Great Lakes and the St. Lawrence River. Each province is the core of one of Canada's two major cultures. A large number of Canada's English-speaking majority live in Ontario. For most French-speaking Canadians, Quebec is home.

Ontario and Quebec are at the center of Canada's political life. Ottawa, Ontario, is the capital of the federal government. Quebec has its own political importance as the heart of French Canadian life.

Ontario and Quebec also power Canada's economy. Together, they account for more than 35 percent of Canada's agricultural production, 45 percent of its mineral output, and 70 percent of its manufacturing.

Toronto, located on the shores of Lake Ontario, is not only the country's most populous city but also its banking and financial center. Montreal, located on the St. Lawrence River, is Canada's second largest city. It is also the heart of economic and political activity in Quebec province.

2. How do the cultures of these provinces differ?

The Prairie Provinces (page 168)

How *diverse is this region?*

The **Prairie Provinces**—Manitoba, Saskatchewan and Alberta—lie to the west of Ontario and Quebec. They are part of the Great Plains of North America. The three provinces are the center of the nation's agricultural region. They are responsible for 50 percent of Canada's agricultural production. In addition, about 60 percent of Canada's mineral output comes from this region. Alberta itself has the nation's largest known deposits of coal and oil and produces 90 percent of Canada's natural gas.

The people of the Prairie Provinces are a diverse group. Manitoba has large numbers of Scots-Irish, Germans, Scandinavians, Ukrainians, and Poles. The population of Saskatchewan also includes immigrants from south and east Asia and is home to the métis. Alberta is perhaps the most diverse of all. In addition to European immigrants, this province also has significant numbers of people from India, Japan, Lebanon, and Vietnam.

3. How important is the region's mineral output?

The Pacific Province and the Territories (pages 168–169)

When *was Nunavut created?*

Canada's westernmost province is **British Columbia**. Nearly all of it lies within the Rocky Mountains. As a result, three-fourths of the province is 3,000 feet or more above sea level. Over half of the land is heavily forested. About one-third is frozen tundra, snowfields, and glaciers.

Most of the population lives in the southwest. This is where British Columbia's two largest cities, Victoria and Vancouver, are located. The economy is built on logging, mining, and the production of hydroelectric power. Vancouver is Canada's largest port and has a successful shipping trade.

Canada's three territories—Yukon Territory, Northwest Territories, and Nunavut—make up 41 percent of the country's land area. Yet, they do not have large enough populations to be provinces.

The Yukon Territory is largely unspoiled wilderness. The Northwest Territories is directly east and extends into the Arctic. **Nunavut** was carved out of the eastern half of the Northwest Territories in 1999. It is home to many of Canada's Inuit.

4. Why is British Columbia so far above sea level?

Name _____ Date _____

Glossary/After You Read

consumption the process of using up; the using of economic goods to satisfy wants

domestic relating to and limited to the country being considered

dominate to have the number one place or position

mainstay a chief support

monarch a person who reigns over a kingdom, such as a king or queen

severe inflicting hardship or discomfort; harsh

significantly in important ways

terrain a piece of earth; environment

Places & Terms

A. Write the place or term in each blank that best completes the meaning of the paragraph.

Nunavut	Ontario
First Nations	prime minister
British Columbia	parliament

Canada was originally settled by people from Asia. They became Canada's native peoples, now known as the (1)_____. Some of them migrated south or east, but a group called the Inuit stayed in the north. Today, many of Canada's Inuit live in the territory of (2)_____. There are three territories in Canada and ten provinces. The westernmost province of Canada is (3)_____. These provinces and territories are governed from the capital of Ottawa. Canada has a legislature called a (4)_____. The leader of the government is the (5)_____.

B. Write the letter of the place or term next to the description that explains it best.

a. métis   d. Atlantic Provinces

b. reserve   e. Prairie Provinces

c. confederation

_____ 1. public land set aside by the government for Canada's native peoples

_____ 2. four provinces—Prince Edward Island, New Brunswick, Nova Scotia, and Newfoundland—located in eastern Canada

_____ 3. people of mixed French and native peoples descent

_____ 4. provinces of Manitoba, Saskatchewan, and Alberta

_____ 5. political union

Main Ideas

1. What are two ways in which settlement by the French and the English affected Canada's development?

   _____

   _____

2. How did Canada's climate affect the distribution of the population?

   _____

   _____

3. What abundant natural resources have contributed to Canada's economic strength?

   _____

   _____

4. What are the Core Provinces? Why is this region sometimes called Canada's heartland?

   _____

   _____

5. Which subregion is the center of Canada's agricultural production?

   _____

   _____

Thinking Critically

Answer the following questions on a separate sheet of paper.

1. What are some of the advantages of having a bilingual nation? What are some of the disadvantages?

2. What are three or more elements of the development, culture, economy, and life of Canada that are similar to those in the United States? Explain.

Name _____ Date _____

The Fight Against Terrorism

BEFORE YOU READ
In the last section, you read about the uniqueness of each of Canada's four subregions.

In this section, you will read about the fight against terrorism in the United States and around the world.

AS YOU READ
Use this chart to take notes about terrorism in the United States and around the world.

	Causes	Effects
Issue 1: Terrorism		

PLACES & TERMS
terrorism the surprise use of violence by an individual or group to intimidate a government or civilian population for social or political ends

global network worldwide interconnected group

coalition alliance

biological weapons bacteria and viruses that cause diseases

The September 11 Attacks
(pages 173–174)

***What** happened during the September 11 attacks?*

<u>Terrorism</u> is the surprise use of violence by an individual or group to intimidate a government or civilian population to achieve social or political ends. On the morning of September 11, 19 Arab terrorists hijacked four airplanes. They crashed two planes into the World Trade Center towers in New York City. They crashed one plane into the Pentagon in Washington, D.C. Another plane crashed in Pennsylvania. The hijackers may have been overtaken by a group of passengers who had learned about the World Trade Center attacks from their cellular phones.

The hijacked planes became missiles as they crashed into the twin towers. Thousands of people were able to escape before the towers eventually crumbled. The plane that crashed into the Pentagon tore a 75-foot hole into the building. Over 3,500 people died in the attacks. This number includes 350 New York City firefighters who died while trying to rescue people in the twin towers. Eight

buildings were either destroyed or partially collapsed. The disaster area in New York covered 16 acres.

After the attacks, investigators worked to find those responsible for the attacks. Investigators pointed to a <u>global network</u> of Islamic terrorists known as al-Qaeda. Saudi millionaire Osama bin Laden leads al-Qaeda. Al-Qaeda opposed American involvement in Muslim lands. Al-Qaeda has planned and carried out many terrorist attacks to oppose this involvement.

1. Who is responsible for the attacks of September 11?

_____

_____

Aftermath of the Attacks (pages 174–175)
***How** did the United States and the world react to the attacks?*

The attacks shocked Americans and its allies. George W. Bush called the attacks "acts of war." He promised to punish those responsible. He also pushed for new security measures.

The United States sought to build a **coalition** of nations to fight terrorism. These nations pledged to share information on terrorists, arrest terrorists, and seize financial assets of terrorists. The group also supported U.S.-led air strikes in Afghanistan where Osama bin Laden was based. In October, 2001, the United States also sent in ground forces to hunt down bin Laden and destroy al-Qaeda.

New airport security measures were put into place after the attacks. Also, extra steps were taken at public places such as sports stadiums and mass transit. The Office of Homeland security was also created to organize homeland security measures.

2. What new security measures were enacted after September 11?

_____

_____

Facing Terrorist Threats
(page 175)

What other terrorist threats exist?

Terrorism has been a problem for many years. Preventing terrorism is difficult. Terrorists move in secret. Some terrorist groups want territory, like the Palestinian extremists in Southwest Asia. Others want to change government policies like the domestic terrorists who bombed the federal building in Oklahoma City in 1995.

Biological weapons are bacteria or viruses that cause diseases. After September 11, letters containing anthrax were sent to members of the news media and members of Congress. Investigators believe that the letters may have been the work of a lone terrorist rather than an organized group.

The United States and its allies want to eliminate the threat of terrorism. They want to break up terrorist groups and increase security. This fight could last many years. The United States and its allies also have to balance security with maintaining peoples' freedoms and individual rights.

3. What are some of the goals of terrorist groups?

_____

_____

Urban Sprawl

BEFORE YOU READ

In the last section, you read about the issue of managing natural resources in the United States and Canada.

In this section, you will learn how these countries are addressing the problem of urban sprawl.

AS YOU READ

Use this chart to take notes about the issue of urban sprawl in the United States and Canada.

	Causes	Effects
Issue 2: Urban Sprawl		

PLACES & TERMS

urban sprawl poorly planned development that spreads a metropolitan population over a wider and wider area

infrastructure basic facilities, services, and installations needed for a community to function

smart growth efficient use and conservation of land and other resources in growing cities

sustainable community community where residents can live and work

Growth Without a Plan (pages 176–177)

Where *does urban sprawl occur?*

North Americans often choose to work in a city but live in its suburbs. They are attracted to the suburbs by new housing and open spaces. As outlying areas become more populated, the land between them and the city fills in as well.

Metropolitan areas become larger and more difficult to manage as suburbs become more numerous. Poorly planned development that spreads population over a wider and wider geographical area is called **urban sprawl**.

Urban sprawl is a matter of increasing concern in North America. From 1970 to 1990, people who worked in U.S. cities moved farther and farther from urban centers. The population density of cities in the United States decreased by more than 20 percent. About 30,000 square miles of rural lands were gobbled up by housing developments.

Canada is less populated than the United States but has similar problems. In the 1990s, more than 75 percent of all Canadians lived in urban areas.

Sprawl occurs in metropolitan areas that allow unrestricted growth or that have no plans to contain it. Other factors also contribute to sprawl. These include unlimited use of automobiles and the growth of expressways.

Autos and relatively cheap gasoline allow Americans to drive many miles to and from their jobs. Despite clogged highways and long commutes, Americans have been *reluctant* to use mass transit.

Many Americans try to recapture the sense of community they experienced while growing up. They want their children to know their neighborhoods and have a backyard in which to play. Most American cities only recently have begun to plan neighborhoods with a sense of community. Traditionally, city dwellers have sought this way of life in the suburbs.

1. How does the unlimited use of automobiles contribute to urban sprawl?

_____

_____

Urban Sprawl's Negative Impact
(page 177)

How *can urban sprawl affect costs?*

Urban sprawl has a negative impact on the quality of life in many ways. As the perimeters of cities grow, more commuter traffic strains the infrastructure. **Infrastructure** consists of the basic facilities, services, and installations needed for a community to function. Sources of water, such as rivers or underground aquifers become depleted. More cars on the road add to air pollution, too.

Urban sprawl causes housing costs to rise. The cost of providing streets, utilities, and other public facilities is often at least 25 percent higher in suburbs. Urban sprawl also separates the well-off from the poor. Lower-income residents can become isolated in inner city areas.

2. How does increased commuting affect infrastructure?

_____

_____

Solutions to Sprawl (page 178)

What *is smart growth?*

More and more cities are developing plans for **smart growth**—the efficient use and conservation of land and other resources. Most often this involves encouraging development close to or inside the city limits. Good public transportation systems make smart growth possible.

In 1971, the city of Portland, Oregon, drew a line around itself to create its urban growth boundary. Building was allowed inside the boundary. The surrounding green space was off limits to developers. This decision caused *controversy* but has paid off. Portland has contained urban sprawl.

Since 1961, Vancouver, British Columbia, has seen the population of its metropolitan area double. The growth of outlying suburbs often took place at the expense of forests, farms, and flood plains. In 1995, the Greater Vancouver Regional Board adopted a plan to manage growth. It involved turning suburbs into **sustainable communities**. These are communities where residents can live and work.

Not all city governments respond to the concerns of their citizens. So, people often band together to offer their own solutions. For example, the citizens of Durham, North Carolina, opposed additional commercial development along a *congested* area of nearby interstate highway.

Urban sprawl has had a major impact on the quality of life for North America's increasingly urban population. It challenges us to plan wisely for continued growth and development in the 21st century.

3. Which problems do sustainable communities solve? Which remains unsolved?

_____

_____

Diverse Societies Face Change

BEFORE YOU READ

In the last section, you read about efforts to deal with urban sprawl in the United States and Canada.

In this case study, you will examine the challenge of balancing cultural diversity with national unity.

AS YOU READ

Use this chart to help you understand the diversity of the United States and Canada.

	Causes	Effects
Case Study: Diverse Societies		

PLACES & TERMS

immigrant person who comes to a country to take up permanent residence

mosaic design created from many smaller pieces

domestic relating to one's own country

assimilation when minority people adopt the language, customs, and lifestyles of the dominant culture

"Mosaic" or "Melting Pot"

(pages 180–181)

What task has diversity created?

North America is culturally diverse. <u>Immigrants</u> have come from all over the world. Asian, Eastern European, and Latin American neighborhoods are found in most large cities in the United States and Canada. In New York City alone, immigrant schoolchildren speak more than 100 different languages.

The arrival of so many peoples created the difficult task of forming unified societies. Each of these two countries has approached the task in a different way.

Canada created a cultural "<u>mosaic</u>," composed of many different pieces. In addition to its native peoples, Canada's early settlers were French and English. As Canada developed, its peoples kept their separate identities.

The Canadian government encouraged immigrants to come. It wanted to fill Canada's empty lands. It also wanted to expand its workforce and <u>domestic</u> markets—the markets in the country.

Immigrants were encouraged to retain their cultural identities. As a result, Canadians have strong ethnic ties.

In 1988, the Canadian government enacted the Canadian Multiculturalism Act. This was designed to protect and promote diversity. Many people believe that this policy ensures equality for people of all origins. Others feel that this multicultural policy promotes difference at the expense of national unity. There is no sense of "Canadianness."

The United States has often been described as a "melting pot." For many years, people in the United States thought assimilation was the best way to create unity. <u>Assimilation</u> occurs when people from a minority culture adopt the language, customs, and lifestyles of the people from the dominant culture.

People expected immigrants to assimilate. Those who did not could face prejudice because of their differences. Immigrants who assimilated underwent "Americanization." Most of these immigrants came from Europe. Many wanted to assimilate. They wanted to adopt the language and culture—to become Americans.

1. How do opinions about Canada's multicultural policy differ?

_____

_____

New Immigrants Challenge Old Ways
(page 181)

How did things change in the late 20th century?

Immigrants to the United States in the last half of the 20th century brought different attitudes. These immigrants came mainly from Latin America and Asia. They were culturally or racially unlike earlier immigrant groups. These later immigrants were less willing to give up their traditions and languages.

Some Americans felt that these people did not understand what made the United States unique. The strength of the United States comes from blending its diverse cultures to create something new—an American. They also believed that keeping different languages and customs would promote separation and not unity. Other Americans thought that American society would benefit by stressing multiculturalism, as the Canadians do.

2. What are the two views on diversity in the United States?

_____

_____

The Concerns Are Real (page 182)

Can unity be maintained?

Newspaper Article: It appears that the idea of "One nation, indivisible" is now history. The immigrants of today are coming from still-developing nations in Asia and Latin America. Soon, no one ethnic group will be in the majority, including whites of European descent. Once, there was a yearning to be an American, to be part of the culture. Today, people want to preserve their ethnic identities.

Political Commentary: With the current influx of immigrants, the United States may not survive as "one nation." We need to halt illegal immigration. We need to teach newly adopted Americans our history, traditions, and language.

3. Why do people think that the United States will no longer be "one nation?"

_____

_____

Diversity Is Here (page 183)

What evidence is there of growing multiculturalism?

Social Commentary: The melting pot concept spoke of all Americans being part of the United States. Many people saw the United States as being a place where historical hurts from their homelands could be erased. In contrast to the melting pot, multiculturalism encourages us to take pride in our own roots first. By appreciating our own cultures, we develop an interest in others' origins.

U.S. Government Document: The 2000 census form contained detailed racial and ethnic classifications. This form showed the diverse make up of the population of the United States.

Canadian Law: According to the Canadian Multiculturalism Act, it is the policy of the Government of Canada to recognize and promote multiculturalism. The government sees multiculturalism as a fundamental part of Canada's heritage and identity. The law states that understanding and creativity will come from the interaction between individuals and communities of different origins.

4. How does the Canadian Multiculturalism Act view multiculturalism?

_____

_____

Name _____   Date _____

Glossary/After You Read

congested clogged   **reluctant** unwilling

controversy discussion marked by expression of opposing
views; dispute

Places & Terms

A. If the statement is true, write "true" on the line. If it is false, write the word or words that
would replace the underlined words to make the statement true.

_____   1. Planning for the efficient use and conservation of land and other resources
is called <u>smart growth</u>.

_____   2. The basic facilities, services, and installations needed for a community to
function is called <u>urban planning</u>.

_____   3. President Bush formed a <u>coalition</u>, or alliance, after the attacks of September 11.

_____   4. Poorly planned development that spreads a city's population over a wider
and wider geographical area is called <u>sustainable community</u>.

_____   5. <u>Terrorism</u> is the surprise use of violence to achieve a political or social end.

B. Write the name or term in each blank that best completes the meaning of the paragraph.

smart growth   urban sprawl

sustainable communities

infrastructure

In North America, as people leave the cities and rural lands are gobbled up by housing

developers, (1)_____ is becoming a matter of increased concern. As

cities spread out, more commuter traffic strains the (2)_____. To reduce

the amount of commuting, Vancouver created (3)_____, where

residents could live near their work. People are becoming more aware of the problems

that unlimited growth can cause. As a result, more and more cities are developing plans

for (4)_____, the efficient use of and conservation of land and other

resources.

Main Ideas

1. What was the damage caused by tthe attacks of September 11?

   _____

   _____

2. What steps is the United States taking to end terrorism?

   _____

   _____

3. How does the Canadian Multicultural Act differ from the American policy of assimilation?

   _____

   _____

4. Which of the suggestions for containing urban growth do you think make the most sense?

   _____

   _____

Thinking Critically

Answer the following questions on a separate sheet of paper.

1. How might changes in cities and increasing population be contributing to urban sprawl?

2. To contain urban sprawl, what impact would there be both on the economy and on people's lives if they were limited to working near where they lived?

LATIN AMERICA
Landforms and Resources

BEFORE YOU READ

In the last chapter, you read about resources and urban sprawl in the United States and Canada.

In this section, you will learn about the physical features and resources of Latin America, and how they shape life in the region.

AS YOU READ

Use this chart to take notes about the landforms and resources of Latin America.

Landforms	
Resources	

PLACES & TERMS

Andes Mountains mountains in South America; part of a chain of ranges that runs down the Pacific coast of North, Central, and South America

llanos grassy plains in Colombia and Venezuela; used for grazing and farming

cerrado grassy plains in the interior of Brazil; undeveloped, but suitable for grazing and farming

pampas grassy plains in Argentina and Uruguay; used for grazing and farming

Orinoco River river that winds through the northern part of the continent, mainly in Venezuela

Amazon River one of the world's greatest river, flows about 4,000 miles from west to east across the continent

Paraná River a river with origins in the highlands of southern Brazil

Mountains and Highlands (pages 201–202)

Where are the Andes Mountains?

Latin America stretches from the southern borders of the United States down to the southernmost tip of South America—almost 7,000 miles. It is bounded by the Atlantic and Pacific oceans, the Gulf of Mexico, and the Caribbean Sea.

The <u>Andes Mountains</u> of South America are part of a chain of mountain ranges that runs down the Pacific coast of North, Central, and South America. There are many active volcanoes throughout the Andes.

The Andes Mountains have made settlement along the Pacific coast more difficult. They are a barrier to movement from the coast into the interior. As a result, more settlement in South America has occurred along the eastern and northern coasts.

Highlands are the mountainous or hilly sections of a country. The Guiana Highlands are in the

northeast of South America. The Brazilian Highlands are in southeastern Brazil.

1. How did the Andes Mountains affect settlement of South America?

_____

_____

Plains for Grain and Livestock
(page 202)

How are the llanos, cerrado, and pampas alike?

South America has areas of wide plains. The plains offer rich soil for growing crops and abundant grasses for grazing livestock. The vast, grassy, and treeless plains of Colombia and Venezuela are called <u>llanos</u>.

In Brazil the plains are called <u>cerrado</u>. A flat terrain and moderate rainfall make them suitable for farming. The government of Brazil is encouraging settlers to move into the interior and develop this land.

In Argentina and Uruguay, the plains are known as **pampas**. The main products are cattle and wheat grain.

2. Why does Brazil's government want people to move into the country's interior?

_____

_____

The Amazon and Other Rivers
(pages 202–203)

What are South America's major rivers?

South America has three major river systems. The **Orinoco River** flows more than 1,500 miles to the Atlantic. It flows partly along the Colombia-Venezuela border.

The **Amazon River** is one of the world's greatest rivers. It flows about 4,000 miles eastward, across the central lowlands. The Amazon River is fed by more than 1,000 smaller rivers. The Amazon carries more water to the ocean than the next seven largest rivers of the world combined.

The **Paraná River** has its origins in the highlands of southern Brazil. It travels about 3,000 miles south and west through Paraguay and Argentina. It empties into the Atlantic.

3. Why is the Amazon one of the world's greatest rivers?

_____

_____

Major Islands of the Caribbean
(page 203)

What are the largest islands of the Caribbean?

The Caribbean islands consist of three major groups: the Bahamas, the Greater Antilles, and the Lesser Antilles. These islands together are sometimes called the West Indies.

The Bahamas are made up of hundreds of islands. They lie off the southern tip of Florida and north of Cuba. They extend southeast into the Atlantic Ocean

The Greater Antilles are made up of the larger islands of the Caribbean. These include Cuba, Jamaica, Hispaniola, and Puerto Rico.

The Lesser Antilles are the smaller islands in the region southeast of Puerto Rico.

4. Why are Cuba, Jamaica, Hispaniola, and Puerto Rico part of the Greater Antilles?

_____

_____

Resources of Latin America
(pages 204–205)

What resources exist in Latin America?

The mineral resources of Latin America include gold, silver, iron, copper, bauxite, tin, lead, zinc, and nickel. In addition, mines in this region produce precious gems, titanium, and tungsten. Many of these minerals are exported to other parts of the world.

Oil, coal, natural gas, uranium, and *hydroelectric* power are plentiful. Venezuela and Mexico have major oil reserves. Mexico is able to export oil to other countries.

Brazil is rich in hydroelectric power because of its many rivers and waterfalls. It is also rich in oil and gas. Trinidad has discovered vast reserves of natural gas. These have attracted manufacturers to the island.

In addition, Latin America is rich in agricultural resources and timber.

5. What resources does Latin America's export?

_____

_____

Name _____   Date _____

LATIN AMERICA
Climate and Vegetation

BEFORE YOU READ

In the last section you read about Latin America's landforms and resources.

In this section, you will learn how climate and vegetation affect life in Latin America.

AS YOU READ

Use this chart to take notes about the climate and vegetation of Latin America.

Climate	
Vegetation	

PLACES & TERMS

rain forest dense forests, made up of different species of trees, that grow in areas of high rainfall

A Varied Climate and Vegetation
(page 207)

What *climate regions are found in Latin America?*

The climate of Latin America ranges from the hot and *humid* to the dry and desert-like. Rain forest, desert, and savanna are all found in the region.

The vegetation is varied. It includes rain forests, grasslands, and desert *scrub*. It ranges from the thick trees of the rain forests to the mosses of the tundra.

This variety of climate and vegetation is due to several factors. First, Latin America spans a great distance on either side of the equator. Second, there are massive mountains in the region. This creates big changes in altitude. Third, ocean currents affect the climate. The currents of the Atlantic are warm, and the currents of the Pacific are cold.

1. What three factors are responsible for the varied climate and vegetation of this region?

_____

_____

Tropical Climate Zones (pages 207–208)

What *creatures live in the rain forest?*

The tropical climate zones of the region produce both rain forests and grasslands.

<u>Rain forests</u> are dense forests made up of different species of trees. Rain forests form an ecosystem in the region. An ecosystem is a community of plants and animals living in balance. Rain forests are found in the tropical wet climate zones. The climate in these areas is hot and rainy year round.

Rain forests are abundant in Central America, the Caribbean, and South America. The largest rain forest is the Amazon rain forest. It covers more than two million square miles of South America. Much of this rain forest is located in Brazil.

Rain forests contain many *exotic* plants and animals. Scientists have counted more than 2,500 varieties of trees in the Amazon rain forest. One of these trees is the Brazil nut tree, which grows 150 feet high. Living in these rain forests are anacondas, which are the among the largest snakes in the world. There are also jaguars, the great cats of Latin

America. In the water are piranhas, sharp-toothed, meat-eating fish.

Tropical wet and dry climate zones are found mainly in South America. Savannas are grasslands dotted with trees. They are common in tropical and subtropical regions. Savannas are found in Brazil, Colombia, and Argentina.

2. Where are rain forests abundant?

_____

_____

Dry Climate Zones (pages 208–209)

***Where** is the Atacama Desert?*

Dry climate zones are found in Mexico and in some countries in South America. Neither Central America nor the Caribbean has dry climate zones.

A semiarid climate is dry, with some rain. Vast grass-covered plains are often found in semiarid climate zones. Desert *shrubs* may also grow in semiarid regions. Such regions are found in Mexico, Brazil, Uruguay, and Argentina.

Parts of northern Mexico are classified as desert. So is much of the coast of Peru. The Atacama Desert is in northern Chile. Argentina's southern zone, Patagonia, contains a desert.

3. What vegetation grows in the semiarid regions?

_____

_____

Mid–Latitude Climate Zones (page 209)

***Which** climate zones are found in Argentina?*

Latin America's mid-latitude, moderate climate zones are located south of the equator.

Humid subtropical areas have rainy winters and hot, humid summers. Parts of Paraguay, Uruguay, southern Brazil, and northern Argentina are located in humid, subtropical climates. The vegetation is varied.

Part of Chile along the west coast has a Mediterranean climate. There are hot, dry summers and cool, moist winters. The climate is similar to that of California. The vegetation in this climate is mainly chaparral (drought-resistant trees and shrubs).

A marine west coast climate runs along the coast of southwestern South America. This climate is similar to that of Oregon or Washington. It has cool, rainy winters and mild, rainy summers. Parts of southern Chile and Argentina have this climate. Forests are the typical vegetation.

Highland climate zones vary depending on the altitude. They can be moderate to cold. Highland climates are also influenced by sunlight, the wind, and the landscape. Highland climates are found in the mountains of Mexico and South America.

4. What factors can affect highland climates?

_____

_____

Name _____ Date _____

LATIN AMERICA
Human-Environment Interaction

BEFORE YOU READ

In the last section you read about Latin America's climate and vegetation.

In this section, you will learn about the impact humans have had on the environment in Latin America.

AS YOU READ

Use this graphic to take notes about the human-environment interaction in Latin America.

Human-Environment Interaction

PLACES & TERMS

slash-and-burn technique of cutting and burning trees, brush, and grasses to clear fields for planting

terraced farming ancient technique of cutting step-like fields for growing crops on hillsides or mountain slopes

push factors factors that push people to leave rural areas

pull factors factors that pull people to the cities

infrastructure things that contribute to making a place livable, such as sewers, roads, electricity, and housing

Agriculture Reshapes the Environment (pages 210–211)

What *is the slash-and-burn technique?*

Native peoples in the Western Hemisphere changed their environment to grow food. They changed the course of streams to irrigate their crops. They built raised fields in swampy areas.

Native peoples in Latin America cleared fields to grow crops. They used the <u>slash-and-burn</u> technique. That means they cut trees, brush, and grasses, and burned them to clear a field to plant. This method was particularly effective in humid and tropical areas.

Today, farmers practice the same method in the Amazon River basin in Brazil. They clear land for farming in the rain forest. But the people use destructive farming practices. After a few years, they find that the soil is exhausted—all the nutrients have been drained from the land. When that happens, they move on and clear a new patch to farm.

<u>Terraced farming</u> is an ancient technique for growing crops on hillsides or mountain slopes. Terraces are like wide steps cut into hillsides or slopes. Each wide step creates a flat area where crops can grow. Terraced farming allows steep land to be *cultivated*. Farmers and workers living in the mountainous areas of Latin America create these terraces. The technique also reduces soil erosion. The Inca of Peru practiced this technique hundreds of years ago.

1. How can farmers plant crops in mountainous areas?

_____

_____

Urbanization: The Move to the Cities (pages 211–212)

What *factors "pull" people to the cities?*

Throughout Latin America, people are moving from

rural areas into the cities. People leave farms and villages in search of jobs and a better life. Cities have grown rapidly.

Argentina, Chile, and Uruguay are the most highly urban countries in South America. More than 85 percent of the people live in cities.

Many people in rural areas struggle to make a living. They grow barely enough to keep themselves and their families alive.

Both push and pull factors are at work. **Push factors** are factors that "push" people to leave rural areas, such as poor medical care, poor education, and low-paying jobs. **Pull factors** are factors that "pull" people toward cities, such as higher paying jobs, better schools, and better medical care.

Six cities in South America rank among the region's largest. These include São Paulo and Rio de Janeiro in Brazil, Buenos Aires in Argentina, Lima in Peru, Bogatá in Colombia, and Santiago in Chile. But the biggest city in Latin America is Mexico City.

Similar problems *afflict* cities throughout the region. Slums spread over larger and larger areas. Often, unemployment and crime increase. In addition, there are many environmental problems. These include high levels of air pollution. Some cities have shortages of drinkable water.

Local governments cannot afford facilities—also called the **infrastructure** (including sewers, transportation, electricity, and housing)—to handle the population increase.

2. What problems are created by rapid urbanization?

_____

_____

Tourism: Positive and Negative Impacts (pages 212–213)

How *does tourism create jobs?*

Tourism is a growth industry for Latin America. Every year, millions of tourists visit the resorts of Latin America. They spend money and help create jobs. New hotels, restaurants, boutiques, and other businesses have sprung up on Caribbean islands and in Mexico. Local people are hired to staff the ships, hotels, and restaurants. They profit from the visitors.

In this way, tourism can play a part in reducing the income gap between rich and poor. Jobs in hotels, restaurants, and resorts raise incomes and give people a stake in society.

Though tourism brings income and jobs to Latin America, it causes problems as well. Resorts may be built in previously unspoiled settings. Congestion and pollution begin to increase. Also, the gap between rich tourists and less well-off local residents can produce resentment and hostility.

More important, local governments can run up large public debts. They borrow money to build tourist facilities. Airports and harbors must be constructed. Hotels and resorts must be built. Sewage systems and shopping areas must be expanded.

Often, the profits go to the country of the owners and investors. These absentee owners often make decisions that are not in the tourist country's best interest. They may also influence such things as local politics, elections, and business decisions.

3. What has created resentment in some tourist areas?

_____

_____

Chapter **9** From the Andes to the Amazon   ***Reading Study Guide***

Glossary/After You Read

afflict to trouble, to injure

cultivate to prepare and use for raising crops

exotic strikingly or excitingly different

humid damp, characterized by moisture

hydroelectric relating to production of electricity by waterpower (hydro comes from the Greek for water)

scrub vegetation that consists mostly of stunted trees and shrubs

shrub a low, woody plant, usually with several stems

Places & Terms

A. Write the name or term in each blank that best completes the meaning of the paragraph.

Paraná River	terraced farming
rain forest	cerrado
Andes Mountains	slash-and-burn

In South America, the (1)_____ have made settlement along the Pacific coast more difficult. They are a barrier to movement from the coast into the interior. Because these mountains were steep, the native peoples developed (2)_____ to make it possible to grow plants. Inland, the Amazon River flows across northern Brazil. The Amazon River basin contains vast plains. These savannas, or (3)_____, are suitable for farming but are largely undeveloped. Also in Brazil is the largest (4)_____ in the world. It covers more than two million square miles and is home to many exotic plants and animals. Unfortunately, the poor often use the (5)_____ technique to clear small farms, which is hurting the rain forest and its variety of species.

B. Write the letter of the place or term next to the description that explains it best.

a. Amazon River	d. terraced farming
b. Orinoco River	e. pull factors
c. pampas	f. infrastructure

_____ 1. grassy plains of northern Argentina and Uruguay

_____ 2. flows 4,000 miles from east to west and carries more water to the ocean than any other river in the world

_____ 3. a technique of cutting steps into hillsides or mountains to create step-like fields for planting crops

_____ 4. the facilities needed to make a community work, such as sewers, transportation, electricity, and housing

_____ 5. issues or circumstances that pull people to a place

Main Ideas

1. What use has been made of the wide plains in South America?

_____

_____

2. What are two impressive facts about the Amazon River?

_____

_____

3. What factors contribute to the great variety of climate zones in Latin America?

_____

_____

4. Who first began to alter the land to meet their needs? What two techniques did they develop that are still in use?

_____

_____

5. What are some of the largest cities in Latin America?

_____

_____

Thinking Critically

Answer the following questions on a separate sheet of paper.

1. What steps could be taken to keep poor farmers from using the slash-and-burn technique in the rain forest?

2. Tourism is a mixed blessing. What do you think might happen if tourism left the region?

Mexico

BEFORE YOU READ

In the last chapter you, read about the physical geography of Latin America.

In this section, you will learn about the history and culture of Mexico.

AS YOU READ

Use this graphic organizer to take notes about what you discover in this section.

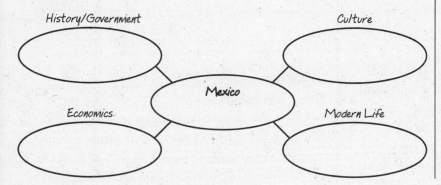

PLACES & TERMS

Tenochtitlán Aztec capital city, the site today of Mexico City

Spanish conquest the conquest of the Aztecs by Cortés

Institutional Revolutionary Party (PRI) political party that arose in Mexico in 1929

mestizo people of mixed Spanish and Native American heritage

maquiladoras factories in Mexico that assemble imported materials into finished goods for export

NAFTA North American Free Trade Agreement among Mexico, Canada, and the United States

Colonialism and Independence

(pages 217–218)

Who *were this region's early inhabitants?*

The area that became Mexico was originally occupied by many different native peoples. There were the residents of Teotihuacán, an early city-state. The Yucatán Peninsula was home to the Maya. There were also Toltecs, Aztecs, and other smaller groups or tribes.

In 1519, Hernando Cortés landed on the coast. He and his men marched to the Aztec capital, **Tenochtitlán**. By 1521, Cortés, his soldiers, and their native allies had conquered the Aztecs. This is known as part of the **Spanish conquest**. For three centuries, Mexico was part of Spain's empire.

In 1821, Mexican soldier Agustín de Iturbide helped Mexico achieve independence. Beginning in the mid-1800s, Benito Juárez led a reform movement and became president of Mexico. He worked for separation of church and state, better educational opportunities, and a more even distribution of land.

A corrupt politician named Porfirio Díaz took over from Juárez. Díaz ruled Mexico for 30 years. His harsh rule led to revolution and civil war. A new constitution was adopted in 1917.

In 1929, a new political party arose in Mexico. This was the **Institutional Revolutionary Party (PRI)**. It helped to introduce democracy and maintain political stability for much of the 20th century. However, *fraud* and corruption hurt the democratic process. In 1997, two parties opposed the PRI and won a large number of seats in the congress. In 2000, Vincente Fox was elected president of Mexico. Finally, Mexico was a democratic state with more than one political party.

1. For how long was Mexico part of Spain's empire?

_____

_____

A Meeting of Cultures (pages 218–219)

Who *was Frida Kahlo?*

Before the Spanish arrived, Mexico was home to many advanced native cultures. The Aztec Empire arose in the Valley of Mexico. Their capital of Tenochtitlán held temples, palaces, gardens, and lakes. Canals linked the city. People grew food on islands in Lake Texcoco. When the Spanish conquered the Aztec Empire, they destroyed the capital and built Mexico City in its place.

The Spanish brought their language and Catholic religion, both of which dominate modern Mexico. However, Mexico's native heritage remains strong. In fact, the name of the country comes from *Mexica,* an older name for the Aztecs. Mexico has a large population of **mestizos**—people of mixed Spanish and Native American descent.

Mexico has a long heritage of architecture and art. The Native Americans constructed temples and public buildings. The Spanish built simple but beautiful missions throughout the territory.

In the 20th century, many of Mexico's best painters portrayed Mexico's history on the walls of public buildings. Among the most important of these mural painters were José Orozco, Diego Rivera, David Siqueiros, and Juan O'Gorman. Frida Kahlo was an important painter known for her self portraits.

2. Where did Mexico's name come from?

_____

_____

Economics: Cities and Factories
(pages 219–220)

What *are maquiladoras?*

Mexico is attempting to close the gap between rich and poor. Mexico has been an *agricultural* society, but it started to industrialize in the mid-20th century.

Mexico's population is young and growing rapidly. The population of about 52 million in 1970 almost doubled by 2000. Mexicans are moving to cities because they see economic opportunities there.

Mexico has a large industry based on its oil reserves. Profits from oil have helped to finance development. Many new factories are located in Mexico's north. **Maquiladoras** are factories where imported materials are assembled into finished goods for export, mostly to the United States.

Mexico is a member, along with the United States and Canada, of **NAFTA**. This agreement has created a huge zone of cooperation on trade and economic issues. It is expected to contribute to the prosperity of the member nations, creating jobs for millions of people.

3. What is NAFTA expected to accomplish?

_____

_____

Mexican Life Today (page 221)

Why *do people emigrate?*

A rapidly growing population and misguided government policies have contributed to a shortage of jobs. Many workers leave Mexico and travel to the United States in search of work. Often, after a year or two working in the United States, they return to Mexico. They use the money to improve conditions for their families.

Without education and training, young workers cannot find good jobs. In recent years, attendance of eligible students at schools has improved. Mexico will have to invest money in education to provide a better life for its citizens. Education will become even more important as Mexico becomes more industrial.

4. Why is education important to Mexico?

_____

_____

Central America and the Caribbean

BEFORE YOU READ

In the last section, you read about the history and development of Mexico.

In this section, you will learn about the culture, economics, and life of Central America and the Caribbean.

AS YOU READ

Use this graphic organizer to take notes about what you discover in this section.

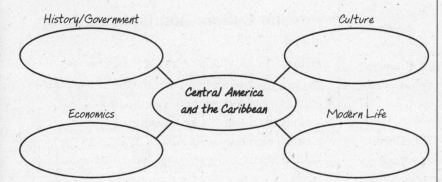

PLACES & TERMS

cultural hearth the heartland or place of origin of a major culture

United Provinces of Central America the name adopted by Central America when it declared independence form Mexico

Panama Canal shipping canal that cuts across Central America, connecting the Atlantic and Pacific oceans

calypso music, originally from Trinidad, that combines musical elements from Africa, Spain, and the United States.

reggae music developed in Jamaica in the 1960s

informal economy jobs without benefits, such as street vending and shining shoes, that provide people with a small income

Native and Colonial Central America
(pages 222–223)

Who were the Maya?

Central America is a cultural hearth. A **cultural hearth** is the heartland or place of origin of a major culture. The Maya built a great civilization in the region.

The Maya built cities with temples and palaces. Each independent city was ruled by a *god-king* and served as a center for religious ceremony and trade.

The Spanish conquest of Mexico opened the door to Central America. Spanish settlers and native peoples are the dominant groups in this region. People from Africa make up a *sizable* percentage of the population in some Central American countries.

In 1823, Central America declared its independence from Mexico. It took the name of the **United Provinces of Central America**. By the late 1830s, the United Provinces had split into separate nations. These became El Salvador, Nicaragua, Costa Rica, Guatemala, and Honduras.

1. What changes occurred in the 1830s?

_____

_____

Native and Colonial Caribbean
(pages 223–224)

What countries claimed this region?

The original inhabitants of the Caribbean islands called themselves the Taino. The Spanish settled the islands and established sugar plantations. Many Taino died from disease and mistreatment on the plantations.

European slave traders brought Africans to the Caribbean to work on the plantations. By the 1800s, the Spanish, French, British, Dutch, and Danish claimed islands. Most used slave labor on sugar plantations.

In the 1700s, Haiti was a French colony. African slaves worked on Haiti's sugar plantations. In the 1790s, Toussaint L'Ouverture led a slave rebellion.

By 1804, Haiti was independent.

As a result of the Spanish-American War in 1898, Cuba achieved independence from Spain. After occupation by U.S. forces, Cuba became self-governing in 1902.

2. Who was Toussaint L'Ouverture?

_____

_____

Cultural Blends (pages 224–225)

How did Africans influence life in the region?

The Spanish were the most important group of European settlers in Central America. Their language is still *dominant*. Catholicism is the major religion.

In the Caribbean, a greater variety of influences were at work. The Spanish, French, British, Danish, and Dutch mixed with Africans and Native Americans.

Religions of the Caribbean include Catholicism and Protestantism. There is also Santeria, which combines Catholic and African elements. Voodoo is practiced in Haiti. Rastafarianism is found in Jamaica.

Spanish is spoken on the most populous islands in the Caribbean. There are also many French speakers. English dominates in Jamaica. There is also some Dutch and Danish spoken in the region.

3. What languages are spoken in this region?

_____

_____

Economics: Jobs and People

(pages 225–226)

Why is the Panama Canal important?

Sugar cane is the Caribbean's largest export crop. Other export crops are bananas, citrus fruits, coffee, and spices. Many people work on farms and plantations. However, the average income is low.

In Central America, too, the main source of income is farming. Plantations here produce ten percent of the world's coffee and bananas.

Trade is important because of the **Panama Canal**. This great shipping canal cuts across Central America, connecting the Atlantic and Pacific oceans.

In Central America, because most people make their living on farms, the population is largely rural. In the Caribbean, most people live in urban areas. They hope to find good jobs, but many end up living in slums.

4. What are the region's important export crops?

_____

_____

Popular Culture, Tourism, and Jobs

(pages 226–227)

What is the informal economy of the Caribbean?

In both Central America and the Caribbean, music has been influenced by the local cultures.

Calypso music began in Trinidad. It combines musical elements from Africa, Spain, and the United States. Calypso songs have *improvised* lyrics.

Reggae began in Jamaica in the 1960s. Many of the songs deal with social problems and religion. African, Caribbean, and American music fed into reggae.

Education and jobs are major concerns in Central America and the Caribbean. Rapid population growth helps cause high unemployment.

Tourism is important. Island residents can work in hotels and restaurants. There is also an **informal economy**. People may work as street vendors or offer small services such as shoe shining to earn income.

5. What influenced calypso and reggae music?

_____

_____

Spanish-Speaking South America

BEFORE YOU READ

In the last section, you read about the culture, economics, and life of Central America and the Caribbean.

In this section, you will learn about the history and development of Spanish-Speaking South America.

AS YOU READ

Use this graphic organizer to take notes about what you discover in this section.

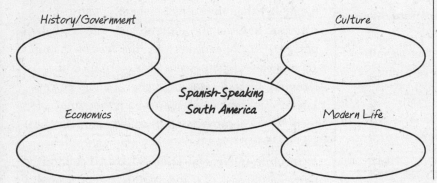

PLACES & TERMS

Inca descendants of people who came from Asia and crossed into South America, where they created a great civilization in the Andes Mountains of Peru

Quechua language of the Inca

Mercosur economic common market that began operating in southern South America in 1995

Conquest and the End of Spanish Rule (pages 230–232)

Where *did the Inca build their empire?*

The Inca built a great civilization in the Andes Mountains of Peru. The **Inca** were descendants of people who came across a land bridge from Siberia. They crossed the *Isthmus* of Panama into South America.

From their capital at Cuzco in Peru, the Inca conquered other tribes. By 1500, the Inca Empire extended 2,500 miles along the west coast of South America. A system of roads linked the empire.

Then, in 1532–1533, Francisco Pizarro and his soldiers invaded and conquered the Inca Empire. Spanish settlers forced the natives to work in mines and on farms and ranches. Many settlers abused the natives or worked them to death. The Inca were forced to move from their villages to large plantations. This broke down families and communities.

Spanish rule in the region lasted for almost 300 years. The **Quechua** language of the Inca was largely replaced by Spanish. The Inca religion was replaced by Catholicism. However, millions of native peoples still speak Quechua.

The people of South America sought independence from Spain in the early 1800s. Two great leaders of the region's independence movement were Simón Bolívar and José de San Martin.

Oligarchy (government by the few) and military rule have been common in many South American countries.

1. Which two leaders helped win the region's independence?

_____

_____

A Cultural Mosaic (pages 232–233)

What *elements make up the cultural heritage of Latin America?*

South America is one of the most culturally complex regions in the world. Societies with different cultures live near each other but do not mix.

Spanish-Speaking South America has a strong literary heritage. Among the most famous of this region's writers is Gabriel García Márquez of Colombia. He won the Nobel Prize for literature in 1982.

Popular music and folk music are important traditions. Street musicians can be heard everywhere. Classical music is also important. Many cities have symphony orchestras.

Beautiful craftwork and handmade items can be found throughout Latin America. Pottery, textiles, glasswork, and metalwork combine beauty and usefulness.

2. Who is Gabriel García Márquez?

_____

_____

Economics: Resources and Trade
(pages 233–234)

Which *country has been most successful?*

Many people in Latin America are poor. However, economic development hopes to improve people's lives.

Different resources, landforms, climate, and vegetation enable the region to create a variety of products. Guyana, Suriname, and French Guiana grow crops for export. Colombia and Venezuela have huge oil reserves. Peru has an important fishing industry.

Ecuador exports shrimp. Bolivia mines tin, zinc, and copper. Argentina produces grain and livestock. Uruguay has major farming and grazing areas. Paraguay exports soybeans, cotton, and animal hides.

Chile is South America's greatest success story. It trades products worldwide. The export of fruit and vegetables to North America is an important part of the economy. But copper remains Chile's largest export.

3. Which countries have huge oil reserves?

_____

_____

Education and the Future (pages 234–235)

Who *is General Pinochet?*

Literacy rates in Spanish-speaking South America are higher than they are elsewhere in Latin America. In Chile, the adult literacy rate is about 95 percent. For Chileans between the ages of 15 and 19, it is close to 98 percent. In Argentina and Uruguay, literacy rates are higher than 90 percent. Literacy rates for women are about the same as for men. Most countries support colleges, universities, and technical schools.

In Chile, public education is free. All children between the ages of 6 and 13 must attend school. Higher education has suffered because of political unrest. Salvador Allende's government was overthrown by General Augusto Pinochet in 1973. The military introduced reforms that *undermined* higher education. Since Pinochet's departure from power in 1990, universities have regained some independence and standards.

4. What are the literacy rates in Chile?

_____

_____

Brazil

BEFORE YOU READ

In the last section, you read about the history and development of Spanish-Speaking South America.

In this section, you will learn about the culture, economics, and life of Brazil.

AS YOU READ

Use this graphic organizer to take notes about what you discover in this section.

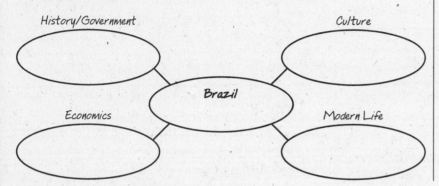

PLACES & TERMS

Treaty of Tordesillas agreement between Spain and Portugal that gave Portugal control over the land that became Brazil

Carnival the most colorful feast day in Brazil

samba a Brazilian dance with African influences

capoeira martial art and dance that developed in Brazil from African origins

History: A Divided Continent

(pages 236–237)

When *did Brazil become independent?*

Spain and Portugal reached an agreement to divide South America. In the resulting <u>Treaty of Tordesillas</u> (1494), Portugal gained control over the land that was to become Brazil. Brazil is the largest country in South America.

The first Portuguese colonists hoped to find gold or silver, but they were disappointed. They cleared areas of forest and created sugar plantations. The demand for sugar soon made Brazil a source of wealth for Portugal.

Settlement occurred along the coast. Here, cities such as Rio de Janeiro grew up. Land farther west was cleared to produce more sugar. The Portuguese conquered some of the region's tribes and put them to work on the sugar plantations. Unfortunately, Europeans diseases killed many of the natives. The Portuguese brought slaves from Africa to replace them.

In 1807, Napoleon's forces invaded Portugal. The Portuguese royal family sailed to Brazil. For 14 years, Brazil was the heart of the Portuguese Empire. After Napoleon's defeat in 1815, many Brazilians demanded independence. A petition signed by thousands of Brazilians asked Dom Pedro, son of Portugal's King John, to rule Brazil. In September 1822, he declared Brazil's independence.

1. What was the Treaty of Tordesillas?

_____

_____

_____

A National Culture (page 237)

What *city became the capital in 1960?*

The dominant influences in Brazilian culture are Portuguese, Native American, and African. When Europeans began arriving in 1500, millions of native peoples lived in the region. Today, only about 200,000 survive in the Amazon rain forest. Many natives died from diseases that the Europeans had.

Brazil has become home to many immigrants. There are immigrants from Portugal, Germany, Italy, Spain, Lebanon, Syria, and Japan.

The Portuguese brought their language and Catholicism with them. Brazil today has the largest Catholic population in the world. Protestants make up almost 20 percent of the population. Many others practice local religions.

A new capital, Brasília, was built in the interior of Brazil beginning in 1957. Part of the reason for locating the capital 600 miles inland was to draw people to the interior.

2. From what countries did Brazil's immigrants come?

_____

_____

An Economic Giant Awakens (page 238)

What *is the cerrado?*

Brazil's economy is the tenth largest in the world. Natural resources help make Brazil an industrial power. There are deposits of many minerals used in manufacturing, such as iron and bauxite.

More than a thousand rivers, including the Amazon, wind through Brazil. Power plants along these rivers produce electricity. Brazil also has large reserves of oil and natural gas.

Brazil is one of the most industrialized nations in South America. It has one of the largest steel plants in the region. It is a leading maker of automobiles. More than half of Brazil's cars use ethanol.

Despite economic success, there is still a wide gap between rich and poor in Brazil. Increasing urbanization reflects people's desires to improve their lives. By 1996, more than 75 percent of the people lived in cities.

About 80 percent of Brazil's population lives within 200 miles of the sea. But there has been a move west as the government encourages settlement in the interior.

3. What are some of Brazil's industries?

_____

_____

Brazilian Life Today (page 239)

What *are favelas?*

Brazil is a country of great variety in its city life, music, and holidays.

The most colorful feast day in Brazil is **Carnival**. In Rio de Janeiro, people in costumes ride floats through the streets of the city. The celebrations of Carnival take place to the music of the <u>samba</u>, a Brazilian dance with African influences.

<u>Capoeira</u> is a martial art and dance that developed in Brazil from African origins. Angolans who were taken to Brazil by the Portuguese brought this martial art and dance with them.

Brasília is the political capital of Brazil. São Paulo is Brazil's economic heart and largest city. But Rio de Janeiro is considered the cultural center of Brazil.

There is a darker side to life in Rio. It is caused by the widening gap between rich and poor. Desperately poor slums, called *favelas*, dot the hillsides. Crime waves and drug abuse are two results of the terrible poverty. Recently, however, government officials have launched programs to bring in electrical power, paved streets, and sewers.

4. What influenced Brazil's music and dance?

_____

_____

Name _____   Date _____

Glossary/After You Read

agricultural having to do with farming, such as producing crops and raising livestock

dominant being the primary one in action or use; most common because it has gained influence over others

fraud trickery, cheating, twisting the truth to get someone to surrender a legal right

god-king a political leader in some ancient cultures who was also believed to be divine and was worshipped by his people

improvise to make, arrange, or invent offhand

isthmus a narrow strip of land connecting two larger land areas

sizable fairly large; big enough to take into consideration

undermine to weaken or ruin slowly; to take away support from

Places & Terms

A. Write the letter of the place or term next to the description that explains it best.

a. Spanish conquest

b. United Provinces of Central America

c. Institutional Revolutionary Party (PRI)

d. NAFTA

e. Treaty of Tordesillas

_____ 1. the new political party that arose in Mexico in 1929

_____ 2. trade agreement between Mexico, the United States, and Canada

_____ 3. agreement between Spain and Portugal that gave Portugal control of Brazil

_____ 4. the taking over of Mexico from the Aztecs

_____ 5. what the region of Central America was called after it declared its independence of Mexico

B. Circle the place or term that best completes each sentence.

1. The language of the Inca was _____.

   Tenochtitlan   Quechua   Maquiladoras

2. _____ is the music played in Brazil during Carnival.

   samba   reggae   calypso

3. The native people who built a great civilization in the Andes Mountains were the _____.

   Quechua   Calypso   Inca

4. _____ are factories where imported materials are assembled into finished goods.

   maquiladoras   cultural hearth   capoeira

5. The heartland or place of origin of a major culture is a _____.

   Panama Canal   carnival   cultural hearth

Main Ideas

1. What language and religion are dominant in Mexico, and why?

_____

_____

2. For what reason are there African elements in the culture of the Caribbean?

_____

_____

3. What are the two areas in which Chile has done better than most other countries in Spanish-Speaking South America?

_____

_____

4. What geographical factors kept the countries of Spanish-speaking South America from uniting or cooperating in the past?

_____

_____

5. Why is the cerrado—the vast grasslands of Brazil—being increasingly settled?

_____

_____

Thinking Critically

Answer the following questions on a separate sheet of paper.

1. Why is democracy an important element of economic development?

2. What areas of life in Latin America have been influenced by the region's original inhabitants?

Rain Forest Resources

BEFORE YOU READ

In the last section, you read about the culture and development of Brazil.

In this section, you will learn about the valuable resources of the rain forest.

AS YOU READ

Use this chart to help you take notes about the resources of the rain forest.

	Causes	Effects
Issue 1: Resources		

PLACES & TERMS

biodiversity a wide range of plant and animal species

deforestation the cutting down and clearing away of trees and forests

global warming a rise in the temperature of the atmosphere

debt-for-nature swap arrangement in which an organization pays off part of government debt, and the government agrees to protect a certain portion of the rain forest

Rain Forest Land Uses (pages 245–246)

***Why** is the rain forest important?*

The rain forest is an important global resource. Its vegetation helps to clean the earth's atmosphere and regulate the climate. It also shelters several million species of plants, insects, and wildlife.

Scientists have begun to investigate and understand the rain forest's **biodiversity**. This is its wide range of plant and animals species. And yet, this variety of life is being destroyed at a breathtaking pace. At the end of the 20th century, nearly 50 million acres of rain forest were being destroyed every year.

The Amazon rain forest contains tropical hardwoods such as mahogany and cedar. These are harvested for export by the timber industry. The world's demand for timber is great.

Native peoples, living in poverty, travel into the rain forest in search of land to grow crops. They clear the forest, not realizing that the soil is not very fertile. Also, cutting down the trees exposes the land to erosion. After a few years, this new farmland

becomes less productive. The people move to a new area and clear more timber.

Livestock, too, have been introduced into the rain forest. Ranchers need land on which to graze their cattle. By clearing the forests for pasture, they can gain a steady supply of beef for the export market.

More than half of the Amazon rain forest is located in Brazil. That country's growing population is contributing to the rain forest's decline. The estimated population of Brazil in 2000 was about 173 million people. Brazil's population is expected to reach 200 million by 2020. With that many people to shelter, some developers are looking to build homes on land now covered by rain forest.

1. What effect will destruction of the rain forest have on biodiversity?

_____

_____

The Price of Destruction (page 246)

***What** is global warming?*

There is a cost to pay for the destruction of the rain forest. <u>Deforestation</u> means the cutting down and clearing away of trees and forests. There are short-term benefits for this to the local people. But these are offset by the high price Latin America and the world are paying as the rain forests are destroyed.

Forests help to regulate the earth's climate. They do this by *absorbing* carbon dioxide and producing oxygen. As the forests disappear, much less carbon dioxide is absorbed. The carbon dioxide that is not absorbed builds up in the atmosphere. This buildup prevents heat from escaping into space. The temperature of the atmosphere begins to rise. Weather patterns start to shift. This rise in temperature is called <u>global warming</u>. By the beginning of the 21st century, evidence of global warming appeared around the world. A common method for clearing rain forest, known as slash-and-burn, produces even more carbon dioxide.

The world's rain forests cover about six percent of the earth's surface. However, they are home to at least 50 percent of the world's plant and animal *species*. Medical researchers are just beginning to understand and make use of rain forest plants. Rain-forest dwellers have harvested these plants for thousands of years. They have used these plants to make medicines that heal wounds and cure disease. The rain forest holds secrets of nature that might improve and extend the quality of people's lives.

2. How do rain forests help regulate the climate?

_____

_____

Moving Toward Solutions (page 247)

***What** competing interests make finding solutions difficult?*

Saving the rain forests of Latin America is an issue that affects people around the world. Creative solutions will be required to make sure that the forests are not sacrificed to economic development.

The central issue facing Latin American countries is how to balance competing interests. Some Latin American countries are trying to find the right balance between economic development and preservation of the rain forest.

For example, *grassroots* organizations are closely watching development projects in the forests. Their mission is to educate people about the value of the rain forests.

Economic gain is at the heart of rain forest destruction. So some people offer money to preserve the forests. One such plan is known as a <u>debt-for-nature swap</u>.

Many Latin American nations are burdened with debt. Now they are struggling to pay it back. In a debt-for-nature swap, an organization agrees to pay off a certain amount of government debt. In return, the government agrees to protect a certain portion of the rain forest. Governments get debt relief. Environmentalists get rain forest preservation.

The movement to preserve the rain forests has many supporters. The battle to preserve the rain forests may be one in which everybody wins.

3. What are some of the things people have done to help preserve the rain forests?

_____

_____

Giving Citizens a Voice

BEFORE YOU READ

In the last section, you read about the valuable resources of the rain forest.

In this section, you will learn about the pursuit of democracy in Latin America.

AS YOU READ

Use this chart to help you take notes about this section.

	Causes	Effects
Issue 2: Democracy		

PLACES & TERMS

oligarchy government by the few

junta harsh government formed by the military and run by the generals

caudillo rule by a military dictator or political boss

land reform the process of breaking up large landholdings and giving land to peasant farmers

A Struggle to Be Heard (pages 249–250)

Who *governed Latin America countries after they won independence?*

Latin Americans today seek more democratic governments. Democracy depends on several things. There must be free and fair elections. Citizens need to participate. There should be majority rule with protection for minority rights. And there must be constitutional freedoms. Latin American history, however, has often stood in the way of democracy.

The Spanish conquered the region in the 16th century. After that, Native Americans in Central and South America were ruled by governors. These governors took their orders from the king and queen of Spain. Latin American countries won their independence during the 1800s. However, they were still governed mainly by small groups of Spanish colonists.

This government by the few is called an **oligarchy**. It was not democratic. The government censored the press, limited free speech, and punished *dissent*. It also discriminated against

everyone who was not part of the Spanish ruling class. Elections were held, but there was never any doubt who was in charge.

If the government was unable to control the people, the military would step in. They would seize power and form a new, harsher government known as a **junta**. A junta was run by the generals.

Throughout the 20th century, many Latin American countries were ruled by a caudillo. A **caudillo** is a military dictator or political boss. The caudillo's support came from the military and the wealthy. Surprisingly, the caudillo was sometimes elected directly by the people.

For example, from the 1920s until the turn of the century, Mexico was governed by the *Partido Revolucionario Institucional* (PRI), or Institutional Revolutionary Party. For 71 years, the PRI dominated Mexican politics.

Opposition parties were legal, but the PRI used fraud and corruption to win elections. Opposition parties made big gains in the 1997 congressional elections. In 2000, Vincente Fox became the first non-PRI president since the adoption of Mexico's constitution in 1917. Finally, it seemed Mexico was ready to fully embrace a *stable* democracy.

1. How was a junta formed?

_____

_____

Establishing Stable Democracies
(pages 250–251)

What *does land reform accomplish?*

Creating stable democracies in Latin America requires political, economic, and land *reforms*.

The goal of political reform is to establish a constitutional government. A freely elected government that respects the rule of law is important to a democratic nation.

At the same time, the participation of citizens in political affairs is critical. This requires that people be well educated and provided with economic security.

Political and economic stability are two sides of the same coin. A lack of prosperity is usually accompanied by social and political unrest.

Another element of reform is the increasingly important role of women in politics. Throughout the region, women are running for office. They are taking an active role in government. For example, in 2000, Marta Suplicy was elected mayor of São Paulo, Brazil. This city is the financial center and economic engine of Brazil.

Latin America had been ruled by a wealthy *elite*. Economic power, including land, was in the hands of the few. To spread the wealth more fairly, some governments set up a program of land reform. **Land reform** is the process of breaking up large landholdings and giving the land to land-poor peasant farmers.

In Mexico, for example, the process of land reform began with Benito Juarez. He was from a small farm. He was elected Mexico's president in 1858. One of his main reform goals was to redistribute land. He did not want rich landowners to keep other Mexicans in a cycle of poverty. After the Mexican Revolution in the early part of the 20th century, there was another attempt at land reform. This gave people a better chance of economic equality.

All of these reforms have been aimed at creating stability. With a sound foundation, democracy has a better chance of taking root.

2. What is required in order to get citizens to participate in political affairs?

_____

_____

Name _____ Date _____

The Income Gap

BEFORE YOU READ

In the last section, you read about efforts to create democracies in Latin America.

In this case study, you will learn about efforts to narrow the gap between rich and poor.

AS YOU READ

Use this chart to help you take notes about this case study.

	Causes	Effects
Case Study: Income Gap		

PLACES & TERMS

income gap the difference between the quality of life enjoyed by the rich and the poor

ethical having to do with moral duty and what is good and bad

The Nature of the Problem

(pages 252–253)

What ethical questions does the income gap raise?

In Rio de Janeiro, gleaming office buildings and hotels line the boulevards. A few blocks away, dreadful slums are home to Rio's poor. These opposites are evidence of what economists call an **income gap**. This is the difference between the quality of life enjoyed by the rich and the poor. In many Latin American countries, the income gap is widening.

Some people argue that Latin America's income gap raises important **ethical** questions. How can a caring society justify vast wealth in the hands of a few while most people live in poverty? The Catholic Church and other religious faiths in Latin America argue that narrowing the income gap is a matter of social justice.

Most Latin American countries now have free-market economies with a minimum of government rules. However, in Latin America, the poor often lack basic skills. Because of this, they cannot take part in the economy.

Often, the poor have little education. Many cannot read. Most cannot find jobs. To the poor of Latin America, the doors of economic equality appear to be shut.

Poverty can make people desperate. Those who have nothing to lose are sometimes willing to take great risks. Civil wars and revolutions may occur if people feel society is unjust.

1. What keeps the poor from taking part in the economy?

_____

_____

Possible Solutions (page 253)

How does democracy contribute to prosperity?

The income gap in Latin America varies from one country to another. For example, nearly 45 percent of Brazilians live in poverty. However, in Ecuador, Paraguay, and Uruguay, the income gap is much narrower than in Brazil.

Many of the countries of Latin America now have free-market economies. Free-market economies provide economic opportunity and stability for all citizens. People hope this will eventually narrow the income gap.

Along with free-market economies, democracy is now seen by many countries as an essential part of achieving prosperity. Democracy provides an outlet for protest and opposition. Policies can be adjusted to reflect the will of the people.

Finally, education is an important part of the mix. A literate, well-educated population will be needed to fill jobs in an increasingly complex society.

2. Why can the introduction of free-market economies help close the income gap?

_____

_____

Poverty is Widespread (pages 254–255)

Where is the poverty worst?

Graph: The relative percentages of households in poverty throughout Latin America in 1997 shows a wide range of statistics. At the high end is Bolivia, with nearly 60 percent of its population living in poverty. At the low end is Uruguay, with less than five percent of its population living in poverty.

Cable News Story: Brazil has 2,000 to 3,000 street children. These children are homeless and live on the streets of Rio de Janeiro. Their greatest fear is to be murdered by the death squads. The death squads shoot the children while they sleep. Official police estimates say about 500 of Rio's homeless children are murdered each year.

Newspaper Report: In Caracas, Venezuela, there is a huge shopping mall with 450 stores. However, a hamburger there costs about half a day's pay for the average Venezuelan worker. A few miles to the west of the mall, there is a slum. Here, open sewers run alongside tin shacks. Inequality of wealth and opportunity is a huge obstacle to development in Latin America. The large numbers of poor people threaten the success of democracy and free markets. Most economists say that the problem is misguided policies of local governments. They deprive the poor of a decent education, fail to collect taxes, and encourage corruption.

3. What part do economists say local governments play in keeping people poor?

_____

_____

Programs are Helping (page 255)

What is being done?

Magazine Article: In Porto Alegre, Brazil, the municipal council has introduced programs to help the children on its streets. Street children can sleep in council-run dormitories and attend the city's "Open School." They hope to create something like a normal life for children and help them get an education. There are a handful of cities that are trying to help. The programs are modest. They offer shelter, food, a place to wash. They supply teachers and drug counselors. Some patrol the streets looking for children in need.

4. What is currently being offered by these programs?

_____

_____

Name _____   Date _____

Glossary/After You Read

absorbing taking in, soaking up

dissent difference of opinion

elite a socially superior group; a powerful minority

grassroots at the local level, especially in rural areas, as distinguished from the centers of political leadership

reform to improve by changing the form or removing faults and abuses

species kind, sort, a biological classification of related organisms

stable firmly established, steady, not fluctuating

Places & Terms

A. If the statement is true, write "true" on the line. If it is false, make it true by changing the underlined word or words and placing the new word on the line.

_____ 1. Government by the few is called a <u>democracy</u>.

_____ 2. A <u>junta</u> is when the military steps in and forms a harsher government run by the general.

_____ 3. Scientists have begun to investigate the rain forest's <u>population</u>, that is, its wide range of plant and animal species.

_____ 4. A <u>caudillo</u> was a military dictator or political boss.

_____ 5. Breaking up large landholdings that once belonged to a wealthy elite in order to aid land-poor peasant farmers is called <u>deforestation</u>.

B. Write the name or term in each blank that best completes the meaning of the paragraph.

global warming   debt-for-nature swap

land reform   deforestation

oligarchy

Changes are taking place in Latin America. Many old problems are being addressed.

Because (1)_____ has reduced the number of trees that are absorbing

carbon dioxide, we may experience the greenhouse effect. This can lead to higher

temperatures in the atmosphere, or (2)_____. But people are coming

up with plans to battle this problem. One such plan is known as a

(3)_____—governments receive financial aid and promise to protect

the rain forest. Economic and political improvements are being made as well. Many

countries that were once ruled by a small group of Spanish colonists have escaped this

age of (4)_____ and replaced it with more democratic governments.

Some governments have set up programs of (5)_____, which

redistribute land so that people have a better chance of economic equality.

Main Ideas

1. What are medical researchers learning that rain-forest dwellers have long known?

_____

_____

2. Why does Brazil's increasing population threaten the rain forest?

_____

_____

3. What are some actions that organizations have taken to preserve the rain forest?

_____

_____

4. What are some reforms that were used in Argentina to try to battle inflation?

_____

_____

5. What is the goal of reform in Latin America?

_____

_____

Thinking Critically

Answer the following questions on a separate sheet of paper.

1. Why is it necessary to create a balance between economic development and preserving the rain forest?

2. Why is education important to the building of a democracy?

Name _____ Date _____

EUROPE
Landforms and Resources

BEFORE YOU READ
In the last chapter, you read about issues regarding resources and politics in Latin America.

In this section, you will learn how Europe's landforms and resources shape Europe's economy and life.

AS YOU READ
Use this chart to take notes on the landforms and resources of Europe.

Landforms	
Resources	

PLACES & TERMS
fjord a steep, glacier-carved, U-shaped valley that connects to the sea

upland a hill or low mountain that may also contain a mesa and high plateau

Meseta central plateau of Spain

Massif Central uplands in France; about one-sixth of French land

peat partially decayed plant matter found in bogs; it is used as fuel

Peninsulas and Islands (pages 273–274)

Why *might Europe be called a "peninsula of peninsulas"?*

Europe is a large *peninsula* west of Asia. It contains many smaller peninsulas. Europe is sometimes called a "peninsula of peninsulas." Most locations in Europe are no more than 300 miles from the sea.

In the north is the Scandinavian Peninsula. It is home to Norway and Sweden. The Norwegian Sea, the North Sea, and the Baltic Sea surround this peninsula. *Glaciers* moved across the Scandinavian Peninsula during the last Ice Age. In Norway, the glaciers carved out <u>fjords</u>, deep U-shaped valleys connected to the sea.

Across from Scandinavia is the Jutland Peninsula. Jutland forms the largest part of Denmark and a small part of Germany.

Southern Europe contains three major peninsulas. The Iberian Peninsula is home to Spain and Portugal. Italy occupies the boot-shaped Italian Peninsula. The Balkan Peninsula is very mountainous. The Adriatic, Mediterranean, and Aegean seas surround it.

Europe also has many islands. The larger islands are Great Britain, Ireland, Iceland, and Greenland.

The smaller islands include Corsica, Sardinia, Sicily, and Crete.

1. What are the five major peninsulas of Europe?

_____

_____

Mountains and Uplands (pages 274–275)

Why *might the mountains and uplands of Europe be viewed as walls?*

The mountains and uplands of Europe separate groups of people and make travel difficult. These landforms also influence the climate. For example, the Alps block cold winds, which makes Italy warmer.

The Alps arc across France, Germany, Switzerland, Italy, Austria, and the northern Balkan Peninsula. The Alps cut Italy off from the rest of Europe.

The Pyrenees make it hard to move from France to Spain and Portugal. The Apennine Mountains divide the Italian Peninsula from east to west. The

Balkan Mountains separate the Balkan Peninsula from the rest of Europe. They also *isolated* the region's various ethnic groups from each other.

Europe also has several regions of <u>uplands</u>. Uplands are hills or low mountains that may also contain mesas or high plateaus. The <u>*Meseta*</u>, Spain's central plateau, is an upland region. So is the <u>*Massif Central*</u>, which makes up about one-sixth of France.

2. How do mountains and uplands affect the movement of people and goods?

_____

_____

Rivers: Europe's Links (page 275)

What are two of Europe's major rivers?

The rivers that cross Europe help bring people and goods together. Rivers are used to transport goods to the coast. This aids economic growth. Historically, they have also aided the movement of ideas.

The Danube and Rhine rivers have served as waterways for centuries. The Rhine flows 820 miles from the center of Europe to the North Sea. The Danube touches 9 countries over its 1,771-mile length. It links Europe to the Black Sea. These rivers helped to connect Europe to the rest of the world.

3. How have rivers affected life in Europe?

_____

_____

Fertile Plains: Europe's Bounty
(page 275)

Where does Europe grow its food?

One of the most fertile regions of the world is the Northern European Plain. It has good farmland that has produced vast quantities of food over the centuries. But the plain's flatness allowed invaders to use it as an easy route into Europe.

Smaller fertile plains exist in Sweden, Hungary, and northern Italy. These, too, are farming regions.

4. Why has the Northern European Plain been both useful and dangerous?

_____

_____

Resources Shape Europe's Economy
(pages 276–277)

What are Europe's primary resources?

Europe has *abundant* supplies of coal and iron ore. Having both of these resources makes it possible to produce steel. One negative result is that regions with industry often suffered from pollution.

In 1959, oil and natural gas were found beneath the stormy North Sea. Even so, technology made it possible to build oil rigs there. Now the North Sea is a major source of petroleum.

About 33 percent of Europe's land can be used for farming. The land produces crops such as grains, grapes, olives, and cork. Timber is cut from vast forests. These forests are on the Scandinavian Peninsula and in the Alps.

5. How did the presence of coal and iron contribute to pollution in some regions?

_____

_____

Resources Shape Life (page 277)

Why do the Irish cut peat?

The resources found in Europe helped shape the lives of Europeans. Resources affect food, fuel, jobs, and housing.

The distribution of resources cause differences between regions. Ireland lacks energy sources. In Ireland, <u>peat</u> beds are cut up and burned for fuel. In contrast, coal is plentiful in other parts of Europe. For example, Poland has had coal mines for generations.

6. How do resources affect the jobs people have?

_____

_____

Name _____   Date _____

EUROPE
Climate and Vegetation

BEFORE YOU READ

In the last section you read about Europe's landforms and resources.

In this section, you will learn how climate and vegetation affect life in Europe.

AS YOU READ

Use this chart to take notes on the climate and vegetation of Europe.

Climate	
Vegetation	

PLACES & TERMS

North Atlantic Drift a current of warm water from the tropics that flows near Europe's west coast

mistral a cold, dry wind that blows from the north to the southern coast of France

sirocco a hot, steady wind that blows from North Africa across the Mediterranean Sea into southern Europe

Westerly Winds Warm Europe
(pages 278–279)

What is the North Atlantic Drift?

A marine west coast climate covers much of Europe. It stretches from northern Spain across most of France and Germany. It reaches western Poland. It also exists in the British Isles. Some coastal areas of Scandinavia have this climate, too. In this region, summers are warm and winters are cool.

The influence of the ocean and the winds create this mild climate. The **North Atlantic Drift** is a current of warm water from the tropics. It flows near Europe's west coast. The *westerlies* are winds that blow from west to east. These winds pick up warmth from this current and carry it over Europe. The wind also carries moisture, so the area has enough rain.

Because of their high elevation, the Alps have a harsher climate. They are cold and snowy.

Mixed forests once covered much of this region. But for centuries, people have cut trees. They did so to get firewood and clear farms. Today, farmers in the region grow grains, sugar beets, livestock feed, and potatoes.

1. What effect do oceans currents and winds have on much of Europe?

_____

_____

_____

Harsher Conditions Inland (page 279)

How does the climate change as you go inland?

The winds do not carry the ocean's warmth far inland. So the climate there is not mild. Parts of Sweden, Finland, Poland, the Czech Republic, Hungary, and Romania have a humid continental climate. Winters are cold and snowy. Summers range from warm to hot. In general, the region has enough rainfall, and rain helps farming.

This region has lost many of its forests. The forests that still stand are mainly fir trees. The region also has broad fertile plains. Grasses once covered these plains. Today, farmers there grow grains such as wheat, rye, and barley. Potatoes and sugar beets are also major crops.

The Peninsula of Peninsulas **105**

2. Why does the inland region of Europe have a harsher climate?

_____

_____

_____

The Sunny Mediterranean
(pages 279–280)

What *special winds affect the Mediterranean?*

The region bordering the Mediterranean Sea has a mild climate. Summers are hot and dry with clear, sunny skies. Winters are mild and wet. This climate includes southern Spain and France. It stretches through Italy to Greece and other parts of the Balkan Peninsula. Mountain ranges protect most of this region from cold north winds.

Not all of the Mediterranean is protected. High mountains do not shield the southern coast of France. As a result, it receives the **mistral**. This is a cold, dry wind from the north.

Most Mediterranean countries experience the **sirocco**. This is a hot, steady wind that blows from North Africa into southern Europe. Some siroccos pick up moisture as they pass over the Mediterranean Sea and produce rain. Others carry dust from the desert. The sirocco blows mostly in the spring.

The Mediterranean region has mostly evergreen shrubs and short trees. They can stand the hot, dry summers. Major crops include citrus fruits, olives, grapes, and wheat. The Mediterranean has sunny beaches. Tourism is a major industry in the region.

3. How does climate affect life in the Mediterranean?

_____

_____

_____

Land of the Midnight Sun (page 280)

What *does "midnight sun" mean?*

A band of tundra climate lies in far northern Scandinavia. It is along the Arctic Circle. In this region, the land is often in a state of *permafrost*. This means that the subsoil stays frozen all year. No trees grow there—only mosses and lichens.

To the south of this lies a *subarctic* climate. It is cool most of the time and has harsh winters. Little grows there except short trees. Because of the climate, farming is limited to southern Scandinavia.

The region north of the Arctic Circle receives very different amounts of sunshine through the year. In far northern Scandinavia, there are winter days when the sun never rises. There are summer days when the sun never sets. As a result, the region is often called the Land of the Midnight Sun.

4. Why is farming limited to southern Scandinavia?

_____

_____

_____

EUROPE
Human-Environment Interaction

BEFORE YOU READ

In the last section you read about Europe's climate and vegetation.

In this section, you will learn about the relationship between humans and the environment in Europe.

AS YOU READ

Use this graphic to take notes on human-environment interaction in Europe.

Human-Environment Interaction

PLACES & TERMS

dike earthen banks that hold back water

polder land reclaimed by diking and drainage

seaworks structures used to control the sea's destructive impact on human life

terpen high earthen platforms that provide a place of safety during floods and high tides

Zuider Zee an arm of the North Sea that the Dutch transformed into a freshwater lake

Ijsselmeer name of the freshwater lake created from the Zuider Zee

Polders: Land from the Sea

(pages 282–283)

***How** did the Dutch get more land?*

The Dutch needed land for their growing population. So they reclaimed land from the sea. To do this, the Dutch built <u>dikes</u>, earthen banks to hold back the sea. Then they drained the water off the land. Land that is reclaimed by diking and drainage is a <u>polder</u>.

At least 40 percent of the Netherlands was once under the sea. Because of this, much of the Netherlands is below sea level. As a result, if a dike breaks, the sea floods in and causes destruction.

The Dutch erected <u>seaworks</u>. These are structures that help reduce the destruction that the sea causes. The seaworks include dikes and terpen. <u>Terpen</u> are high earthen platforms that are safe places to go during floods and high tides.

Over the centuries, the Dutch found ways to make dikes stronger. They also learned to control water in low-lying lands. One way was to pump water from the land. In the 1400s, the Dutch added *windmills* to power the pumps. Today, electric motors power the pumps.

The Dutch also changed their environment by changing the <u>Zuider Zee</u>. This was once an arm of the North Sea. Now it is a freshwater lake. The idea was first proposed in 1667. In the 1800s and 1900s, the Dutch finally made a plan to build dikes all the way across the entrance to the Zuider Zee. The dikes stopped saltwater from flowing into that body of water. In time, it became a freshwater lake called <u>Ijsselmeer</u>. The land around the lake was drained. This created several polders that added hundreds of square miles to the Netherlands.

1. Why were windmills important to the Netherlands?

_____

_____

_____

Waterways for Commerce: Venice's Canals (pages 283–284)

How *did Venice grow?*

Humans also created a unique environment in Venice, Italy. The city is on about 120 islands and part of the Italian *mainland*. Venice has more than 150 canals that snake around and through the islands. Venetians use the canals to move people or goods.

People escaping invaders founded Venice. They took shelter on a cluster of islands in a *lagoon*. The land was swampy and hard to live on. But it was located on the Adriatic Sea, so it was a good site for a port. Trade helped Venice grow.

To build on swampy land, Venetians sank wooden *pilings* into the ground. They constructed buildings on top of the pilings. Venetians needed so much wood, they completely cut down oak forests in northern Italy and Slovenia. Over time, the weight of Venice's buildings squeezed the ground underneath. This is one reason why Venice is slowly sinking. Another reason is that the sea level is rising. And people have pumped too much water from the ground, which also makes the city sink.

Industrial waste and sewage have created severe water pollution in Venice. This pollution and saltwater eat away the *foundations* of buildings. In addition, floods threaten the city.

Another problem is agricultural runoff. Farm chemicals run into Venice's harbor. The chemicals make algae grow too much. When the algae die, they create conditions that kill fish, and dead fish create a stench.

2. Why did people choose to build Vencie in this location?

_____

_____

_____

A Centuries-Old Problem: Deforestation (pages 284–285)

What *is deforestation?*

Deforestation is the clearing of forests from an area. People have been clearing the forests of Europe since ancient times.

Forests provided wood to burn for fuel. People also used wood to build ships and houses. Europeans began to develop industry in the 1700s and 1800s. As a result, they used even more wood to make charcoal, which industries used in blast furnaces. In time, people used coal as a fuel in place of wood. By then, it was too late. Huge areas of Europe had lost their native forests.

In the 1960s, people noticed that many trees in Germany's Black Forest were discolored. Those trees were losing needles and leaves, and dying. Scientists found that acid rain was one cause of tree death. Factories put out high amounts of sulfur dioxide and nitrogen oxide. These combine with water vapor and oxygen to form acid rain or snow. Winds carry the *emissions* to other parts of Europe. About one-fourth of European forests have been affected.

3. What has caused the deforestation of much of Europe?

_____

_____

_____

Name _____   Date _____

Glossary/After You Read

abundant plentiful

emission a substance discharged into the air

foundation the basis on which a building stands

glacier a huge mass of ice slowly moving over land

isolate to cut off from others

lagoon a shallow body of water separated from a sea by sandbars, coral reefs, or islands

mainland the biggest landmass of a continent

peninsula a piece of land projecting into a body of water

permafrost subsoil that remains frozen all year

piling a heavy beam driven into the earth to support a structure

subarctic belonging to the region just south of the Arctic Circle

westerlies winds that blow from west to east

windmill a machine that has a wheel with blades that turn when the wind blows, generating power

Places & Terms

A. In each blank, write the place or term that best completes the meaning of the paragraph.

fjords   North Atlantic Drift

Massif Central   uplands

mistral

In Norway, glaciers carved (1)_____, steep U-shaped valleys that connect to the sea. In many places in Europe, there are (2)_____, hills or very low mountains that may also contain mesas and high plateaus. One such region, called the (3)_____, covers about one-sixth of French lands. In the winter, a cold wind called the (4)_____ blows across the Mediterranean coast of France. Much of Europe enjoys a mild climate because winds pick up warmth from the (5)_____.

B. Write the letter of the name or term next to the description that explains it best.

a. sirocco   d. dike

b. peat   e. terpen

c. polder

_____ 1. earthen banks that hold back the sea

_____ 2. a hot, steady wind that blows from North Africa into southern Europe

_____ 3. land reclaimed by diking and drainage

_____ 4. partially decayed plant matter found in bogs, which is cut and burned as fuel

_____ 5. high earthen platform that provides safety during floods and high tides

Main Ideas

1. What are five or more of the peninsulas or islands that make up Europe?

   _____

   _____

2. How do ocean currents affect the climate in much of Western Europe?

   _____

   _____

3. How does being farther from the Atlantic Ocean affect much of Eastern Europe?

   _____

   _____

4. In what ways have Europeans interacted with land and sea to improve their lives?

   _____

   _____

5. How have the causes for deforestation changed over time?

   _____

   _____

Thinking Critically

Answer the following questions on a separate sheet of paper.

1. What are the ways in which rivers and mountains affected the movement of people and development of different cultures in Europe?

2. Which of the problems facing Venice—sinking, pollution, flooding, agricultural runoff—do you think should be tackled first? What suggestions would you make for resolving these problems?

Name _____   Date _____

Mediterranean Europe

BEFORE YOU READ
In the last chapter, you read about the physical geography of Europe.

In this section, you will learn about the history and development of Mediterranean Europe.

AS YOU READ
Use this graphic organizer to take notes on the human geography of Mediterranean Europe.

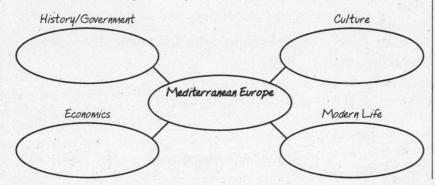

PLACES & TERMS
city-state a political unit made up of a city and its surrounding lands

republic a government in which citizens elect representatives to rule in their name

Crusades a series of wars in which European Christians tried to take Palestine from Muslims

Renaissance a time of renewed interest in learning and the arts, lasting from the 14th through 16th centuries

aqueduct structure that carried water for long distances

A History of Ancient Glory
(pages 289–290)

What types of governments arose in this region?

The Mediterranean was the birthplace of European *civilization*. Two geographic advantages helped cause this. The mild climate made survival easier. The Mediterranean Sea encouraged trade.

The rise of Greece began about 2000 B.C. People from the north moved onto the Balkan Peninsula and built villages. Mountains isolated the villages, so they grew into separate **city-states**. A city-state is a political unit made up of a city and its surrounding lands.

The city-state of Athens had the first democracy, a government in which the people rule. Greek science, *philosophy*, drama, and art shaped modern culture.

In the 400s B.C., conflict weakened Greece. Several city-states fought wars with Persia. In 338 B.C., Macedonia (a kingdom to the north) conquered Greece. Alexander the Great of Macedonia then conquered Persia and part of India. He spread Greek culture.

As Greece lost power, Rome grew. Rome ruled

most of the Italian Peninsula by 275 B.C. At that time, Rome was a **republic**. That is a government in which citizens elect representatives to rule in their name.

Rome conquered the Iberian and Balkan peninsulas. In Italy, turmoil caused the end of the republic. Emperors began to rule Rome.

One of Rome's territories was Palestine, where Jesus was born. Christianity spread from there across the empire.

In A.D. 395, the empire split in two. The Western Roman Empire fell to German invaders in 476. The Eastern Roman Empire lasted nearly 1,000 years longer.

1. What political ideas come from ancient Greece and Rome?

_____

_____

Moving Toward Modern Times
(pages 290–291)

How did the three Mediterranean peninsulas differ?

The Balkan Peninsula was part of the Eastern Roman Empire for 1,000 years. (The Eastern Empire was also called the Byzantine Empire.) Germanic tribes overran the Italian Peninsula. Italy became divided into several small states.

The **Crusades** began in 1096. European Christians fought these wars to take Palestine from the Muslims. Italians grew wealthy by supplying ships to Crusaders. Banking and trade made Italian city-states rich.

The **Renaissance** was a time of renewed interest in learning and the arts. It began in Italy's city-states. It lasted from the 14th through 16th centuries.

Muslims conquered the Iberian Peninsula in the 700s. The Catholic rulers Isabella and Ferdinand retook Spain from them in 1492. Queen Isabella also paid for Christopher Columbus's first voyage. Both Spain and Portugal set up colonies. They spread their languages and the Catholic Church around the world.

2. How did Italy become wealthy?

_____

_____

A Rich Cultural Legacy (pages 291–292)

How were language and religion spread?

The past shaped Mediterranean Europe's languages, religions, and culture. Greece kept its own language. Portuguese, Spanish, and Italian came from Latin, the language of Rome.

The two halves of the Roman Empire had different forms of Christianity. Eastern Orthodox Christianity is the main religion of Greece. Roman Catholicism is strong in Italy, Spain, and Portugal.

Greece and Italy have ancient ruins from classical times. Spain has Roman **aqueducts**, structures that carried water for long distances. Spain also has Muslim mosques.

3. Why would Spain have both Roman aqueducts and Muslim mosques?

_____

_____

Economic Change (page 292)

How has Mediterranean Europe's economy changed?

The region's sunny climate and historic sites encourage tourism. Through history, the economy of the Mediterranean region was based on fishing and farming. But the region's economy changed in the late 20th century.

Manufacturing and service industries, such as banking, are increasing. In the 1980s, Greece, Portugal, and Spain joined the European Union (EU). This promoted trade. Trade leads to growth.

Southern Italy has had less growth than northern Italy. The north is closer to other regions of Europe. Poor transportation and bad planning hurt the south.

4. What slowed the development of southern Italy?

_____

_____

Modern Mediterranean Life
(pages 292–293)

What recent problems have affected Mediterranean Europe?

Dictators ruled Spain and Italy for long periods during the 20th century. In 1975, Spain set up a *constitutional* government. After World War II, Italy became a republic but has had dozens of governments. Greece has also been unstable.

In 1970, Spain granted the Basque people self-rule. The Basques live in the western foothills of the Pyrenees and speak their own language. Some Basques want total independence and continue to fight Spain.

As farming decreases, more people move to cities. Urban growth has created housing shortages, pollution, and traffic jams.

5. What conflict exists between Spain and the Basques?

_____

_____

Chapter 13 Section 2 (pages 296–301)   *Reading Study Guide*

Western Europe

BEFORE YOU READ

In the last section, you read about the history and development of Mediterranean Europe.

In this section, you will learn about the culture, economics, and life of Western Europe.

AS YOU READ

Use this graphic organizer to take notes on the human geography of Western Europe.

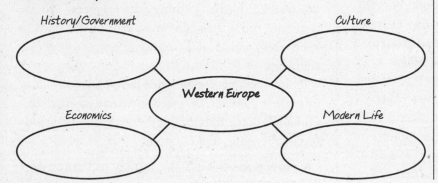

PLACES & TERMS

Benelux the countries of Belgium, the Netherlands, and Luxembourg

Reformation a period when many Christians broke away from the Catholic Church and started Protestant churches

feudalism a political system in which powerful lords owned most of the land

nationalism the belief that people should be loyal to their nation

Holocaust the Nazis' program of mass murder of European Jews

Berlin Wall the wall that divided Berlin into two zones

A History of Cultural Divisions
(pages 296–297)

What shaped language and religion in the region?

France and Germany are *dominant* countries in Western Europe. They have influenced Austria, Liechtenstein, Monaco, Switzerland and the **Benelux** countries of Belgium, the Netherlands, and Luxembourg.

Western Europe is divided by language. French is a Romance language. It evolved from the language of Rome. Rome never fully conquered the Germanic tribes in the lands east of France. Germanic languages are still spoken there.

In the late 700s, a Germanic king conquered most of the region. His name was Charlemagne. His empire fell apart after his death. Western Europe remained a region of small, competing kingdoms.

Religion also divides the region. In 1517, Martin Luther published 95 statements that criticized the Catholic Church. This began the Reformation. During the **Reformation**, many Christians left the Catholic Church and started Protestant churches.

Today, France is mostly Catholic. Germany, the Netherlands, and Switzerland have both Protestants and Catholics.

1. What are two elements that divide cultures in this region?

_____

_____

The Rise of Nation-States
(pages 297–298)

What is nationalism?

After Rome fell, **feudalism** evolved. It was a system in which lords owned most of the land. They gave land to nobles who served in their armies.

Over time, strong kings gained power over feudal lords, and nationalism evolved. **Nationalism** is the belief that people should be loyal to their nation.

Nationalism caused modern nation-states to form. A nation-state is an independent nation of people with a common culture. France was one of the first nation-states. French kings abused their power, so in 1789, the people began the French Revolution. They *deposed* the king and started a republic. Later, Napoleon Bonaparte seized power. In 1804, he made himself emperor. He tried to conquer Europe but was defeated.

In the 1800s, a wave of nationalism swept Western Europe. Industrial growth also took place. Europeans wanted raw materials and markets. To get them, European nations set up colonies in other lands.

Nationalism and competition for colonies helped start World War I. The Allied Powers, including France, fought the Central Powers, including Germany. The Allies won and treated Germany harshly. German anger helped cause World War II. Germany, led by the Nazis, tried to conquer Europe. The Nazis carried out the **Holocaust**, a program to murder all European Jews. In 1945, the Allies defeated Germany.

After the war, Germany was split in two parts. East Germany was *Communist*. West Germany was non-Communist. The **Berlin Wall** cut the capital city of Berlin in two. In 1989, anti-Communist reforms swept Europe. East Germany opened the Berlin Wall. In 1990, the two Germanys united under a democratic government.

2. What effects did nationalism have on this region?

_____

_____

Economics: Diversity and Luxury
(pages 298–300)

What products come from this region?

Western Europe has long been rich in agriculture. In the 1800s, it was one of the first regions to develop industry. France, Germany, and the Netherlands are still three of Europe's top manufacturing nations.

High-tech and service industries are important. The Netherlands makes electronics. Germany produces electronics and scientific instruments. France has high-speed trains and a space program. Switzerland specializes in banking.

Tourism is also a major part of the economy. And the region is famous for luxury goods. These include

German cars, French fashions, and Swiss watches.

Germany's reunification caused economic problems. West Germany has a higher standard of living. East Germany's factories are outdated. Germany is trying to foster growth in the East.

3. Why would such economic diversity be beneficial?

_____

_____

Great Music and Art (page 300)

Which art forms were characteristic of the region?

Western Europe has a strong artistic legacy. Germany and Austria are famous for music. Bach, Beethoven, and Mozart were composers from those countries.

France and the Netherlands have had many important painters. Vermeer and Rembrandt were famous Dutch artists. Major French painters include Monet, Cézanne, and Gauguin.

4. How does the artistic legacy of France and Germany differ?

_____

_____

Modern Life (page 301)

What are cities like in Western Europe?

Most Western Europeans live in cities. Most have good public transportation systems and cultural attractions. Europeans spend time in parks and cafés.

There have been conflicts. In the 1980s, many people from Yugoslavia and Turkey came to West Germany for jobs. When the economy grew worse, some Germans committed violence against immigrants.

5. What led to recent conflicts?

_____

_____

Northern Europe

BEFORE YOU READ

In the last section, you read about the culture, economics, and life of Western Europe.

In this section, you will learn about the history and development of Northern Europe.

AS YOU READ

Use this graphic organizer to take notes on the human geography of Northern Europe.

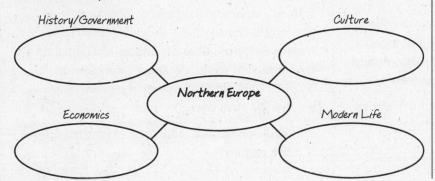

PLACES & TERMS

Nordic countries Denmark, Finland, Iceland, Norway, and Sweden

parliament a representative lawmaking body, whose members are elected or appointed

Silicon Glen a section of Scotland, between Glasgow and Edinburgh, that has many high-tech companies

euro a common European currency proposed by the European Union

A History of Seafaring Conquerors

(pages 302–303)

Who *were the Vikings?*

Northern Europe includes the United Kingdom and Ireland. It also includes the <u>Nordic countries</u> of Denmark, Finland, Iceland, Norway, and Sweden.

Celts lived in ancient Great Britain. Romans conquered southern Britain by about A.D. 80. In the 400s, Germanic tribes invaded. They drove out the Romans and pushed the Celts north and west.

Beginning about 795, many *seafaring* warriors raided Europe. They were from Denmark, Norway, and Sweden. These Norsemen, or Vikings, conquered parts of Britain. They settled in Normandy, a part of France named for them. They also went many other places.

In 1066, William the Conqueror of Normandy invaded England and began to rule it. The Normans spoke French. Over time, English acquired many French words.

Denmark, Sweden, and Norway each became a

kingdom in the 900s. Sweden was powerful in the 1600s but never created an empire.

Great Britain did build an empire. First, England won control of Wales, Ireland, and Scotland. In 1801, the nation became known as the United Kingdom.

Britain's island location helped protect it. After 1066, no enemy successfully invaded Britain. Britain built a navy and developed trade. By the 1800s, Britain had colonies around the world.

1. What groups affected the development of Britain?

_____

_____

Moving into the Modern Age

(pages 303–305)

How *did representative government develop?*

Britain's government has a monarch and a <u>parliament</u>. A parliament is a *representative* lawmaking body. Its members are elected or appointed. In 1215, English nobles forced the king to sign the Magna Carta. This document inspired many of today's political ideas. Over time, English rulers lost power to Parliament. The government grew more representative.

The Nordic countries also have representative governments. Iceland has the oldest parliament in the world. It has been meeting since 930.

Britain had iron ore and coal. This helped it to be the first nation to industrialize. The growth of industry led Britain to build an empire. Colonies could supply raw materials and buy finished goods. In the 1800s, the industrial revolution spread to other nations. Sweden developed the most industry of the Nordic countries.

After World War II, nearly all of Britain's colonies gained independence. The British have problems in Northern Ireland. Conflicts between Protestants and Catholics and anti-British violence occur there.

2. What three things characterized Britain as it moved toward modern times?

_____

_____

Economics: Diversity and Change
(page 305)

Where *are technology industries growing?*

Sweden and the United Kingdom have strong motor vehicle and *aerospace* industries. Both produce paper products, food products, and pharmaceuticals.

Technology is changing the economy. Ireland now makes computer software and hardware. A section of Scotland is called <u>Silicon Glen</u> because of its high-tech companies.

Most nations of the region joined the European Union (EU). EU members have mixed feelings about using the euro. The <u>euro</u> is a common currency to be used by EU members.

3. What are the strengths of Northern Europe's economy?

_____

_____

Cultural Similarities and Modern Art
(page 306)

How *is the United Kingdom changing?*

The Nordic nations have populations that consist mostly of one ethnic group. The United Kingdom has grown more diverse in recent years.

Most people in Northern Europe speak a Germanic language. Of non-Germanic languages, Sami is spoken only in the far north. Celtic languages survive only on the edges of the British Isles.

The Reformation swept through the region. Several Protestant churches took root. Only Ireland is mainly Catholic.

The Nordic countries helped to influence modern culture. Important artists were Norwegian playwright Henrik Ibsen and Swedish director Ingmar Bergman. Great Britain and Ireland also contributed to world literature. Many people consider William Shakespeare the greatest playwright of all time.

4. What cultural similarities exist throughout the region?

_____

_____

Life in Northern Europe (pages 306–307)

How *are women treated in Northern Europe?*

In Northern Europe, most people live in cities. The standard of living is high. Northern European women have made great political progress.

The governments of Northern Europe offer many welfare services to their people. For example, the Nordic countries and Britain have national health insurance programs. To pay for these programs, the people in these countries pay high taxes.

5. How do Northern European governments treat their citizens?

_____

_____

Name _____ Date _____

Eastern Europe

BEFORE YOU READ

In the last section, you read about the history and development of Northern Europe.

In this section, you will learn about the history, culture, and economy of Eastern Europe.

AS YOU READ

Use this graphic organizer to take notes on the human geography of Eastern Europe.

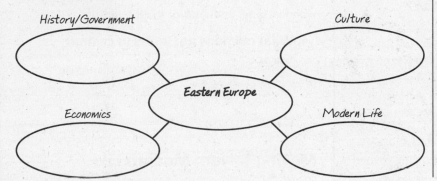

PLACES & TERMS

cultural crossroads a place where various cultures cross paths

balkanization the process of a region breaking up into small, mutually hostile units

satellite nation a nation dominated by another country

market economy an economy in which industries produce goods that consumers want to buy

folk art arts and crafts produced by rural people with traditional lifestyles, rather than by professional artists

anti-Semitism discrimination against Jewish people

History of a Cultural Crossroads

(pages 310–311)

Why *is Eastern Europe called a cultural crossroads?*

Eastern Europe is a cultural crossroads. A **cultural crossroads** is a place where various cultures cross paths. For example, many world powers have tried to control Eastern Europe. Ancient Rome, the Byzantine Empire, and the Ottoman Empire all held parts of the region.

Various Slavic groups moved into the region from the 400s through the 600s. They formed kingdoms such as Poland and Serbia. In the late 800s, a non-Slavic group called the Magyars swept into Hungary.

In the 1400s, the nation of Austria drove the Ottomans out of Hungary. In the late 1700s, Austria, Prussia (a German state), and Russia divided up Poland. Poland ceased to exist.

1. What major empires ruled parts of Eastern Europe?

_____

_____

Turmoil in the 20th Century

(pages 311–313)

What *triggered the two world wars?*

By 1908, several Balkan nations had broken free from the Ottoman Empire. In 1912, the Ottomans lost the rest of their territory in Europe. The Balkan countries fought over that land. The conflict gave rise to the word **balkanization**. The term refers to the process of breaking up a region into small, hostile units.

Serbia wanted to free the Slavs in Austria-Hungary. In 1914, a Serb assassinated an Austrian noble. That act started World War I. After the war, Austria and Hungary split apart.

In 1939, Germany seized Poland. That started World War II. After the war, the Soviet Union set up Communist governments in Eastern Europe. It became a region of satellite nations. <u>Satellite nations</u> are nations that another country controls.

The Soviet Union controlled Eastern Europe for four decades. In the late 1980s, a new Soviet leader made reforms. By 1990, most Eastern European nations had ended Communist rule.

Without Communist control, the region grew unstable. In the 1990s, four of Yugoslavia's six republics declared independence. Civil war followed.

2. What happened to Eastern Europe after World War II?

_____

_____

Developing the Economy (page 313)

***What** is a market economy?*

After 1948, the Soviet Union tried to start industry in Eastern Europe. Communist governments owned all the factories and told them what to make. Factories had no reason to cut costs or please customers. Eastern European nations could trade only with the Soviet Union or each other. They did not keep up with new technology.

After 1989, most of Eastern Europe began to change to a <u>market economy</u>. In market economies, industries produce goods that *consumers* want to buy. Private citizens began to own many factories in Eastern Europe.

Some nations in the region have economic problems. Albania has old equipment and uneducated workers. Few Romanians have money to invest. The war in Yugoslavia caused destruction. It also killed workers or caused them to flee the country.

3. How did Communist control affect industry?

_____

_____

A Patchwork Culture (page 314)

***What** differences exist in the region?*

Eastern Europe contains many ethnic groups. These groups speak a variety of languages. Some of the languages are unrelated to others in the region.

Catholicism and Eastern Orthodox Christianity are widespread in the region. Some countries have small groups of Protestants. Some countries have people who practice Islam. The region also has a small Jewish minority.

Eastern Europe is known for its folk art. In general, <u>folk art</u> is produced by rural people with traditional lifestyles, rather than by professional artists. Folk artists create items such as pottery, woodcarving, and embroidered clothing.

4. What religions are found in Eastern Europe?

_____

_____

Moving Toward Modern Life
(pages 314–315)

***What** is rule of law?*

Eastern Europe is less urban than the rest of Europe. As the region develops industry, its cities will grow. Cities offer more jobs, education, and culture. They also usually have pollution and traffic jams.

Many Eastern Europeans still have ethnic loyalties. These loyalties can create conflict. For example, many Serbs hate Croats, who helped the Nazis in World War II. Jews have suffered from <u>anti-Semitism</u>, which is discrimination against Jewish people.

5. How might urban growth change Eastern Europe?

_____

_____

Name _____ Date _____

Glossary/After You Read

aerospace relating to the science or technology of flight

civilization a society with an advanced state of cultural development

Communist a system in which the government plans and controls the economy and a single party holds all power

constitutional based on a document that sets up the nature of the government

consumer one who buys goods or services

depose to remove from power

dominant exercising the most influence

philosophy the study of the meaning of life

representative having officials who are authorized to act as the people's agents

seafaring living at sea

Places & Terms

A. Write the letter of the place or term that best answers the questions.

a. euro   d. Reformation

b. parliament   e. Silicon Glen

c. Renaissance   f. aqueduct

_____ 1. What was the time of renewed interest in learning and the arts?

_____ 2. What is a structure that carried water for long distances?

_____ 3. Which term applies to a representative lawmaking body whose members are elected or appointed?

_____ 4. What is the name for the common currency proposed by the European Union?

_____ 5. Which term is applied to a section of Scotland where high-tech companies are located?

B. Circle the place or term that best completes each sentence.

1. A nation that is dominated by another country is a _____.

   republic   city-state   satellite nation

2. Denmark, Finland, Iceland, Norway, and Sweden are _____.

   Benelux   Nordic countries   satellite nations

3. The belief that people should be loyal to their nation is called _____.

   feudalism   balkanization   nationalism

4. The _____ was a period when many Christians broke away from the Catholic Church and started Protestant churches.

   Reformation   Crusades   Renaissance

5. Discrimination against Jewish people is called _____.

   balkanization   anti-Semitism   Holocaust

Main Ideas

1. What two geographic advantages helped the Mediterranean to become the birthplace of European civilization?

   _____

   _____

2. Why did France and the Germanic countries end up with such different languages?

   _____

   _____

3. Beginning in about 795, warriors from the Nordic countries took to the sea. What were they called and what did they do?

   _____

   _____

4. How has being a cultural crossroads affected the history of Eastern Europe?

   _____

   _____

5. Why have the countries of Eastern Europe had so little experience with self-rule?

   _____

   _____

Thinking Critically

Answer the following questions on a separate sheet of paper.

1. What do you think will be the most difficult problems for Eastern Europe to overcome? Why?

2. What are some cultural and historic similarities between Western and Northern Europe?

Turmoil in the Balkans

BEFORE YOU READ
In the last chapter, you read about the human geography of Europe.

In this section, you will learn about conflicts in the Balkan region of Eastern Europe.

AS YOU READ
Use this chart to help you take notes on the Balkan conflict.

	Causes	Effects
Issue 1: Conflict		

PLACES & TERMS
South Slavs Slavic people who migrated from Poland and Russia and settled on the Balkan Peninsula

Slobodan Milošević Serbian leader who tried to increase Serbia's power over the rest of Yugoslavia

ethnic cleansing the policy of violently trying to eliminate an ethnic group

KLA the Kosovo Liberation Army

Vojislav Kostunica reform leader elected president of Yugoslavia in 2000

Roots of the Balkan Conflict
(pages 319–320)

What *happened at the Battle of Kosovo Polje?*

One conflict in the Balkans is that different groups want control of the same land. The causes of this conflict go back centuries. Starting in the 500s, Slavic people migrated from Poland and Russia to the Balkan Peninsula. They were the <u>South Slavs</u>. The South Slavs included Croats, Slovenes, and Serbs. Each group formed its own kingdom.

In 1389, the Muslim Ottoman Empire defeated Serbia at the Battle of Kosovo Polje. The Ottomans began to rule Serbia. They also ruled Bosnia and Herzegovina. Austria ruled Slovenia, and Hungary ruled Croatia. These influences created differences among the South Slavic groups.

Though ruled by Muslims, the Serbs clung to Christianity. Many Bosnians converted to Islam. In addition, many Serbs fled Kosovo, where both Serbs and Albanians had lived. Kosovo became more Albanian in culture.

In 1878, Serbia broke free of the Ottoman Empire. Many Serbs wanted all the South Slavs to be free of foreign rule. They also want the South Slavs to unite in one nation. That desire helped spark World War I.

After the war, the Kingdom of the Serbs, Croats, and Slovenes was formed. To help end ethnic divisions, the king renamed the nation Yugoslavia in 1929.

During World War II, Germany and Italy invaded Yugoslavia. The Croats worked with the Nazis. Their leader ordered the murder of Jews and Serbs. Many other Yugoslavs joined the Chetniks or the Partisans. Those were two rival groups fighting the Nazis. One Partisan leader, Josip Broz Tito, was also a Communist. After the war, he became the *dictator* of Yugoslavia.

In 1946, a new constitution set up Yugoslavia as a nation of six republics. The republics were Bosnia and Herzegovina, Croatia, Macedonia, Montenegro, Serbia, and Slovenia. Serbia had two provinces, Kosovo and Vojvodina. Croatia and Bosnia had mixed populations with many Serbs.

1. How did the South Slavic groups develop cultural differences?

_____

_____

_____

Ethnic Tension Boils Over (pages 320–321)

What is ethnic cleansing?

In 1980, Tito died. Leaders from Yugoslavia's republics and provinces took turns serving as president.

Slobodan Milošević was a Serbian leader who tried to increase Serbia's power. He proposed the creation of Greater Serbia. Serbia would expand its borders to include other lands where Serbs lived. This plan alarmed Croats and Bosnians. Then in 1991, Serbia stopped a Croat from becoming president.

In response, Slovenia and Croatia declared their independence. In June 1991, the Serbian-led Yugoslav army invaded both republics. Slovenia quickly won its freedom. But Croatia had a large Serbian minority. Past Serb-Croat hatreds exploded in war. In January 1992, the United Nations arranged a *cease-fire*. Slovenia and Croatia remained free.

Bosnia and Herzegovina declared independence in March 1992. Bosnia's Muslims and Croats favored the move. Bosnia's Serbs and Serbia started a war to stop it. They also used murder and violence to get rid of Muslims and Croats. The policy of trying to *eliminate* an ethnic group is called **ethnic cleansing**. Over 200,000 people died. Over 2 million fled their homes.

In 1995, the United States set up peace negotiations. In December, a peace treaty was signed. Bosnia remained independent.

The Serbs saw Kosovo as an important part of Serbia. But in the 1990s, mostly Albanians lived in Kosovo. Albanians spoke a non-Slavic language. Their religion was Islam.

Serbia, led by Milošević tried to assert control over Kosovo. He wanted to wipe out the Albanian culture there. In response, Kosovo demanded independence. A group called the Kosovo Liberation Army (**KLA**) began to attack Serbian officials. In response, the Serbian government started to bomb villages.

In March 1999, NATO started bombing Serbia. NATO wanted Serbia to stop the violence. In June, Milošević pulled his troops out of Kosovo. An international court accused Milošević of *war crimes*. Many countries stopped trading with Yugoslavia.

In 2000, the Yugoslav people voted Milošević out of office. They elected **Vojislav Kostunica**, a reform leader, president. But the outlook for peace was unclear. Ethnic loyalties still caused tension. The wars had created millions of refugees. Poverty was widespread. Also, Kosovo and Montenegro wanted independence.

2. Why did Serbia's plans alarm Croatia and Slovenia?

_____

_____

_____

Cleaning Up Europe

BEFORE YOU READ

In the last section you read about tensions and conflicts in the Balkans

In this section, you will learn about the causes of pollution in Europe and some solutions Europeans are taking to cleanup pollution.

AS YOU READ

Use this chart to help you take notes about pollution in Europe.

	Causes	Effects
Issue 2: Pollution		

PLACES & TERMS

European Environmental Agency agency created to provide the European Union with reliable information about the environment

particulate a very small particle of liquid or solid matter

smog a brown haze that occurs when the gases released by burning fossil fuels react with sunlight creating harmful chemicals

ozone a form of oxygen that causes health problems

Saving Europe's Water (pages 323–324)

What *is polluting Europe's water?*

Mines and factories create much of Europe's water pollution. Industries often dump chemicals into streams and rivers. Factories sometimes bury solid waste. Poisons from this waste seep into the ground water and *contaminate* wells and rivers. And the burning of coal and other fuels causes acid rain. Acid rain not only hurts trees. It also changes the chemistry of lakes and rivers, often killing fish.

The link between industry and pollution creates a hard choice. Most countries want to develop industry. Some accept environmental damage as the price they must pay for progress. Other nations force industry to use pollution controls, but these are usually expensive.

Industry is not the only source of water pollution. Other sources include the following:

• **Sewage** Treatment plants remove harmful substances from *sewage* before it is released into bodies of water. But not all cities have such plants. In Poland, from 1988 to 1990, 44 percent

of the cities had no sewage treatment plants. The water in most of Poland's rivers is unsafe to drink. It has also poisoned the soil so that some crops are unsafe.

• **Chemical Fertilizers** Rain washes *fertilizers* from fields into bodies of water, where they cause algae and plants to grow faster than fish can eat them. The plants and algae die and decay, using up oxygen. The lack of oxygen kills the fish.

• **Oil Spills** In 1999, a tanker sank of the coast of France and spilled 10,000 tons of oil. That oil spread along 250 miles of coastline. It killed thousands of shorebirds.

Pollution spreads easily, so many countries must work together to solve the problem. For example, the Rhine River grew much more polluted after the mid-1900s. To correct this, five nations formed the International Commission for the Protection of the Rhine. Since it began meeting in 1950, the commission has recommended many programs. One program was sewage treatment. Today, the Rhine is less polluted.

In addition, the European Union (EU) has passed environmental laws that its member nations must obey. The EU also set up the **European Environmental Agency**. The purpose of this agency is to provide the EU with reliable information about the environment.

1. How are chemical fertilizers creating problems?

_____

_____

_____

Improving Europe's Air Quality
(pages 324–325)

What *problems are caused by air pollution?*

Air and water pollution are often studied separately. But they are linked. For example, water pollution can be caused by air pollution when rain washes chemicals out of the dirty air.

Air pollution is made up of gases and particulates. **Particulates** are very small particles of liquid or solid matter. Many human activities expel gases and particulates into the atmosphere.

- **Using Fossil Fuels** The burning of petroleum, gas, and coal causes much air pollution. It often leads to the formation of smog. **Smog** is a brown haze. It occurs when the gases released by burning fossil fuels react with sunlight to form harmful chemicals. One such chemical is **ozone**, a form of oxygen that causes health problems.
- **Fires** Forest fires and the burning of garbage release smoke and particulates into the atmosphere.
- **Chemical Use** Many activities release harmful chemicals into the air. These include dry cleaning, refrigeration, and the spraying of pesticides.

- **Industry** Factories discharge chemicals, such as sulfur and ammonia, into the air. The factories in former Communist countries have been heavy polluters. For example, air pollution is worse in the former East Germany than in the United States.

Breathing polluted air can cause *respiratory* diseases. These include asthma, bronchitis, and emphysema. Air pollution may cause lung cancer. It also harms livestock, stunts plant growth, and causes acid rain.

Individual countries are working to cleanup the air. France has passed laws that require new buildings to use better *insulation*. Insulation reduces the need to burn fossil fuels for heat. Other nations in Europe are also passing laws to protect the air.

Members of the EU agreed to begin reducing emissions from cars and vans. The EU will help lead the effort to restore Europe's environment.

2. What steps are being taken to clean the air?

_____

_____

_____

The European Union

BEFORE YOU READ

In the last section, you read about efforts in Europe to cleanup pollution.

In this case study, you will examine the pros and cons of a united Europe.

AS YOU READ

Use this chart to help you take notes on the European Union.

	Causes	Effects
Case Study: The European Union		

PLACES & TERMS

unification the act or result of uniting

alliance an association designed to advance the common interests of members

European Economic Community (EEC) a general alliance of European nations, also called the Common Market

European Union (EU) alliance of 15 nations that replaced the European Community

Steps Toward Unity (page 326)

What *was the EEC?*

After World War II, many people in Europe wanted to rebuild the economy and prevent further wars. Some thought that the way to reach these goals was for separate European nations to join together.

In 1951, several nations began the process of <u>unification</u>, or uniting together. Those countries were France, Germany, Italy, and the Benelux nations. They signed a treaty that gave control of their coal and steel resources to a common group. That group was the European Coal and Steel Community (ECSC). The countries' leaders thought this <u>alliance</u>, or association, would have positive results.

The nations would depend on each other for resources. Because of this, their industries would suffer if they fought again. Each country knew what the other was manufacturing. So no country could prepare for war secretly.

In 1957, a more general alliance was formed. It was the <u>European Economic Community (EEC)</u>. It was also known as the Common Market. The EEC removed trade barriers and set economic goals. It also allowed people to live and work in any member country. Between 1958 and 1968, trade among EEC nations increased four times.

In 1967, the EEC, the ECSC, and another alliance merged to become the European Community (EC). In 1973, the EC began to admit other European nations.

1. How did the EEC affect trade in Europe?

_____

_____

_____

The European Union Today (page 327)

What *is the euro?*

In 1993, the <u>European Union (EU)</u> replaced the EC. With 15 members, the EU faces several issues. One issue is settling differences between member nations. Two other issues are replacing national *currencies* with a single currency, the euro, and expanding EU membership.

EU members wonder how the union will affect their national economies. For example, workers may move to areas with higher wages. This would cause shifts in population.

Several countries are worried about using the euro. Some feel that they will lose control of interest rates. Others do not want to lose their national identities. Currency is often a symbol of national identity.

But many people believe that the euro has benefits. These include greater business efficiency and increased trade between countries. Banks and credit companies have started using euros to figure money exchanges. By 2002, euros will be used in everyday life.

One complex issue facing the EU is growth. In time, it might expand to 28 countries, with about 475 million people. Running such a large alliance would be hard. Many of the proposed new members are former Communist nations. In general, they are less wealthy and have little practice in democracy.

2. Why are some countries reluctant to adopt the euro?

_____

_____

_____

Primary Sources: The Euro
(page 328–329)

How do people feel about a single currency?

Political Commentary: The United Kingdom is part of the EU. But it has not adopted the euro. A British group expresses concerns about losing control of Britain's economy. It fears having poorer countries empty British banks and losing the benefits of money exchange rates. In addition, it points out that getting ready for the euro has helped to cause joblessness in Germany, France, and Italy. In these countries, the jobless rates are three times as high as in Britain.

Political Cartoon: A political cartoonist shows the leaders of the EU standing on a euro, as if it were a raft. A tattered shirt is the only sail. A small creature on the raft says that this is the steering committee. But no one is steering and everyone points in a different direction. The waves are high. It looks like the raft may sink.

3. What are some of the possible negative effects of the euro?

_____

_____

_____

Primary Sources: Integrating Nations
(page 328–329)

What are people saying about this?

Speech: Germany is an original member of the EU. One German leader favors letting countries from Central and Eastern Europe into the EU. He claims that the EU is the only way to create stability in Europe.

Political Analysis: Central Europeans remain suspicious of Germany. Adults raised under communism do not understand the way things are done in the West. Also, if the nations of Central Europe join the EU, Germans could buy up much of their land. But joining the EU might make more jobs available to people from Central Europe.

Data: Surveys show that people living in current EU countries disagree about who else should join. Most people wish to see nations such as Norway or Switzerland join. Many oppose membership for former Communist countries and for Turkey.

4. What concerns have people expressed about integrating some countries into the EU?

_____

_____

_____

Chapter **14** **Today's Issues in Europe**   *Reading Study Guide*

Glossary/After You Read

cease-fire a halt to a war or conflict

contaminate to make impure or unclean

currency money

dictator a ruler who governs without limits on power

eliminate to get rid of

fertilizer a material added to soil to make it better able to grow plants

insulation a material used to prevent the loss of heat

respiratory related to breathing

sewage liquid and solid waste matter carried in drains

war crimes murder, violence, or other crimes against civilians or prisoners during wartime

Places & Terms

A. If the statement is true, write "true" on the line. If the statement is false, make it true by changing the underlined word or words and placing the new word on the line.

_____ 1. <u>Particulates</u> are very small particles of liquid or solid matter.

_____ 2. <u>Algae</u> is a form of oxygen that causes health problems.

_____ 3. The policy of violently trying to eliminate an ethnic group is called ethnic <u>loyalty</u>.

_____ 4. The <u>South Slavs</u> moved into the Balkan Peninsula from Russia and Poland.

_____ 5. Slobodan Milošević was a leader of the <u>Ottomans</u>.

B. Write the latter of the place, name, or term next to the description that explains it best.

a. smog   d. European Environmental Agency

b. KLA   e. South Slavs

c. Vojislav Kostunica   f. Slobodan Milošević

_____ 1. a group in Kosovo that carried out attacks against Serbian officials

_____ 2. elected president of Yugoslavia in 2000

_____ 3. tried to increase Serbia's power

_____ 4. agency designed to provide the EU with reliable information about the environment

_____ 5. a brown haze that occurs when the gases released by burning fossil fuels react with sunlight

Main Ideas

1. Why did the king rename his kingdom Yugoslavia in 1929?

   _____

   _____

2. Why did the Serbs try to assert control over Kosovo?

   _____

   _____

3. Why do most countries want to develop industry, even though it causes pollution?

   _____

   _____

4. How are water pollution and air pollution connected?

   _____

   _____

5. Why is cooperation among European nations important to the environment?

   _____

   _____

Thinking Critically

Answer the following questions on a separate sheet of paper.

1. Why would Serbia want to discourage the republics of Yugoslavia from becoming independent?

2. Why would the former Communist nations of Eastern Europe have worse pollution than other countries?

RUSSIA AND THE REPUBLICS
Landforms and Resources

BEFORE YOU READ
In the last chapter, you read about political turmoil and problems with pollution in Europe.

In this section, you will learn about the physical features and resources of Russia and the Republics.

AS YOU READ
Use this chart to take notes about the landforms and resources of Russia and the Republics.

Landforms	
Resources	

PLACES & TERMS
chernozem fertile soil found on the Northern European Plain; means black earth

Ural Mountains mountains that separate the Northern European and West Siberian plains; also a boundary between Europe and Asia

Eurasia the name for the combined continents of Europe and Asia

Transcaucasia region that consists of the republics of Armenia, Azerbaijan, and Georgia

Central Asia region that includes the republics of Kazakhstan, Kyrgyzstan, Tajikistan, Turkmenistan, and Uzbekistan

Siberia the part of Russia that lies on the continent of Asia

Northern Landforms (pages 345–346)
***What** is Eurasia?*

Russia and the Republics occupy more than 8,500,000 square miles of land. That is nearly one-sixth of the earth's land surface. The northern two-thirds of this region can be divided into four different areas. Moving from west to east, they are the Northern European Plain, the West Siberian Plain, the Central Siberian Plateau, and the Russian Far East.

The Northern European Plain is an extensive lowland area. Incredibly rich soil—**chernozem**, or black earth—is abundant on the plain.

Almost three quarters of the region's 290 million people live on the plain. The **Ural Mountains** separate the Northern European and West Siberian plains. Some geographers recognize the Urals as a dividing line between Europe and Asia. Others consider Europe and Asia to be a single continent. They call it **Eurasia**.

The West Siberian Plain tilts northward. As a result, its rivers flow toward the Arctic Ocean,

taking water away from the arid lands to the south.

High *plateaus*—with average heights of 1,000 to 2,000 feet—make up the Central Siberian Plateau. This plateau lies between the Yenisey and Lena rivers.

1. Where does water from the West Siberian Plain go?

_____

_____

Southern Landforms (pages 346–347)
***What** landforms dominate this region?*

The Caucasus Mountains stretch across the land between the Black and Caspian seas. The mountains form the border between Russia and Transcaucasia. **Transcaucasia** is a region that consists of the republics of Armenia, Azerbaijan, and Georgia.

Farther east, there is a great wall of mountains. Some of these mountains are located along the southeastern border of **Central Asia**. This is a region

A Land of Extremes **129**

that includes the republics of Kazakhstan, Kyrgyzstan, Tajikistan, Turkmenistan, and Uzbekistan.

An extensive lowland called the Turan Plain lies between the Caspian Sea and the mountains and uplands of Central Asia. Two major rivers cross the plain. These are the Syr Darya and Amu Darya. Even so, much of the lowland is very dry. Two large deserts stretch across the plain. These are the Kara Kum (black sand desert) and Kyzyl Kum (red sand desert).

2. Why is Central Asia dry?

_____

_____

Rivers and Lakes (pages 347–348)

Which *river is the longest?*

The rivers of this region flow through large drainage basins. You may remember that a drainage basin is an area drained by a major river and its *tributaries*. The main drainage basins in Russia and the Republics are named for where the major river empties out. The Arctic Ocean basin is the region's largest.

The Volga River is the longest river on the European continent. It drains the Caspian Sea basin. It flows southward for about 2,300 miles. This important waterway carries about 60 percent of Russia's river traffic.

The Caspian Sea is really a saltwater lake. It is the largest inland sea in the world. The Aral Sea, also a saltwater lake, lies east of the Caspian Sea. Extensive irrigation projects have *diverted* water away from the Aral, causing it to shrink.

Lake Baikal is a freshwater lake. It is the deepest lake in the world. At its deepest point, it is more than a mile from the surface to the bottom. This lake holds nearly 20 percent of the world's fresh water. Lake Baikal is remarkably clean. Thousands of species of plants and animals live in the lake.

3. Why is Lake Baikal special?

_____

_____

Regional Resources (pages 348–349)

Where *is Siberia?*

Russia and the Republics are rich in natural resources. However, regional leaders have found it difficult to properly manage the resources.

This region has huge coal reserves, deposits of iron ore, and other metals. It also is a leading producer of oil and natural gas. Russia's vast forests hold one-fifth of all the world's timber resources. And the region's rivers have made it one of the world's largest producers of hydroelectric power.

Harsh climates, rugged terrain, and great distances make it difficult to *extract* these resources. Many of the region's resources are located in the frigid arctic and subarctic regions of <u>Siberia</u>. This is the part of Russia that lies on the continent of Asia.

Businesses have had some success extracting regional resources. But this has often caused damage to the environment. Mining operations and hydroelectric power plants have caused damage. When hot water is discharged from the hydroelectric plants, it often causes damage to plant and animal habitats. This is known as thermal pollution.

4. What is thermal pollution?

_____

_____

Chapter 15 Section 2 (pages 350–352)   *Reading Study Guide*

RUSSIA AND THE REPUBLICS
Climate and Vegetation

BEFORE YOU READ
In the last section you read about the landforms and resources of Russia and the Republics.

In this section, you will learn how climate and vegetation affect life in this region.

AS YOU READ
Use this chart to take notes on the climate and vegetation of Russia and the Republics.

Climate	
Vegetation	

PLACES & TERMS
continentality the influence on the climate of being far from the moderating influence of the sea

taiga the largest forest on earth

A Climate of Extremes (pages 350–351)

Where *are the region's warmer climates?*

Humid continental and subarctic climates dominate much of Russia and the Republics. These climates reflect the effects of the region's high latitude. They also reflect the effects of the wall of mountains in the southeast.

Another major influence is **continentality**. This refers to the effect on the climate of being far from the moderating influence of the sea. Because of its enormous size, much of the region is hundreds of miles away from surrounding oceans.

Continentality affects the amount of *precipitation* a region gets. It also affects its temperatures. Most of the region's moisture comes from the Atlantic Ocean. But the air coming from the ocean loses moisture as it travels inland.

Distance from the ocean also results in extreme temperatures. In Siberia, average monthly temperatures rarely get higher than 50°F and sometimes drop below -90°F.

The long stretches of cold weather in the region have a unique impact on daily life. For example, Siberians use frozen rivers as roads for part of the year.

Temperatures in the region are so consistently low that the region is covered by a layer of permanently frozen subsoil called permafrost. This frozen layer can reach depths of up to 1,500 feet.

Russia and the Republics have warmer climates, too. A wall of mountains in the southeastern areas of the region block moist air traveling northward. The mountains contribute to the semiarid and desert climates of Central Asia.

In Transcaucasia, moist air from the Mediterranean Sea helps create a subtropical climate zone.

1. What effect does continentality have on climates?

_____

_____

Vegetation Regions (pages 351–352)

What *is the taiga?*

Russia and the Republics have four major vegetation regions. These regions run east to west in wide strips. Moving from north to south, these regions are the tundra, forest, steppe, and desert.

The tundra region of Russia and the Republics is located mostly in the arctic climate zone. Only specific types of vegetation are able to survive in the tundra's climate. These types include mosses, *lichens,* small herbs, and low shrubs.

South of the tundra lies the largest forest on the earth—the **taiga**. The taiga is composed primarily of coniferous trees. Many fur-bearing animals live in the taiga. These include the sable, fox, and ermine. The taiga is also home to elk, bear, and wolves.

The steppe is the name of the temperate grassland. It extends from southern Ukraine through northern Kazakhstan to the Altay Mountains. The highly fertile chernozem soil is found in the steppe. It has helped to make the grassland a major source of grain for Russia and the Republics.

Deserts and semideserts occupy the wide plains in the west and central areas of Central Asia. There are two main deserts. One is the Kara Kum, which covers most of the republic of Turkmenistan. The other is the Kyzyl Kum, which is located in western Uzbekistan. Together the two deserts occupy an area of about 230,000 square miles.

2. What are the four major vegetation regions of Russia and the Republics?

_____

_____

RUSSIA AND THE REPUBLICS

Human-Environment Interaction

BEFORE YOU READ

In the last section you read about the climate and vegetation of Russia and the Republics.

In this section, you will learn about human-environment interaction in the region.

AS YOU READ

Use this graphic to take notes about human-environment interaction in Russia and the Republics.

Human-Environment Interaction

PLACES & TERMS

runoff rainfall not absorbed by the soil that runs off into rivers

Trans-Siberian Railroad the railroad the connects Moscow with the Pacific port of Vladivostok

The Shrinking Aral Sea (pages 353–354)

How *has runoff affected the Aral Sea?*

Between 1960 and the present, the Aral Sea lost about 80 percent of its water.

The Aral Sea receives most of its water from two rivers, the Amu Darya and the Syr Darya. However, in the 1950s, officials began to take large amounts of water from the rivers to irrigate cotton fields in Central Asia. Soon, the water reaching the sea was reduced to a trickle. The Aral began to evaporate.

Reducing the flow of water into the Aral caused other problems. Cotton growers used pesticides and fertilizers. These chemicals were being picked up by the **runoff**. This is rainfall not absorbed by the soil that runs into streams and rivers. The runoff carried the chemicals into the rivers that feed the Aral Sea. The effects were *devastating*. Every one of the 24 native species once found in the sea are now gone.

Soon, the retreating waters of the Aral exposed the fertilizers and pesticides, as well as salt.

Windstorms began to pick up these *residues* and dump them on nearby populations.

This pollution has caused a sharp rise in diseases. The incidence of throat cancer and respiratory diseases has risen. Dysentery, typhoid, and hepatitis have also become more common.

Scientists estimate that just to keep the lake at its present levels would take drastic measures. People would have to remove 9 of the 18 million acres that are now used for farming. This would create terrible economic hardship for the farmers. But many argue that it is the only way to save the Aral.

1. When did drastic changes in the Aral begin? Why?

_____

_____

The Russian Winter (pages 354–355)

How *did winter help to save Russia from Napoleon?*

Most of Russia's population lives west of the Ural Mountains. But more than 32 million people make their homes in Siberia. The climate of Siberia presents unique challenges to its inhabitants.

Scientists have recorded the most *variable* temperatures on Earth in Siberia. In the city of Verkhoyansk, temperatures have been as low as −90°F and as high as 94°F. But most of the time it is cold. Temperatures drop so low that basic human functions, such as breathing and opening your eyes, become painful.

Little relief is brought by the change of seasons. Warmer weather melts ice and snow and leaves pools of water. Also, northward flowing rivers, swollen with spring rain, are stopped by the still-frozen water in the north. The water can't flow, so it spreads out, creating swamps. These pools and swamps become breeding grounds for mosquitoes and black flies.

The climate also affects construction in Siberia. Permafrost makes the ground iron hard. However, heated buildings thaw the permafrost. As the ground thaws, buildings sink, tilt, and even fall over. To prevent this problem, builders raise their structures a few feet off the ground on concrete pillars.

Russia's harsh climate has also, at times, come to their aid. In the early 1800s, the armies of the French leader Napoleon Bonaparte were taking control of Europe. In the spring of 1812, Napoleon decided to extend his control over Russia. He gathered his army and marched from Poland to Moscow.

Napoleon arrived in Moscow in September. The Russian winter was coming. The citizens of Moscow had burned the city. Napoleon's army had no shelter.

Napoleon retreated from Moscow. He left with 100,000 French soldiers. But by the time his army arrived back in Poland, the harsh Russian winter had helped to kill more than 90,000 of his soldiers.

2. What problem does building on permafrost present?

_____

_____

Crossing the "Wild East"
(pages 355–356)

How *many workers did it take to build the railway?*

At the end of the 1800s, Siberia was in many ways similar to the "Wild West" of the United States. Travel through the region was dangerous and slow. For these reasons, Russia's emperor ordered work to start on a railroad. The railroad would go from Moscow east to the Pacific port of Vladivostok.

The railway was a huge project. The distance to be covered was more than 5,700 miles. The tracks would have to cross seven time zones. Approximately 70,000 workers were involved in creating the railway. Between 1891 and 1903, the workers moved 77 million cubic feet of earth and cleared more than 100,000 acres of forest.

Russian officials wanted a faster way to cross the country. They also wanted to populate the region so that they could profit from its many resources.

The railway line was completed in 1904. Within the next ten years, nearly five million settlers took the railway from European Russia to settle in Siberia. Most of these settlers were peasant farmers.

As migrants streamed into Siberia, resources began to pour out. Coal and iron ore were among the resources Siberia supplied.

3. What were two reasons for building the railway?

_____

_____

Name _____ Date _____

Glossary/After You Read

devastating ruining; laying waste; causing desolation over a wide area

diverted turned from one course or use to another; turned aside

extract to withdraw; to pull out, especially by force

lichen a complex, cold-tolerant, almost flat plant that grows on solid surfaces such as rocks or frozen ground

plateau a land area, usually large and with a relatively flat surface, that is considerably higher than the surrounding land

precipitation moisture released from the air or from clouds and deposited on the earth in the form of hail, mist, rain, snow, or sleet

residue something that remains after something else is taken away, for example, ash is the residue after wood is burned

tributaries streams feeding a larger stream, river, or lake

variable changeable; characterized by variations

Places & Terms

A. Write the place or term in each blank that best completes the meaning of the paragraph.

runoff   chernozem   Siberia

taiga   continentality

Russia and the Republics have many resources. In the broad plains, there is rich soil called

(1)_____. The great forest, called the (2)_____,

holds one-fifth of the world's timber resources. The part of Russia that lies in Asia,

(3)_____, has important reserves of coal and iron ore. The weather in

this region is harsh. One reason is because of (4)_____, that is, the

effect of being so far from the moderating influences of the ocean. Governments and

businesses must balance their desire for economic progress with their responsibility to

protect the environment. In the past, for example, problems have been caused by the use

of pesticides and fertilizers that (5)_____ has carried into rivers and

lakes.

B. Write the letter of the name or term next to the description that explains it best.

a. Eurasia   c. runoff   e. Trans-Siberian Railroad

b. Transcaucasia   d. Ural Mountains

_____ 1. southern region that consists of the republics of Armenia, Azerbaijan, and Georgia

_____ 2. they form the boundary between the Northern European and West Siberian plains

_____ 3. a transportation link between Moscow and Vladivostok

_____ 4. the name for the combined continents of Europe and Asia

_____ 5. rainfall not absorbed by the soil that runs off into rivers

Main Ideas

1. Why is so much of the agriculture of Russia and the Republics found on the Northern European Plain.

   _____

   _____

2. What challenges face leaders who manage the region's natural resources.

   _____

   _____

3. How is the region affected by continentality?

   _____

   _____

4. Which areas of Russia and the Republics have warmer climates?

   _____

   _____

5. How has the harsh climate protected the region's people?

   _____

   _____

Thinking Critically

Answer the following questions on a separate sheet of paper.

1. What do you think makes Lake Baikal worth protecting?

2. What do you think might happen if the government of this region simply shut down nine million farms to save the Aral Sea?

Russia and the Western Republics

BEFORE YOU READ

In the last chapter, you read about the physical geography of Russia and the Republics.

In this section, you will learn about the history and culture of Russia and the Western Republics.

AS YOU READ

Use this graphic organizer to take notes about what you discover in this section.

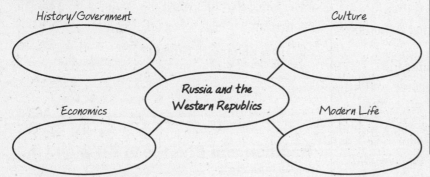

PLACES & TERMS

Baltic Republics the republics of Latvia, Lithuania, and Estonia

czar emperor

Russian Revolution a revolt that put an end to the Russian Empire and the rule of the czars

USSR Union of Soviet Socialist Republics

Cold War the tension between the United States and the Soviet Union that began after World War II

command economy economy in which the central government makes all important economic decisions

collective farm large farms organized by Soviet officials

A History of Expansion (pages 361–363)

What are the Baltic Republics?

In the 800s, Vikings settled in a region between the Baltic Sea and Black Sea. In time, they adopted the customs and language of the local Slavic population.

In the 1200s, fierce invaders arrived from Mongolia. Mongol warriors controlled the region until the early 1500s.

Ivan the Great put an end to Mongol rule. Russia then entered a period of explosive growth. By the end of the 1600s, Russia extended to the Pacific Ocean. The effects of this growth can still be seen in the republics to Russia's west: Ukraine, Belarus, Moldova, and the **Baltic Republics** of Latvia, Lithuania, and Estonia.

Peter the Great was **czar**, or emperor, of Russia from 1682 to 1725. He contributed to modernizing Russia. He moved the capital from Moscow to a city on the Baltic Sea. This provided direct access by sea to western Europe. The new capital was named St. Petersburg.

During World War I (1914–1918), the **Russian Revolution** occurred. By 1917, the Russian Empire and the rule of the czars had ended. The Russian Communist Party, led by V.I. Lenin, took control of the region. They called the new nation the Union of Soviet Socialist Republics (**USSR**), or *Soviet* Union for short.

When World War II broke out, Joseph Stalin was in control. In 1941, he led the Soviet Union in the fight against Nazi Germany. After the war, Stalin installed pro-Soviet governments in the Eastern European countries that his armies had liberated. U.S. leaders feared more Russian expansion. By the late 1940s, tensions between the United States and the Soviet Union led to conflict. Diplomats called this conflict the **Cold War**, because it never grew into open warfare.

The tension began to end in the mid-1980s. Soviet leader Mikhail Gorbachev started to give more economic and political freedom to the Soviet people. This started the process that led to the collapse of the Soviet Union in 1991—and the end of the Cold War.

After the fall of the Soviet Union, the region divided in 15 independent republics.

1. What was the Cold War?

_____

_____

Building a Command Economy
(page 364)

How did Stalin treat protesters?

The Communists who overthrew czarist Russia in 1917 had been inspired by the writings of Karl Marx. Marx was a *philosopher* who believed that capitalism was doomed. He believed that there should be no private property. Everything should be owned by all citizens.

To move their society toward communism, Soviet leaders adopted a **command economy**. In this system, the central government makes all economic decisions. They took control of land, mines, factories, banks, and transportation systems. The government decided what products factories would make, what crops farms could grow, and even what prices merchants could charge.

When Stalin took control, rapid industrialization was his goal. Even farming became an industry. The Soviet government created huge **collective farms** on which large teams of laborers worked together.

Millions starved to death in famines caused by the creation of the collective farms. Also, citizens soon realized that only a few people were benefiting from the economic changes. Doing or saying anything about this injustice was dangerous, however. Protesters were punished. Some historians say that Stalin was responsible for the deaths of more than 14 million people.

2. What is a command economy?

_____

_____

A Rich Culture (pages 365–366)

What artistic traditions does the region have?

Russia has the greatest ethnic diversity of the region's republics. Russians make up about 80 percent of the total, but nearly 70 other peoples live in Russia. The region also has many religious traditions. Russian Orthodox Christians are the largest religious group. But there are other religions, including Buddhism and Islam. Soviet persecution drove many Jews to emigrate, especially to Israel and the United States.

In the early history of the region, religious and artistic expression blended together in art and architecture. During and after the reign of Peter the Great, forms and ideas came in from western Europe.

When the Communist Party took over, they outlawed artists who did not work in the official style. Since the collapse of the Soviet Union, artistic expression has begun to gain strength.

3. How diverse is Russia?

_____

_____

Tradition and Change in Russian Life
(pages 366–367)

What is a banya?

As communication opened up in Russia, people began to enjoy more social and cultural opportunities. Books, magazines, and newspapers now arrive from all over the world.

However, native traditions still survive. For example, many Russians still prefer traditional foods. Russians also cherish their countryside. Nearly 30 percent of the population owns homes in the country. These homes are called *dachas*. They are small, plain houses, often with gardens to grow vegetables.

One custom Russians enjoy is the *banya*. *Banya* means bathhouse. Russians go to the *banya* to enjoy a cleaning ritual that combines dry sauna, steam bath, and a plunge into ice-cold water.

4. What is a *dacha,* and why do Russians like them?

_____

_____

Transcaucasia

BEFORE YOU READ

In the last section, you read about the history and development of Russia and the Western Republics.

In this section, you will learn about the culture, economics, and life of Transcaucasia.

AS YOU READ

Use this graphic organizer to take notes about what you discover in this section.

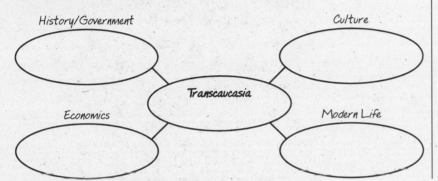

History/Government   Culture

Transcaucasia

Economics   Modern Life

PLACES & TERMS

Red Army the Soviet military

supra a traditional dinner party in the republic of Georgia

A Gateway of Migration (pages 370–371)

What *accounts for the region's ethnic diversity?*

The region of Transcaucasia has long been used as a migration route. It is a gateway between Europe and Asia. As waves of people moved across the region, they made their homes in the region. These new arrivals added to the many cultures already existing in Transcaucasia. Today, more than 50 different peoples live in the region.

Migrants also brought many languages to the area. The Indo-European, Caucasian, and Altaic language families are the region's most common.

The people of Transcaucasia follow a number of different religions. However, most of the region's people are Christian or Muslim. These faiths arrived in the region at an early date.

The region's diverse population has not always lived together in harmony. Under the rigid control of the Soviets, open hostility was rare. After the collapse of the USSR in 1991, tensions between the groups

resulted in violence. Civil war broke out in Georgia. Armenia fought with Azerbaijan.

1. What language families are common in the region?

_____

_____

A History of Outside Control

(pages 371–372)

How *did Transcaucasia live under Soviet control?*

For centuries, Transcaucasia has been a place where the borders of rival empires met. Armies have repeatedly invaded to protect or extend those borders.

In the 1700s, the invading armies came from Russia. The inhabitants of the region resisted the Russians. But the czar's troops *prevailed*. By 1723, Peter the Great's generals had taken control of Baku, the capital of Azerbaijan. In 1801, Russia *annexed* Georgia. In 1828, Russian armies took control of much Armenian land. By the late 1870s, all of Transcaucasia was part of the Russian Empire.

After the Russian Revolution (1917), the Transcaucasia republics enjoyed a brief period of independence. By the early 1920s, however, the **Red Army**—the military of the Soviet Union—had taken control of the region.

In the decades that followed, the people of Transcaucasia experienced the same economic and political problems as the rest of the Soviet Union. Many people lost their lives during the collectivization of farms. More were killed because of their political beliefs. The republics of Transcaucasia regained political independence in 1991, after the fall of the Soviet Union.

2. What was the Red Army?

_____

_____

Economic Potential (pages 372–373)

Which *republic is famous for its wine?*

Much of Transcaucasia is mountainous. Nevertheless, the republics have a significant agricultural output.

The humid subtropical lowlands and foothills of the region are ideal for growing tea and fruit. Grapes are one of the most important fruit crops.

In general, the region's industry was relatively limited before the Russian Revolution. After the revolution, Soviet planners transformed Transcaucasia into an industrial and urban region. Transcaucasia's economic transformation was rapid and ruthless.

Some industrial centers built by the Soviets continue to produce iron, steel, chemicals, and consumer goods. But today, attention is focused on the region's oil industry.

The name Azerbaijan means "land of flames." The republic's founders chose the name because of the fires that erupted from rocks and the waters of the Caspian Sea. These fires were the result of oil and gas.

Since the breakup of the Soviet Union, the Caspian Sea's resources have started geographical arguments. The arguments are about how the resources should be divided among the five states that border the Caspian Sea. The development of the oil industry has given many people in Azerbaijan hope for a better life.

3. Why is Azerbaijan called the "land of flames"?

_____

_____

Modern Life in Transcaucasia
(pages 373–374)

What *is a* supra?

The educational programs of the Soviet Union had a positive impact. At the time of the Russian Revolution, only a small percentage of Transcaucasia's population was literate. Communist leaders wanted to train a new generation of workers. As a result, literacy rates in Transcaucasia rose to nearly 99 percent, among the highest in the world. Today, quality educational systems remain a priority.

Transcaucasians have not forgotten the value of their traditions. Among the most important are the region's mealtime celebrations.

The Georgian *supra*, or dinner party, is one of the best examples of such gatherings. The word *supra* means tablecloth. It also refers to any occasion at which people gather to eat and drink. The *supra* is accompanied by a great number of toasts. Georgians take the toasts very seriously. They show respect for tradition and eloquence. They also show a respect for the importance of bringing people together.

4. Why do Georgians take toasts seriously?

_____

_____

Central Asia

BEFORE YOU READ

In the last section, you read about the culture, economics, and life of Transcaucasia.

In this section, you will learn about the history and cultures of Central Asia.

AS YOU READ

Use this graphic organizer to take notes about what you discover in this section.

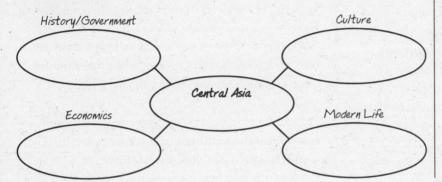

PLACES & TERMS

Silk Road caravan routes that connected China and the Mediterranean Sea

Great Game the struggle between Russia and Britain for the control of Central Asia

nomad a person who has no permanent home and who moves from place to place according to the seasons in search of food, water, and grazing land

yurt a portable tent of felt stretched around a wooden frame

A Historical Crossroads (pages 375–376)

What *is the Great Game?*

Today, Central Asia consists of five independent republics: Kazakhstan, Kyrgyzstan, Tajikistan, Turkmenistan, and Uzbekistan. Travelers first crossed the region in large numbers around 100 B.C. Many of these travelers joined *caravans*. The caravans traveled between China and the Mediterranean Sea.

Traders called the route the caravans took the Silk Road. It had this name because the traders carried silk they *acquired* in China. In addition to silk, traders carried many other goods on their horses and camels. They carried gold, silver, ivory, jade, wine, spice, *amber*, linen, porcelain, grapes, and perfumes. The Silk Road became a channel for the *diffusion* of ideas, technology, and religion.

Traffic on the Silk Road slowed in the 1300s. Traders began to use less expensive sea routes.

Interest in Central Asia exploded again in the 1800s. Great Britain and czarist Russia began to struggle for control of the region. Russian troops were moving southward. British leaders wanted to stop them before they could threaten Britain's possessions in India.

Both sides recruited daring young officers who made dangerous trips through the region in disguise. A British officer named Arthur Connolly named this struggle between the two empires the Great Game.

By the end of the 1800s, the Russian Empire had won control of Central Asia. In the 1920s, the Soviet Union took control. They governed the region until 1991.

1. What was the Silk Road?

_____

_____

An Uncertain Economic Future
(page 377)

What *did Soviet nuclear tests do to the region?*

Until the late 1980s, the Soviet nuclear industry was the economic mainstay of Semey (now called Semipalatinsk). This is a city in northeastern Kazakhstan. Between 1949 and 1989, Soviet scientists exploded 470 nuclear devices near Semey.

The tests were so close to Semey that citizens could see the mushroom clouds of the early above-ground explosions. Winds spread fallout over a 180,000 square mile area. This exposed millions of people to dangerous levels of radiation. Although testing at the site ended in 1989, the harmful effects of radiation will continue for years to come.

Recent exploration has suggested that huge oil fields may lie in Kazakhstan and Turkmenistan. These discoveries have triggered what many are calling the new Great Game. Nations all over the world are beginning to compete for profits from the region's resources.

2. What is the new "Great Game"?

_____

_____

Cultures Divided and Conquered
(pages 377–378)

How *did the Soviets divide up the region?*

Before the Russian Revolution, Central Asians identified with one another according to where they lived, their religion, ethnicity, and way of life. The Soviets exploited the differences between groups to establish their authority over the region.

Soviet planners carved the region into five new nations. These nations corresponded to the region's largest ethnic groups: Kazakh, Kyrgyz, Tajik, Turkmen, and Uzbek. However, the Soviets deliberately divided ethnic groups. They made sure that each republic had a large ethnic minority from the other nations. The legacy of Soviet political geography continues to make the region unstable.

Although the peoples of Central Asia are divided, there are unifying forces, as well. Islam was brought by Muslim warriors in the 700s and 800s. Islam is one of the strongest forces to unite people in the region. Also, most Central Asians speak languages related to Turkish. Many also speak Russian.

3. What unifying forces exist in the region?

_____

_____

The Survival of Tradition (pages 378–379)

What *are nomads?*

The vast grasslands of Central Asia are ideal for nomadic peoples. **Nomads** are people who have no permanent home and move according to the seasons. They travel from place to place in search of food, water, and grazing land.

During the Soviet years, officials forced people onto collective farms. The nomadic population of Central Asia decreased dramatically. Even so, the tradition did not completely vanish from the region. For example, in central Kyrgyzstan, herders still travel with their animals to summer pastures.

Among the most valuable of the nomads' possessions are their tents—called **yurts**. Yurts are light and portable. They usually consist of several layers of felt stretched around a collapsible wooden frame.

The inside of a yurt can be beautiful. Perhaps the most beautiful and useful of the yurt's furnishings are the nomads' hand-woven carpets. Their elaborate designs are famous worldwide. Nomads use them for sleeping, as floor coverings, wall hangings, and insulation.

The nomadic lifestyle of Central Asia is not as widespread as it once was. But many people are working to preserve the tradition.

4. What caused the nomad population to decrease?

_____

_____

Glossary/After You Read

acquire to gain possession of

amber a hard, usually yellow, clear fossil resin that is used in making jewelry and ornamental objects

annex incorporate (a country or other territory) within the domain of a state; take over

caravan a company of travelers on a journey through desert or hostile regions; also, a traveling group of pack animals

diffusion action of spreading out freely; distribution

philosopher thinker; one who proposes theories in a particular area of experience

prevailed triumphed; gained controlling influence by strength or superiority

Soviet Communist political and military leaders of the USSR

Places & Terms

A. Circle the place or term that best completes each sentence.

1. The struggle between Britain and Russia over Central Asia was called the

   _____.

        Red Army   Cold War   Great Game

2. A _____ is a traditional dinner party held in the republic of Georgia.

        supra   yurt   nomad

3. Many people starved to death when the Soviet government tried to reform agriculture by creating vast _____, where large teams of laborers worked together.

        Baltic Republics   collective farms   command economies

4. After Soviet officials organized the different peoples of the Russian Empire into a new nation, they called it the _____.

        Russian Revolution   Baltic Republics   USSR

5. The Communist leaders of the Soviet Union created a _____ in which they decided what could be made, what crops could be grown, and what things would cost.

        collective farm   command economy   Great Game

B. Write the letter of the place or term next to the description that explains it best.

    a. nomads   d. Cold War

    b. St. Petersburg   e. Russian Revolution

    c. Silk Road

_____ 1. Russian city, the capital of Russia during the reign of Peter the Great

_____ 2. tensions between the United States and the Soviet Union after World War II

_____ 3. a revolt that ended the Russian Empire and the rule of the czars

_____ 4. caravan route that connected China and the Mediterranean Sea

_____ 5. people who have no permanent home and move from place to place in search of food, water, and grazing land

Main Ideas

1. How did Ivan the Great make further Russian expansion possible in the 1500s?

_____

_____

2. What are two or more things that Joseph Stalin did that had a negative impact on the USSR?

_____

_____

3. What are the three different governments that have ruled in Russia in the 20th century?

_____

_____

4. What arguments have been triggered by the discovery of oil around and under the Caspian Sea?

_____

_____

5. What did the Soviet government do when carving up Central Asia that has made the region politically unstable?

_____

_____

Thinking Critically

Answer the following questions on a separate sheet of paper.

1. What are the differences between a command economy and a capitalist economy?

2. Why is the diversity of peoples and languages so great in Transcaucasia?

Name _____ Date _____

Regional Conflict

BEFORE YOU READ

In the last section, you read about the history and cultures of Central Asia.

In this section, you will learn about the regional tensions that have flared up in Russia and the Republics since the collapse of the Soviet Union.

AS YOU READ

Use this chart to help you take notes about this section.

	Causes	Effects
Issue 1: Conflict		

PLACES & TERMS

Caucasus a region that straddles the Caucasus Mountains; also called Caucasia

Chechnya a republic in Russia that has experienced the violent upheaval

Nagorno-Karabakh mountainous area in Azerbaijan now controlled by Armenia

A Troubled Caucasus (pages 385–387)

Who are the Chechens?

The Soviet Union once maintained tight control over Russia and the Republics. But when the Soviet Union collapsed in 1991, central authority weakened. In a number of regions, the demands of some ethnic groups has resulted in conflict.

Some of the most violent uprisings have taken place in the Caucasus. The **Caucasus**, or Caucasia, is a region that straddles the Caucasus Mountains.

To the north of the mountains lie republics that are part of Russia. These Russian republics include Chechnya, Dagestan, Ingushetia, and North Ossetia. To the south of the mountains are the republics of Transcaucasia. These were once part of the Soviet Union but are now independent. The republics of Transcaucasia are Armenia, Azerbaijan, and Georgia.

Caucasia is about the size of California. It is a land of great complexity. Inhabitants of the region speak dozens of distinct languages. They belong to approximately 50 different ethnic groups.

The Soviet Union began to break up in the late 1980s. As a result, several of these ethnic groups began to take up arms. They wanted to win their own independent territories. In the following decades, hundreds of thousands of people died in the resulting conflicts.

One republic that remained part of Russia after the collapse of the Soviet Union was **Chechnya**. It has experienced the most violent upheaval. Chechnya's demands for independence from Russia triggered two major invasions. These invasions caused over 100,000 *casualties*.

Russia first invaded Chechnya in 1994. By the spring of 1995, Russian troops controlled much of the republic's territory. But Chechen rebels continued to fight from hideouts in the surrounding mountains.

The Russians could not defeat the rebels. They reluctantly signed a peace agreement with Chechnya. This ended the first phase of the war in August 1996.

There was a series of bombings in Moscow and other Russian cities. The Russian leaders blamed the bombings on Chechen terrorists. This led to another Russian invasion of Chechnya in October 1999. The invasion continued into the winter of 2001. No one is certain when the conflict will end.

Russia is not the only former Soviet republic that has experienced instability. Ethnic tensions in Georgia were causing problems even before the fall of the Soviet Union. South Ossetians in central Georgia had been struggling since 1989 to join North Ossetia. A truce put an end to the conflict in June 1992. Before the truce, this violent struggle resulted in 2,000 deaths and more than 40,000 refugees.

During the truce in South Ossetia, another conflict erupted in Abkhazia. Abkhazia was once a popular resort in northwestern Georgia. Abkhazians declared independence in July 1992. In the following months, they forced Abkhazia's Georgian population to leave the region. More than 250,000 Georgians were forced out. Many died while crossing snow-covered mountains to safer areas. Though Abkhazia won the war, the region still lies in ruins. Also, the fate of the Georgian *refugees* remains to be settled.

Conflict has also plagued the republics to the south of Georgia—Armenia and Azerbaijan. Armenia and Azerbaijan fought for a long time over a mountainous area called **Nagorno-Karabakh**. Leaders in Azerbaijan say that the region's history proves that Nagorno-Karabakh belongs to them. Armenia claims Nagorno-Karabakh because much of the region's population is ethnic Armenian.

Beginning in 1988, open warfare broke out. The fighting continued on and off for nearly six years. Eventually, Armenia won control of the territory. A cease-fire was declared in 1994. However, by that time, hundreds of thousands of people had died.

1. What triggered the second invasion of Chechnya by Russia?

_____

_____

Hope on the Horizon? (page 387)

What could bring an end to the conflict in Chechnya?
Tragedy has struck the Caucasus repeatedly since the fall of the Soviet Union. However, many believe that there is some hope for the future. In April 2001, the leaders of Armenia and Azerbaijan met in Florida. They held talks aimed at creating a lasting peace. In Georgia, the government of President Edvard Sheverdnadze has been a stabilizing force.

Fighting has continued in Chechnya. The human costs of war have continue to mount. In February 2001, Russian officials reported that more than 2,700 Russian troops and 13,000 Chechen *guerrillas* have died since the second war began. Russians supported the war when it began in October 1999. Their support is now weakening.

2. What steps have Armenia and Azerbaijan taken toward creating peace?

_____

_____

The Struggle for Economic Reform

BEFORE YOU READ

In the last section, you about regional conflicts in Russia and the Republics.

In this section, you will learn about the pursuit of economic reform in Russia.

AS YOU READ

Use this chart to help you take notes about economic reform in the region.

	Causes	Effects
Issue 2: Economy		

PLACES & TERMS

privatization the sale of government-owned businesses to individuals and private companies

distance decay the tendency of increasing distances between places to make transportation and communication between them difficult

Steps Toward Capitalism (pages 388–389)

What *happened when price controls were removed?*

After the collapse of Communism, Russia tried to move quickly toward a capitalist system. This meant ending the central government's tight control over economic activity.

In January 1992, Russia removed Soviet-era price controls. The effect was dramatic. Almost immediately, the prices of many goods increased by 250 percent.

In the same year, Russia began to sell government-owned businesses. This process is called **privatization**. But few Russians had enough money to buy large businesses. So leaders offered vouchers to the public. Vouchers could be used to purchase businesses. The businesses' new owners promised to repay the government.

The policy had mixed success. Many of the new businesses were not profitable. Borrowers were unable to repay their vouchers. The failures

contributed to an economic crash suffered by Russia in 1998. In spite of a shaky start, 70 percent of the country's workforce worked in the private sector by the end of the decade.

Since the 1998 crash, Russia's economy has moved slowly toward recovery. But the movement towards a market economy has yet to benefit most Russians. By the end of the 1990s, nearly 40 percent of the Russian population lived below the poverty line. Some wondered whether things were not better under the Soviet Union.

1. How did the voucher program contribute to the economic crash of 1998?

_____

_____

_____

Obstacles to Economic Reform

(pages 389–390)

What *is distance decay?*

Though the steps have been slow, Russians continue to move toward capitalism. However, many *obstacles* remain.

A major obstacle facing economic reformers is distance decay. <u>Distance decay</u> is another way of saying that long distances between places make communication and transportation between them difficult.

Russia stretches across 11 time zones. Spread over this vast area are 89 different regional governments. The interaction and cooperation of these regional leaders is *crucial* for economic success. However, officials far from the capital sometimes refuse to *implement* the government's reform programs.

To gain control, Russian president Vladimir Putin recently created seven large federal districts. Each of the Federal Districts has its own governor-general. Putin hopes that these regional officials will carry out the economic reforms that Moscow wants.

The government must also face a powerful enemy—organized crime. The Russian mafia is a name sometimes given to the region's criminal organizations. These criminal organizations grew rapidly during the 1990s.

By the end of the decade, the Russian Mafia had created its own economy. In 1998, the government estimated that organized criminals controlled 40 percent of the private companies and 60 percent of the state-owned companies. Russian criminal activity also expanded outside of Russia.

The growth of organized crime has slowed economic reform. It often offers more money for illegal activity than can be earned by honest business. And because the activities are illegal, and the criminals do not report earnings. As a result, the government cannot collect taxes on this money.

Russian officials have made efforts to combat organized crime. Officers have been added to the police force. A special tax police has also been created.

In February 2001, Russia's prime minister reported increases in tax and customs revenues. Government officials said the increases are a sign that the Russian economy is on track. If the growth of revenues continues, Russia will be better able to come to terms with the economic *legacy* of the Soviet Union.

2. What has Vladimir Putin done to help ensure the carrying out of economic reform?

_____

_____

The Soviet Union's Nuclear Legacy

BEFORE YOU READ

In the last section, you read about the struggle for economic reform in Russia and the Republics.

In this case study, you will learn about the political, economic, and environmental problems created by the Soviet Union's use of nuclear energy.

AS YOU READ

Use this chart to help you take notes about this case study.

	Causes	Effects
Case Study: Nuclear Legacy		

PLACES & TERMS

warhead the section of a missile that contains the explosive charge

task force a group temporarily brought together to accomplish a specific task

nuclear waste radioactive materials created by or left over from the creation of nuclear energy

fuel rods bars of radioactive material used as fuel in a nuclear reactor

An Unwelcome Legacy (page 392)

Why *was the world worried about the USSR?*

Long before the USSR broke up, there was widespread concern about Soviet Union's nuclear programs. They tested bombs near villages. They placed nuclear <u>warheads</u> on top of missiles. Their nuclear power plants were poorly constructed and badly maintained. They had numerous decaying nuclear waste dumps. All threatened the region's people and environment.

The USSR collapsed in the early 1990s. World leaders were concerned about the region's nuclear weapons. The Soviet Union was now divided into fifteen independent republics. The world wanted to know who was in control of the weapons. They worried about how well protected they were. And they wondered what would happen to the nuclear scientists who had worked on the weapon systems.

The weapons industry was just part of the problem. As the 1986 disaster at Chernobyl had shown, many of the region's nuclear reactors were potentially dangerous. Observers worried that there

would be another incident like the one at Chernobyl.

1. What besides weapon systems was of concern to world leaders?

_____

_____

The Consequences of Collapse
(page 393)

Why *is the lack of security a problem?*

When the Communist government could no longer keep the USSR together, the security of the region's nuclear material became uncertain. This has caused political tensions between this region and other nations, especially the United States.

In January 2000, a **task force** of former U.S. officials issued a report. The report said that there is a chance that Russian nuclear materials could be stolen or misused. It concluded that this is an urgent national security threat. The task force recommended a $30 billion program to help ensure the safety of Russia's nuclear stockpile.

There is a connection between the Soviet Union's nuclear legacy and the region's economic health, too. For example, many regional leaders are reluctant to shut down old Soviet reactors. It is expensive to build new plants that run on alternative fuels, such as natural gas.

Some republics want the nuclear legacy to boost their economies. For example, Russian legislators recently drafted plans to make their country the world's nuclear dump. In January 2001, the Russian legislature gave approval to a plan to import, store, and treat **nuclear waste** from other countries. Officials hope the project will earn Russia as much as $21 billion over the next ten years.

Plans for the disposal of this nuclear waste outraged Russian environmentalists. But other developments have given some hope that things might improve. In December 2000, the government of Ukraine finally shut down the last active reactor at Chernobyl. Officials there pledged to spend millions on a new protective dome for the site.

Help has also come from overseas. The United States funded a treatment plant near the White Sea. It opened in October 2000. The $17 million facility will treat radioactive waste from Russia's fleet of nuclear submarines. Previously, the radioactive waste was just dumped in the sea.

2. What are two signs that things might improve?

_____

_____

Leftovers (pages 394–395)

What *is stored in Murmansk?*

Political Cartoon: A cartoonist illustrates a frightening problem—the collapse of a country with a lot of nuclear weapons. He shows the word "Russia" composed of bricks topped by a vast array of nuclear missiles. The brick "Russia" is falling apart. The missiles are beginning to fall over. A person watching this just says "Uh, oh."

News Report: A retired Russian supply ship sits moored at the Atomplot shipyard in Murmansk. The ship is loaded with a deadly cargo of warped nuclear-reactor parts and spent **fuel rods** that would be sufficient to poison the world's population. About 200 disused nuclear reactors and thousands of fuel rods are stored at bases around Murmansk. A catastrophe in Murmansk could affect the climate of all of Europe, perhaps for hundreds of years.

3. What affect could a catastrophe in Murmansk have?

_____

_____

Some Economic Considerations
(pages 394–395)

What *crisis does Ukraine face now?*

Editorial Commentary: There is no longer any threat of Russia's deliberately attacking the United States. But the nuclear bombs, nuclear ingredients, and biological and chemical weapons Russia still pose a different threat. This material is poorly stored and guarded. It could easily be stolen or sold to an aggressive country such as Iraq, North Korea, or Serbia. Also, the weapons scientists are unemployed. They could be hired by other governments. The United States once spent a lot to keep Russia from using these weapons. It would not take much more than $10 billion to eliminate most of the current risks from those weapons.

News Report: The shutdown of the last reactor at Chernobyl is only the beginning of a new chapter. The radioactive wastes must be guarded for decades. Ukraine faces an acute energy crisis. The country would like to complete two nuclear power plants started before the USSR collapsed. European banks are not offering lending terms the Ukraine can afford.

4. What threat do Russia's weapons pose today?

_____

_____

Name _____ / _____   Date _____

Glossary/After You Read

casualties people seriously injured, lost, or killed

crucial the determining factor in a doubtful issue

guerrilla a person who carries out irregular warfare (*guerra* is Spanish for war), especially as a member of an independent unit that uses sabotage and harassment

implement to carry out; to put into effect and ensure fulfillment of specific measures

legacy something received from an ancestor or from the past

obstacle something that stands in the way or opposes

refugees people who escape to safety, especially those who flee to a foreign country or power to escape danger or persecution

Places & Terms

A. Write the letter of the place or term next to the description that explains it best.

a. privatization   c. Caucasus   e. Nagorno-Karabakh

b. distance decay   d. Chechnya

_____   1. also called Caucasia, a region that straddles the mountains that stretch between the Black Sea and Caspian Sea

_____   2. disputed mountainous area, formerly of Azerbaijan, now controlled by Armenia

_____   3. the selling of previously government-owned businesses

_____   4. among the republics that remained part of Russia, the one that has experienced the most violent upheaval

_____   5. the tendency of increasing distances between places to reduce interactions among those places

B. Fill in the blanks with the correct place or term. Each term is used only once.

privatization   Caucasus   Nagorno-Karabakh

distance decay   Chechnya

1. With no central government exercising total control over Russia and the Republics, ethnic unrest has become more common. The most violent uprisings have taken place in the

   _____.

2. Chechen rebels fought from mountain hideouts when Russians first invaded

   _____.

3. There is hope that fighting over _____ will end, because Armenia and Azerbaijan have met to discuss a lasting peace.

4. In a country the size of Russia, _____ will be a consideration when trying to establish policies.

5. One way the Russians have tried to deal with the economy after the collapse of communism was through the _____ of government-owned businesses.

Main Ideas

1. How did the fall of the Soviet Union contribute to the increase in conflict in the region?

_____

_____

_____

2. Why did Russia invade Chechnya the second time?

_____

_____

_____

3. What reasons have Armenia and Azerbaijan given for their claims to Nagorno-Karabakh?

_____

_____

_____

4. Why did Russia create a voucher program, and how was it supposed to work?

_____

_____

_____

Thinking Critically

Answer the following questions on a separate sheet of paper.

1. Why is Caucasia the focus of much of the conflict in Russia and the Republics?

2. How did the rise of organized crime slow economic reform?

AFRICA
Landforms and Resources

BEFORE YOU READ
In the last chapter, you read about regional conflict and economic reform in Russia and the Republics.

In this section, you will learn about the physical features and resources of Africa, and how they shape life in the region.

AS YOU READ
Use this chart to take notes about the landforms and resources of Africa.

Landforms	
Resources	

PLACES & TERMS
basin a large depression, five large basins are located in Africa

Nile River the world's longest river, flowing through Uganda, Sudan, and Egypt

rift valley a long, thin valley created by the movement of continental plates

Mount Kilimanjaro a volcano; Africa's highest peak, located in Kenya

escarpment a steep slope with a nearly flat plateau on top

A Vast Plateau (pages 415–416)

Why is Africa sometimes called the "plateau continent"?

Africa is the world's second largest continent. A huge plateau covers most of Africa. This plateau rises inland from narrow lowlands along the coast. Much of the continent lies at least 1,000 feet above sea level. This plateau is Africa's most prominent physical feature. It is why geographers sometimes call Africa the "plateau continent."

On top of the plateau, there are five huge <u>basins</u>, or depressions. Each basin is more than 625 miles across and as much as 5,000 feet deep.

The world's longest river is the <u>Nile River</u>. It flows more than 4,000 miles through Uganda and Sudan and into Egypt. The waters of the Nile have provided irrigation for the region for thousands of years. More than 95 percent of Egyptians depend on the Nile for their water.

Africa's rivers contain many waterfalls, rapids, and gorges. These features make Africa's rivers less useful for transportation when compared to shorter rivers on other continents. The 2,900-mile-long Congo River forms the continent's largest network of waterways. But a series of 32 cataracts, or waterfalls, makes large portions of the river *impassable*.

Meandering courses also make Africa's rivers difficult to use for transportation. For example, the Niger River begins in West Africa and flows north toward the Sahara. It forms an interior delta and turns to the southeast. It cuts through Nigeria and forms another delta as it empties into the Gulf of Guinea.

1. Why is transportation difficult on Africa's rivers?

_____

Distinctive African Landforms
(pages 416–417)

What is an escarpment?

The continent's most distinctive landforms are in East Africa. As the continental plates pulled apart over millions of years, huge cracks appeared in the earth. The land then sank to form long, thin valleys.

These are called **rift valleys**. The rift valleys show that the eastern part of Africa is pulling away from the rest of Africa. Africa's rift valleys stretch over 4,000 miles from Jordan in Southwest Asia to Mozambique in Southern Africa.

A cluster of lakes formed at the bottoms of some of these rift valleys. These lakes are unusually long and deep. Lake Tanganyika is the longest freshwater lake in the world. It is about 420 miles long and more than 4,700 feet deep.

Africa contains mainly volcanic mountains. Mount Kenya and **Mount Kilimanjaro** are both volcanoes. Mount Kilimanjaro is the highest peak in Africa.

Volcanic activity also produced the Ethiopian Highlands, the Tibesti Mountains in the Sahara, and Mount Cameroon in West Africa. In addition, volcanic rock covers the Great Escarpment in Southern Africa. An **escarpment** is a steep slope with a nearly flat plateau on top.

2. How do the rift valleys form?

_____

Africa's Wealth of Resources

(pages 417–418)

What resources does Africa have?

Africa's mineral resources make it one of the world's richest continents. The continent contains large amounts of gold, platinum, chromium, cobalt, copper, phosphates, diamonds, and many other minerals. South Africa is the world's largest producer of chromium. Chromium is an element used in stainless steel.

Cobalt is another important resource. Cobalt is used in high-grade steel for aircraft and industrial engines. African nations produce about 42 percent of the world's cobalt, mostly from the Democratic Republic of Congo and Zambia. Ores and minerals account for more than half of the total value of Africa's exports.

Africa's mineral wealth has not meant economic prosperity for most of its population. In the 1800s and 1900s, European colonial rulers developed Africa's natural resources for export back to Europe. As a result, many African nations have been slow to

develop the infrastructure and industries that could turn these resources into valuable products.

Libya, Nigeria, and Algeria are among the world's leading petroleum producers. Other countries, such as Angola and Gabon, also have huge untapped oil reserves. Angola illustrates why valuable resources do not always benefit most Africans. The United States receives more oil from Angola than from Kuwait. American oil companies pay Angola a fee for drilling rights and for the oil. However, the Angolan government spends the money on an ongoing civil war caused in part by ethnic divisions resulting from years of colonialism. They invest little money in schools, hospitals, or other public infrastructure.

3. Why do Angola's resources not benefit the people?

_____

Diversity of Resources (page 418)

What is Africa's most important economic activity?

After oil, coffee is the most profitable *commodity* in Africa. Not many Africans drink coffee, but they grow 20 percent of the world's supply.

Lumber is another important commodity. Nigeria leads Africa in lumber exports. In fact, it ranks eighth worldwide in lumber exports. However, logging is depleting Africa's forests. Other major commodities include sugar, palm oil, and cocoa beans. Côte d'Ivoire is the world's largest exporter of cocoa beans, which are the main ingredient in chocolate.

Agriculture is the most important economic activity in Africa. About 66 percent of Africans earn their living from farming. Farm products account for nearly one-third of the continent's exports.

4. What is one way that Africa's economic activity is harming its environment?

_____

AFRICA
Climate and Vegetation

BEFORE YOU READ

In the last section, you read about the landforms and resources of Africa.

In this section, you will learn how climate and vegetation affect life in this region.

AS YOU READ

Use this chart to take notes about the climate and vegetation of Africa.

Climate	
Vegetation	

PLACES & TERMS

Sahara the largest desert in the world

aquifer natural store of underground water

oasis place in the desert where water comes to the surface, supporting vegetation and wildlife

Serengeti Plain tropical grassland region in Tanzania

canopy uppermost layer of branches in a rain forest

A Warm Continent (pages 420–421)

***How** large is the Sahara?*

The <u>Sahara</u>, in North Africa, is the largest desert in the world. Sahara actually means "desert" in Arabic. The Sahara is about 3,000 miles across. It spans the continent from the Atlantic Ocean to the Red Sea. It is 1,200 miles from north to south. Temperatures can rise as high as 122°F in the summer. But temperatures can also fall below freezing at night.

Only about 20 percent of the Sahara consists of sand. Towering mountains, rock formations, and gravelly plains make up the rest of the landscape.

Extreme conditions make travel in the Sahara risky. Many travelers rely on the camel as transportation. A camel can go for up to 17 days without water. In addition, wind-blown sand has little effect on a camel.

Six thousand feet under this desert lie huge stores of underground water called <u>aquifers</u>. In some places, the water comes to the surface. Such a place is called an <u>oasis</u>. It supports vegetation and wildlife and is a critical resource for people living in the desert.

Africa has a large tropical area—the largest of any continent. In fact, nearly 90 percent of the continent lies within the Tropical Zone. As a result, temperatures are high most of the year.

The hottest places are the parts of the Sahara that lie in Somalia. Daily temperatures in July average between 110°F and 115°F.

1. What effect does Africa's location have on its overall climate?

_____

_____

Sunshine and Rainfall (pages 421–422)

***Where** in Africa is a Mediterranean climate found?*

The amount of rainfall in Africa can vary greatly from year to year, as well as season to season. The rain forest in Central Africa receives the most precipitation. Here, rain falls throughout the year. Most of the rest of Africa, however, has one or two rainy seasons. Africa's tropical savanna stretches through the middle of the continent. It covers nearly half the total surface area of Africa. Rainy seasons in this area can last up to six months. The closer an area is to the equator, the longer the rainy season. The closer to the desert, the longer the dry season.

Africa's west coast also receives a great deal of rain. For example, Monrovia, Liberia, experiences an average June rainfall of more than 40 inches. In contrast, many parts of Africa barely get 20 inches of rain all year. In the Sahara and other deserts, rain may not fall for years at a time.

A Mediterranean climate exists on the northern and southern tips of the continent. Clear, blue skies in these places are normal.

2. What region receives the most precipitation?

_____

_____

A Grassy Continent (page 422)

What animals graze on the Serengeti?

In Africa, the regions north and south of the equator seem to be almost mirror images of each other. This is true for the vegetation, just as it is for the climate.

Tropical grassland covers most of the continent. One example of this grassland is the **Serengeti Plain** in northern Tanzania. Its dry climate and hard soil prevent the growth of trees and crops. However, these conditions are perfect for growing grass. Some of these grasses can grow taller than the average person. The abundance of grass makes Serengeti National Park an ideal place for grazing animals. Huge herds of *wildebeest, gazelles,* and zebras roam there.

3. Why is this region not suited to trees and crops?

_____

_____

Africa's Extremes (pages 422–423)

What is endangering the rain forest?

The major rain forests of Africa sit on the equator in the area of the Congo Basin. One square acre of rain forest can contain almost 100 different kinds of trees. It may also be home to hundreds of species of birds.

The huge number of plants, leaves, and trees block much of the sunlight that would otherwise reach the rain forest floor. Beneath this umbrella of vegetation, the air is hot and filled with moisture.

Most animals in a rain forest live in the canopy. The **canopy** is the top branchy layer of the forest. The canopy is about 150 feet above the ground.

Farmers using slash-and-burn agricultural methods are endangering the rain forest. They cut and burn trees and vegetation to create fields for planting crops. After they have exhausted the soil, they clear another patch. Experts estimate that more than half of Africa's original rain forest has been destroyed.

All of Africa's regions contain a variety of vegetation. In West Africa, mangrove trees sprout up in swamps and river deltas. Mangrove tree roots are breeding grounds for fish.

4. Where are the major rain forests of Africa?

_____

_____

AFRICA
Human-Environment Interaction

BEFORE YOU READ
In the last section, you read about the climate and vegetation of Africa.

In this section, you will learn about the interaction of humans and the environment in this region.

AS YOU READ
Use this graphic to take notes about the human-environment interaction in Africa.

Human-Environment Interaction

PLACES & TERMS
Sahel a narrow band of dry grassland on the southern edge of the Sahara

Niger delta in Nigeria, the delta created by the Niger River, which is the location of rich oil deposits

desertification an expansion of dry conditions to moist areas that are next to deserts; a shifting or spreading of the desert

Aswan High Dam a dam built in Egypt on the Nile River

silt loose sedimentary material, especially that which is deposited by moving water

Desertification of the Sahel
(pages 424–425)

What causes desertification?

<u>Sahel</u> in Arabic means "shore of the desert." The Sahel is a narrow band of dry grassland that runs east to west along the southern edge of the Sahara. People use the Sahel for farming and herding. Since the 1960s, the desert has spread into the Sahel. This shift of the desert is called desertification. Desertification is an expansion of dry conditions to moist areas that are next to deserts. Normally, it results from nature's long-term cycle.

Scientists and geographers have identified several human activities that increase desertification. Overgrazing of vegetation by livestock exposes the soil. Livestock trampling the soil makes it more *vulnerable* to erosion.

Farming also increases the pace of desertification. When farmers clear the land to plant crops, they expose the soil to wind. This can

cause erosion. Also, when farmers drill for water to irrigate crops, they put further stress on the Sahel. More irrigation increases salt levels in the soil, which prevents the growth of vegetation.

Increasing population levels are an indirect cause of desertification. More people require more food. As a result, farmers clear more land or overfarm the land they already have.

Desertification has affected many parts of Africa. For example, large forests once existed around Khartoum, Sudan. Slowing desertification is difficult. Some African countries have increased tree planting and promoted more efficient use of forests and farmland.

1. How can population levels affect desertification?

_____

_____

_____

Harming the Environment in Nigeria
(pages 425–426)

How *has the discovery of oil affected Nigeria?*

In 1956, rich oil deposits were discovered in the **Niger delta**, the delta created by the Niger River in Nigeria. These oil deposits made Nigeria one of Africa's wealthiest countries.

During the 1970s, high oil prices made Nigeria wealthy. As a result, the government borrowed millions of dollars against future oil sales. However, mismanagement, poor planning, corruption, and a decline in oil prices left Nigeria poorer than before the oil boom.

There has been considerable damage to the people and land of the region. More than 4,000 oil spills have occurred in the Niger delta over the past 40 years. Cleanup operations are slow or non-existent. Fires have also occured. The smoke caused acid rain, massive deposits of *soot*, and *respiratory* diseases among the region's people. In addition, between 1998 and 2000, oil pipeline explosions have killed more than 2,000 people. Many of these explosions were not accidents. Government officials have estimated that, in 1999, bandits sabotaged about 500 pipelines.

In May 1999, Olusegun Obasanjo became Nigeria's new president. He has started many economic reforms and fired corrupt government officials. Now he faces the enormous task of finding ways for Nigeria to benefit from oil.

2. **Why did Nigeria end up poorer after the oil boom?**

_____

_____

Controlling the Nile (pages 426–427)

How *has the Aswan High Dam helped Egypt?*

Four miles upriver from the old Aswan Dam, the Egyptians began building the **Aswan High Dam**. It was completed in 1970. Lake Nasser, which Egypt shares with Sudan, is the artificial lake created behind the dam. The lake is nearly 300 miles in length.

The dam gives farmers a regular supply of water. It holds the Nile's floodwaters, releasing them as needed. Farmers can now have two or three harvests per year, rather than just one. The dam has increased Egypt's farmable land by 50 percent. The dam has also helped Egypt avoid floods and droughts.

The dam has provided many benefits but some problems, too. During the dam's construction, many people had to be relocated. This included thousands of Nubians. In addition, one of ancient Egypt's treasures, the temples at Abu Simbel, had to be moved. Other smaller ancient treasures could not be saved.

The dam also decreased the fertility of the soil around the Nile. First, the river no longer deposits its rich **silt**, or sediment, on the farmland. Now, farmers must rely on expensive artificial fertilizers to enrich the soil. Second, this year-round irrigation has resulted in a rising water table in Egypt. As a result, salts from deep in the earth have decreased fertility of the soil. Before the dam, floodwaters flushed out the salt. Now, expensive field drains have to be installed.

Also, the still waters of Lake Nasser and the many irrigation canals provides an ideal breeding ground for mosquitoes and snails, which spread malaria and other diseases. In addition, Egyptians lose millions of gallons of fresh water every year to evaporation.

3. **How has the dam decreased the fertility of the soil?**

_____

_____

Chapter 18 The Plateau Continent

Glossary/After You Read

commodity Something useful or valuable; an article to be sold or bought

gazelle Small, graceful African antelope

impassable Not able to overcome or pass through

meandering Following a winding course

respiratory Having to do with the breathing process or organs (specifically the lungs)

soot A black substance formed when fuel is burned

vulnerable Open to attack or damage

wildebeest A large African antelope with a head like an ox, also called a gnu

Places & Terms

A. Write the place or term in each blank that bests competes the meaning of the paragraph.

desertification	silt
Sahel	Niger delta
Sahara	Nile River

In North Africa is the (1)_____, the largest desert in the world. South of this is the (2)_____, a narrow strip of grassland used for herding and farming. A growing problem on this band of grassland is (3)_____, which is being sped up by farming and grazing. Another area experiencing difficulty is the (4)_____, which Egyptians dammed in order to control the water. Now they have water for irrigation and can avoid floods and droughts, but the river no longer deposits its rich (5)_____ on the farmland.

B. Write the letter of the name or term next to the description that explains it best.

a. escarpment

b. canopy

c. rift valley

d. aquifer

e. oasis

_____ 1. long, thin valleys created by the movement of continental plates

_____ 2. place in the desert where water comes to the surface, supporting vegetation and wildlife

_____ 3. the top branchy layer of a rain forest

_____ 4. steep slope with a nearly flat plateau on top

_____ 5. natural store of underground water

Main Ideas

1. What does the creation of rift valleys indicate about the eastern part of Africa?

_____

_____

2. What attracted Europeans to Africa in the 1800s?

_____

_____

3. Where do travelers rely on camels, and why?

_____

_____

4. What vegetation and animals characterize the Serengeti Plain?

_____

_____

5. What are two serious problems that have come about because of oil drilling in the Niger delta?

_____

_____

Thinking Critically

Answer the following questions on a separate sheet of paper.

1. In what ways have the physical geography of Africa hurt its economic development?

2. Desertification of the Sahel and problems caused by year-round irrigation in Egypt are both triggered by growing populations. What recommendations might you make to people living in these areas?

East Africa

BEFORE YOU READ

In the last section, you read about human-environment interaction in Africa.

In this section, you will learn about the history and culture of East Africa.

AS YOU READ

Use this graphic organizer to take notes about what you discover in this section.

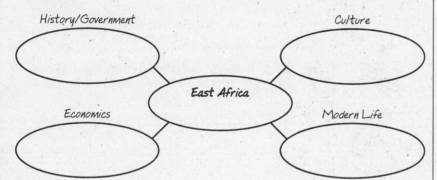

PLACES & TERMS

Olduvai Gorge place in Tanzania where fossils show human occupation dating back two million years

Aksum an important civilization that once existed in the area of present-day Ethiopia

Berlin Conference meeting of Europeans to divide up Africa

cash crop crops grown for direct sale

Masai East African ethnic group

pandemic when a disease affects a large population over a wide geographic area

Continental Crossroads (pages 431–432)

Why was East Africa an important trading center?

East Africa is *bounded* on the east by the Red Sea and Indian Ocean. East Africa includes the countries of Burundi, Djibouti, Eritrea, Ethiopia, Kenya, Rwanda, Seychelles, Somalia, Tanzania, and Uganda.

East Africa is called the cradle of humanity. In 1931, Louis Leakey, an English archaeologist, began doing research in **Olduvai Gorge**. This gorge is located in northern Tanzania. It contains fossils that show human occupation dating back two million years.

East Africa was also a place where early civilizations developed. An important civilization was **Aksum**. Aksum emerged in the area of present-day Ethiopia in the A.D. 100s. Its location on the Red Sea and Indian Ocean made it an important trading center. During the 500s, Aksum lost many trading partners. Trade between the eastern Mediterranean and Asia began passing through the Persian Gulf, rather than the Red Sea. Also, cutting down forests and overuse of the soil led to a population decline.

In the 600s, Arab, Persian, and Indian traders

once again made East Africa an international trading center.

1. Why is this region called the cradle of humanity?

_____

_____

Colonization Disrupts Africa
(pages 432–433)

How did colonization affect Africa?

In the 1800s, Europe's industrialized nations became interested in Africa's raw materials. To prevent European wars over Africa, 14 European nations convened the **Berlin Conference** in 1884–1885. Their purpose was to lay down rules for dividing Africa.

The European nations divided Africa without regard to where ethnic or *linguistic* groups lived. They set boundaries that often put traditional enemies together and separated groups that were not enemies. Europe's division of Africa is one of the root causes of the political violence and ethnic conflicts in Africa during the 20th century.

By the 1970s, most of East Africa had regained its independence. However, internal disputes and civil wars among the region's countries became a serious problem. One cause of these problems was that European colonial powers had not prepared East African nations well for independence.

2. What was decided at the Berlin Conference?

_____

_____

Farming and Tourism Economies
(pages 433–434)

How *do cash crops affect food production in a region?*

East Africa is more than 70 percent rural. Large farms dominate the region. Since European colonization, countries have become more reliant on **cash crops** such as coffee, tea, and sugar. Cash crops are grown for direct sale. They bring in revenue but reduce the amount of farmland devoted to growing food in the region.

Africa's agricultural balance is changing. People are leaving farms for the greater economic opportunities in cities. However, rapid urban growth puts a strain on the city's resources and on agricultural production.

One of the main economic activities in East Africa is tourism. The region's vast wildlife parks are world famous. These parks are an important source of income for Africans. They generate millions of dollars each year.

3. How do wildlife parks benefit Africa?

_____

_____

Maintaining Traditional Cultures
(pages 434–435)

Who *are the Kikuyu?*

East Africa is a melting pot of more than 160 different ethnic groups. Two major ethnic groups in the region are the **Masai** and the Kikuyu.

The Masai live on the grasslands of the rift valleys in Kenya and Tanzania. Most of the Masai herd livestock and farm the land. Typical Masai dress includes clothes made from calfskin or buffalo hide. Women wear long skirtlike robes, while men wear a shorter version of the robe. They often grease their clothes with cow fat to protect themselves from the sun and rain.

The Kikuyu are the largest ethnic group in Kenya. They number around 6.6 million. Their homeland is centered around Mount Kenya. Like the Masai, the Kikuyu traditionally are herders. However, now the Kikuyu live throughout the country and work in a variety of jobs.

During colonial British rule, the Kikuyu organized a society called the Mau Mau. They fought against the British.

4. What is the traditional occupation of the Masai?

_____

_____

Health Care in Modern Africa (page 435)

What *is a pandemic?*

The people of East Africa face many health care problems. The most critical is acquired immune deficiency syndrome (AIDS).

AIDS has become a pandemic. A **pandemic** is when a disease affects a large population over a wide geographic area. AIDS is having a devastating effect on Africa. AIDS education is increasing. However, many doctors in Africa say that more AIDS cases exist than are reported.

Some medical geographers predict that the populations of some African countries could decline by 10 to 20 percent.

5. What is Africa's most critical health care problem?

_____

_____

North Africa

BEFORE YOU READ

In the last section, you read about the history and development of East Africa.

In this section, you will learn about the culture, economics, and life in North Africa.

AS YOU READ

Use this graphic organizer to take notes about what you discover in this section.

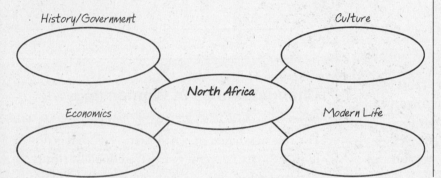

PLACES & TERMS

Carthage one of the great cities of the ancient world

Islam monotheistic religion based on the teachings of the prophet Muhammad

rai a kind of music developed in Algeria in the 1920s by poor urban children

Roots of Civilization in North Africa

(pages 438–439)

What *religion dominates North Africa?*

<u>Carthage</u> was one of the great cities of the ancient world. It was situated on a peninsula on the Gulf of Tunis, in what is now Tunisia, North Africa. Because of its position on the Mediterranean, Carthage became an important trading and commercial force.

North Africa includes Algeria, Egypt, Libya, Morocco, Sudan, and Tunisia. Egypt and the Nile valley formed a cultural hearth. The Nile River made possible the existence of the great civilization of ancient Egypt. The river flooded at the same time every year. This provided the people with water and rich soil for their crops.

Egyptians had been living in farming villages along the Nile River since 3300 B.C. Each village followed its own customs and rituals. Around 3100 B.C., a strong king united all of Egypt and established the first Egyptian *dynasty*. The history

of ancient Egypt would span another 2,600 years and around 30 dynasties.

Egyptians pioneered the use of geometry in farming. They used it to set boundaries after the Nile's annual flood. Egyptian medicine was famous throughout the ancient world. They could set broken bones and treat wounds and fevers.

North Africa lies close to Southwest Asia and across the Mediterranean Sea from Europe. As a result, it has been invaded and occupied by many people and empires from outside Africa. Greeks, Romans, Phoenicians, and Ottoman Turks all invaded from Europe or Southwest Asia.

<u>Islam</u> remains the biggest cultural and religious influence in North Africa. Islam is a religion based on the teachings of the prophet Muhammad. The Muslim invaders from Southwest Asia brought their language, culture, and religion to North Africa. Beginning in A.D. 632, the successors of Muhammad began to spread Islam through conquest. By 750, Muslims controlled all of North Africa and parts of Europe. The Muslims bound their territory together

with a network of sea-trading zones. They used the Mediterranean Sea and Indian Ocean to connect North Africa and Europe with Southwest Asia.

1. How did the Nile River affect civilization in Egypt?

_____

_____

Economics of Oil (pages 439–440)

How *has the region's economy changed?*

North Africa began with an economy based on agriculture. It then developed an economy based on the growth of cash crops and on mining. The discovery of oil has started a new economic phase.

Oil has transformed the economies of some North African countries. In Algeria, oil has surpassed farm products as the major export and source of revenue. Oil makes up about 99 percent of Libya's exports. Libya and Algeria supply the European Union with much of its oil and gas.

Oil has helped the economies of these countries. However, Libya, Algeria, and Tunisia do not have enough skilled labor to carry out this work. Oil companies are forced to give jobs to foreign workers.

Even with the oil industry, unemployment is still a problem. As a result, large numbers of North Africans have migrated to Europe in search of jobs.

2. Why are North Africans migrating to Europe?

_____

_____

A Culture of Markets and Music
(pages 440–441)

Where *did rai originate?*

North African culture is a combination of Arabic people and traditional African ethnic groups. The food and music of the region reflects this diversity.

Souks, or market places, are common features of life in North Africa. A country *souk* begins early in the morning. Tents are set up and filled with a variety of products. Storytellers, musicians, and fortunetellers entertain the crowds. A typical city *souk* is located in the *medina,* or old section, of a North African town or city. The *medina* has narrow, winding streets.

In both the city and the country, *souks* are busy all day. They offer brightly colored clothes, spices, and a variety of foods. It is a place where you can eat traditional foods such as couscous, a kind of steamed grain. In a *souk,* shoppers must bargain for the right price.

Algeria is home to <u>*rai*</u>, a kind of music developed in the 1920s by poor urban children. Carefree and centered around topics for youths, *rai* is fast-paced with danceable rhythms. It is played in discos.

3. Where is a city *souk* is typically located?

_____

_____

Changing Roles of Women (page 441)

What *roles did women traditionally have?*

The role of women in North Africa has changed during the past several years. Traditionally, North African households are centered around the male. Men go out to work in offices or the field. Few women hold jobs after they marry. Men and women generally eat and pray separately. Women are not allowed to pray in the local mosques.

In Tunisia, polygamy has been abolished. Polygamy is having more than one spouse at a time. Once, only men could seek divorce, but now either spouse can. In addition, teenage girls can no longer be given away for marriage. Penalties for spousal abuse have been increased.

Women have made gains outside the home, particularly in cities. Growing numbers have professional jobs. Women hold seven percent of Tunisia's parliamentary seats. And women now manage nearly nine percent of the businesses in Tunis, the capital of Tunisia.

4. What gains have women made outside the home?

_____

_____

Name _____   Date _____

West Africa

BEFORE YOU READ

In the last section, you read about the history and development of North Africa.

In this section, you will learn about the culture, economics, and life in West Africa.

AS YOU READ

Use this graphic organizer to take notes about what you discover in this section.

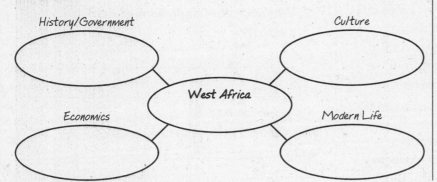

History/Government

Culture

Economics

West Africa

Modern Life

PLACES & TERMS

Gorée Island departure point for slaves during the slave trade

stateless society society in which people use family lineage to govern themselves

Ashanti West African cultural group

A History of Rich Trading Empires
(pages 442–443)

How *has trade affected the development of civilizations in West Africa?*

West Africa includes Benin, Burkina Faso, Cape Verde, Chad, Côte d'Ivoire, Gambia, Ghana, Guinea, Guinea-Bissau, Liberia, Mali, Mauritania, Niger, Nigeria, Senegal, Sierra Leone, and Togo. West Africa is a cultural hearth. Ideas and practices from this region spread to North America and Europe. Often, it was through the slave trade that these practices were spread. <u>Gorée Island</u> off the coast of Senegal was once a busy departure point for slaves. Before the slave trade, many empires flourished in West Africa.

Several empires *thrived* in West Africa. They were located on natural trade routes across the Sahara. Gold and salt were the main products traded. Ghana grew rich from taxing the traders who passed through their territory. Ghana became an empire around A.D. 800 but began to decline in power by the end of the 11th century.

By 1235, the kingdom of Mali *emerged*. Mali's first great leader, Sundiata, conquered Ghana. He promoted agriculture and reestablished the gold and salt trade. Some experts estimate that until 1350, about two-thirds of the world's gold came from West Africa. Around 1400, Mali declined. Around 1400, the empire of Songhai replaced Mali. Sunni Ali ruled for 28 years, beginning in 1464. In 1591, a Moroccan army with cannons invaded Songhai and defeated it.

In many parts of Africa, people govern themselves according to family lineage. Instead of having a central authority, such as an elected government or monarch, the power rests in a family lineage. A lineage is a family or group that has descended from a common ancestor. This system is called a <u>stateless society</u>. Different lineages share the power equally.

The Igbo of southern Nigeria are an example of a stateless society. They lived for centuries in a stateless society. If a conflict arose in an Igbo village, respected elders from the affected lineages settled the problem. However, when Europeans arrived in the 18th century, it created problems. Europeans expected a single ruler to govern a society.

1. How are problems solved in a stateless society?

_____

_____

West Africa Struggles Economically
(pages 443–444)

What *makes Ghana's economy solid?*

Trade is as important to West Africa today as it was in the past. The economy of the region is based on selling products to industrialized countries in Europe, North America, and Asia. The economies of West African countries vary. They range from the solid economy of Ghana to the weak economy of Sierra Leone.

Ghana's transition from colonialism to democracy had some difficulties. There was a period of military rule and a civil war. But Ghana now has free and fair elections. Because of this political stability, the economy is growing and healthy.

The worst economic conditions in West Africa are in Sierra Leone. Sierra Leone once produced some of the world's highest quality diamonds. However, years of political instability and civil wars have left the economy in shambles. The population is largely uneducated. Also, there are no highways and only 800 miles of roads. In contrast, neighboring Benin has about 5,000 miles of roads.

2. What problems hurt Sierra Leone's economy?

_____

_____

Cultural Symbols of West Africa
(pages 444–445)

What *is* kente *cloth?*

West Africa is home to hundreds of different cultures and peoples. West African cultures, such as the Ashanti and Benin, have produced elaborate crafts.

The **Ashanti** live in what is now Ghana. They are known for their weaving. They weave colorful *asasia*—what Westerners usually call *kente* cloth. Woven into the *kente* cloth are colorful geometric figures. These figures all have meanings.

Other crafts include making masks and stools. An Ashanti stool symbolizes the unity between the ancestral spirits and the living members of a family. A father usually gives his son a stool as his first gift.

The kingdom of Benin also produces great works. The people there are famous for making objects made of metal and terra cotta. However, their best works are made of bronze. Benin "bronzes" include masks jewelry and statues.

3. Why is a stool important in Ashanti society?

_____

_____

Music in Daily Life (page 445)

What *is a kora?*

Music is a big part of life in West Africa. West African popular music is a blend of traditional African music and American forms of jazz, blues, and reggae. However, because of the slave trade, even these American forms had their origins in West Africa.

Over the years, West African musicians have cultivated a worldwide following. Musicians from the region write song lyrics in French and English. West African music uses a wide variety of drums. There are also other instruments, such as the kora. The kora is a cross between a harp and a *lute*. The kora originated in what is now Guinea-Bissau.

4. Where did jazz, blues, and reggae have their origins, and why?

_____

_____

Central Africa

BEFORE YOU READ

In the last section, you read about the history and development of West Africa.

In this section, you will learn about the culture, economics, and life in Central Africa.

AS YOU READ

Use this graphic organizer to take notes about what you discover in this section.

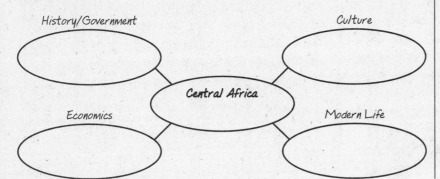

History/Government

Culture

Economics

Central Africa

Modern Life

PLACES & TERMS

Bantu migrations Movements of Bantu people southward through Africa for thousands of years

King Leopold II King of Belgium, and the person most responsible for opening the African interior to Europeans

Mobutu Sese Seko African dictator who exploited the Congo after colonialism ended

Fang sculpture Carved wooden boxes and masks produced by the Fang people

Bantu Migrations and Colonial Exploitation (pages 448–449)

How did King Leopold's exploration affect Central Africa?

Central Africa includes Cameroon, Central African Republic, Democratic Republic of the Congo, Republic of the Congo, Equatorial Guinea, Gabon, and São Tomé and Princípe. Europeans first began colonizing Africa in this region.

The Bantu are a group of peoples and cultures who speak one of the Bantu languages. Around 2000 B.C., the Bantu started in what is now southeastern Nigeria and moved southward throughout Africa. As they moved, they spread their language and culture. This mass movement is called the **Bantu migrations**. They produced a great diversity of cultures, but also helped link the continent together. Today, around 120 million Africans speak one of the hundreds of Bantu languages.

In the 1400s, the Portuguese created a base on the island of São Tomé, off the coast of what is now Gabon. It was the first base for the slave trade. Europeans wanted slaves for their plantations in the Americas.

European traders traveled to Africa and waited on the coast. African merchants brought slaves to them. The merchants traded slaves for guns and other goods. By the end of the slave trade in 1870, Europeans had transported about 9.5 million slaves to the Americas and Europe.

In the mid-1800s, Central Africa consisted of hundreds of different ethnic groups. Politically, they ranged from large empires to small villages.

Europeans had been in Africa since the mid-1400s, but had stayed mainly on the coast. That changed when **King Leopold II** of Belgium developed an interest in the region. Leopold wanted to open the region along the Congo River to European trade. By 1884, Leopold controlled this area. It was called the Congo Free State. Leopold used forced labor to gather rubber, palm oil, ivory, and other resources.

1. What were the Bantu migrations?

_____

_____

The Economic Legacy of Colonialism
(pages 450–451)

Who *was Mobutu Sese Seko?*

Central Africa's economy is still recovering from the effects of colonialism. European colonizers invested little in Africa. They left behind no money to develop more roads, railroads, airports, or a productive educational system. The region is rich in natural resources, including gold, copper, and diamonds. However, money and infrastructure are needed to develop these resources.

After colonialism ended, African leaders hurt the region further. These leaders wanted power and riches and exploited their own countries. **Mobutu Sese Seko** ruled in what is now the Democratic Republic of the Congo from the 1960s until 1997. He brought the country's businesses under national control. He then began taking money for himself. The country's economy, educational system, and social structure began a rapid decline.

Mobutu used the army to hold power. His regime finally gave way in 1997 to Laurent Kabila. Kabila's government led to more violence in Central Africa. In 2001, Kabila was assassinated. His son, Joseph, took over.

2. After Europeans left, why did problems continue?

_____

_____

The Influence of Central African Art
(page 451)

What *themes appear in African art?*

Central African art shares common ideas and themes with art in other parts of Africa. These include expressions of traditional African culture and the struggles against colonialism.

After the 1960s, many countries banned Western influences from their art. Artists wanted to recover the personality of African art by using materials they considered African in origin. Today, a new generation of artists is coming of age. They are focusing on issues of political instability, urban life, and social justice.

Prior to the 20th century, African art was not widely known. In 1907, Spanish artist Pablo Picasso saw a display of African **Fang sculpture** in Paris. After that, he used African themes in some of his work.

The Fang live in Gabon, southern Cameroon, and Equatorial Guinea. They carve wooden masks. Fang masks are painted white with facial features outlined in black. They also carve boxes for the bones of deceased ancestors. They decorate these with figures that represent the person whose remains are inside.

3. How is a Fang mask decorated?

_____

_____

Improving Education (pages 451–452)

How *can education help Central Africa?*

Central African countries hope that education will turn out more skilled workers and citizens better able to participate in democratic governments.

Education in the region suffers from few trained teachers, a high dropout rate, and a shortage of secondary schools. Central Africa's more than 700 languages also pose a barrier.

However, education is improving. In 1991, Cameroon created two new universities. Libreville University in Gabon, founded in the 1970s, now has more than 4,000 students.

4. What problems does education face in this region?

_____

_____

Southern Africa

BEFORE YOU READ

In the last section, you read about the history and development of Central Africa.

In this section, you will learn about the culture, economics, and life of Southern Africa.

AS YOU READ

Use this graphic organizer to take notes about what you discover in this section.

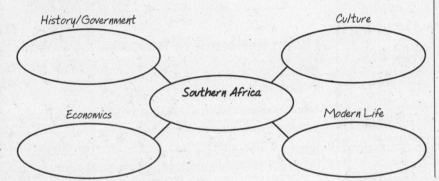

PLACES & TERMS

Great Zimbabwe City established by the Shona people around A.D. 1000

Mutapa Empire Empire founded in the 1400s that extended through most of present-day Zimbabwe

apartheid Policy of separation of races in South Africa

Nelson Mandela Leader of the African National Congress who helped to end apartheid

Gold Trade Builds Empires (pages 453–455)

***What** is apartheid?*

Southern Africa includes the countries of Angola, Botswana, Comoros, Lesotho, Madagascar, Malawi, Mauritius, Mozambique, Namibia, South Africa, Swaziland, Zambia, and Zimbabwe.

The majority of Southern Africans are Bantu-speaking peoples. This includes the Shona. Around A.D. 1000, the Shona established a city called **Great Zimbabwe** in what is now the country of Zimbabwe. From the 1200s to the 1400s, Great Zimbabwe was the capital of a thriving gold-trading area. The Shona abandoned the city around 1450.

Another empire began to grow in a nearby valley. According to local legend, a man named Mutota had left Great Zimbabwe around 1440 to start this empire, the **Mutapa Empire**. Before long, this empire extended throughout most of present-day Zimbabwe. The Mutapa Empire also thrived on the gold trade. In the 1500s, the Portuguese arrived. They interfered in local politics. The Mutapa

Empire began to decline.

Europeans migrated to Southern Africa in the 1700s and 1800s. Their presence led to conflicts with Africans. Many ethnic groups were already in the region, competing for control of the land. Now, they competed with Europeans, too.

In 1948, the white minority government of South Africa created **apartheid**. Apartheid is a policy of separation of the races. The law banned social contact between blacks and whites. Though blacks made up 75 percent of the population, they received only a small percentage of the land.

In 1912, blacks founded the African National Congress (ANC) to fight for their rights. In 1949, **Nelson Mandela** emerged as a leader of the ANC.

F.W. de Klerk became South Africa's president in 1989. He wanted change, and South Africa experienced a peaceful revolution. The government ended apartheid. A new all-race election took place in 1994. Mandela won the election.

1. Why did the Mutapa Empire decline?

Southern Africa Grows Economically
(pages 455–456)

What *resources have brought Botswana wealth?*

The policy of apartheid hurt the economy of South Africa. Economic *sanctions* prevented foreign countries from doing business or investing in South Africa. Also, apartheid led to poor education of blacks.

South Africa has produced great cities, such as Johannesburg and Cape Town. It has created huge industrial complexes and modern farms and ranches. But it also has shantytowns and poor rural areas. The new government faces unequal land distribution and a severe housing shortage.

Botswana gained its independence from Britain in 1966. The country has experienced long-term economic growth. In 1966, its per capita income was $69. In 1997, it was $3,900. Botswana has made a great deal of money from valuable resources. People discovered diamonds shortly after independence. By 1995, Botswana had become the world's third largest diamond producer. However, profits are unevenly distributed. This is a problem in many African countries.

Around 80 percent of the people work as farmers and never benefit from the diamond revenue. The other 20 percent grow wealthy. Poor farm owners often sell their farms for cash, then move to less productive land. As a result, the country now produces half of the food needed to feed its population. The rest must be imported or come from international aid.

2. Why is Botswana unable to feed its population?

Dance and Celebrations in Southern Africa (pages 456–457)

What *do* benji *dances mock?*

Celebrations and festivals are a large part of life in Southern Africa. The Chewa people perform a dance called the *Gule Wamkulu.* It reflects traditional African religious beliefs. Dancers dress in ragged costumes of cloth and animals skins. They wear masks and sometimes walk on stilts.

The Tumbuka people in northern Malawi perform the *vimbuza,* a dance performed by healers to cure people of sickness. The Yao people in southern Malawi perform *benji* dances, which poke fun at European military parades. In Madagascar, the Hira Gasy festival is a huge event. Costumed groups play music, perform dances, or act out stories. The themes of Hira Gasy promote the virtues of honesty and respect for elders.

3. What are the themes of Hira Gasy?

Living in Southern Africa (page 457)

What *role did natural resources play in the growth of Johannesburg?*

Johannesburg began about 100 years ago as a small mining town. There are gold reserves nearby. Today, greater Johannesburg is a city of over six million people. The city center looks like most modern cities. Skyscrapers tower over the city. However, because of apartheid, Johannesburg developed into two different cities. To the north lie spacious suburbs, once all white. To the south are poor black townships.

People in Southern Africa have a wide variety of lifestyles. Some work as doctors, lawyers, businesspeople. Many blacks, though, still have menial or unskilled jobs. Others live traditional lifestyles, as farmers, traders, or herders.

Some Southern African ethnic groups, such as the Zulu, work in jobs such as mining. Other Zulu hold to traditional lifestyles. They farm and do metalwork. The Zulu have a long tradition of making hoes, spears, axes, and other tools and weapons.

4. What are traditional Zulu lifestyles?

Chapter 19 — From Human Beginnings to New Nations   *Reading Study Guide*

Glossary/After You Read

bounded Enclosed; have a boundary formed

convene To come together as a group

dynasty A powerful group or family that maintains its power for a long time, usually over generations

emerge To come into being

linguistic Having to do with language

lute A stringed instrument, a little like a guitar, but with a large, pear-shaped body

sanction An action, often involving a penalty, designed to direct someone toward making a moral judgment

thrive To grow vigorously; to prosper

Places & Terms

A. Write the letter of the place or term next to the description that explains it best.

a. pandemic   d. Bantu migrations

b. stateless society   e. *rai*

c. cash crop   f. Ashanti

_____ 1. mass movement that spread their cultures and languages throughout Africa

_____ 2. society in which people use family lineage to govern themselves

_____ 3. when a disease affects a large population over a wide geographic area

_____ 4. a kind of music developed in Algeria in the 1920s by poor urban children

_____ 5. agricultural products are grown for direct sale

B. Circle the place or term that best completes each sentence.

1. In _____, archaeologists have discovered fossils that show human occupation dating back two million years.

   Great Zimbabwe   Gorée Island   Olduvai Gorge

2. _____ was a policy in South Africa that separated blacks and whites.

   stateless society   apartheid   pandemic

3. Some African leaders were corrupt and exploited their own people for personal gain. _____ was one such leader.

   Mobutu Sese Seko   Nelson Mandela   King Leopold II

4. Europeans gathered to divide up Africa at a meeting called the _____.

   Mutapa Empire   Bantu Migrations   Berlin Conference

5. The biggest religious and cultural influence in North Africa is _____.

   apartheid   Islam   Ashanti

Main Ideas

1. Why is East Africa sometimes called the cradle of humanity?

   _____

   _____

2. How did the Nile River make the great civilization of Egypt possible?

   _____

   _____

3. What were the main products traded by the Ghana, Mali, and Songhai empires of West Africa?

   _____

   _____

4. What was the impact of the Bantu migrations?

   _____

   _____

5. What different lifestyles do people have in Southern Africa?

   _____

   _____

Thinking Critically

Answer the following questions on a separate sheet of paper.

1. One advantage to having reserves that protect Africa's animals from being killed is that Africans gain an income from tourism. What other advantages do you think the reserves offer?

2. How might Africa have been different if Europeans had not colonized it?

Economic Development

BEFORE YOU READ

In the last section, you read about the history and culture of Southern Africa.

In this section, you will learn about the efforts of Africans to create diverse economies.

AS YOU READ

Use this chart to help you take notes on this section.

	Causes	Effects
Issue 1: Economic Development		

PLACES & TERMS

"one-commodity" country Nation with an economy based almost entirely on one principle export

commodity An agricultural or mining product that can be sold

diversify Increase economic variety by promoting manufacturing and developing other industries

Africa's Economy Today (pages 461–462)

Why are there so few paved roads?

As you have already read, European colonizers exploited Africa's resources and people in past centuries. Millions of Africans were sold into slavery. Countless others have died in Africa while obtaining raw materials for foreign interests. In addition, the land has been minded and drilled with little *regard* for the environment. This history of exploitation has limited Africa's economic growth and fostered political instability. Without political stability, consistent economic growth is difficult.

Today, most African countries are worse off economically than they were in the 1960s. In the last 40 years, average incomes in Africa have decreased. Incomes have grown in most of the rest of the world. Africa accounts for only one percent of the total world GNP—a small number compared to Africa's population and natural resources.

The economic infrastructure needed for substantial growth is not in place. One reason is that colonial governments only needed to move raw

materials to the coast. They *neglected* to build roads and railroads in Africa's interior.

In addition, most Africans do not have access to high technology. High technology has fueled economic growth in other parts of the world, such as North America, Europe, and Asia.

1. What has happened to people's incomes in Africa during the last 40 years?

_____

_____

On the Road to Development

(pages 462–463)

How did African nations get into debt?

Despite this legacy of exploitation, African nations are struggling to build economies that based on the careful use of natural and human resources.

When the colonial nations pulled out of Africa, they often left the new nations without money for transportation, education, and business. African countries wanted to build their economies. To do this, they were forced to borrow heavily. By 1997, total public debt of sub-Saharan governments was about $227 billion. As a result, many Western leaders have urged their countries to forgive Africa's debts. This way, Africa's countries have more money to build their economies.

Another way that Africa seeks to improve its economy is through regional cooperation. Two groups were formed—the Economic Community of West African States (ECOWAS) and the Southern African Development Community (SADC). These two groups are *striving* for greater economic *integration*.

The economy of many African nations is based on the export of raw materials. Also, several of Africa's countries rely on one principal export for much of their earnings. These countries are called **"one-commodity" countries**. A **commodity** is an agricultural or mining product that can be sold. The value of a commodity varies from day to day, based on worldwide supply and demand. This is particularly hard on one-commodity countries. Economists believe that African nations must **diversify**, or create variety in, their economies. This means they need to increase economic variety by promoting manufacturing and developing other industries.

2. What is a "one-commodity" country?

_____

_____

Educating Workers (page 463)

***What** are some of the problems with education in Africa?*

A key to developing Africa's economies is improving the educational systems. They need to be able to produce people with a high level of skills.

Africa's unschooled population is a major barrier to economic development. For example, over the last 40 years, the average length of school attendance for African women has only increased by 1.2 years. That's the lowest gain of any place in the world. In some countries, such as Angola and Somalia, civil wars have all but destroyed the school systems.

African nations must also find ways to keep its educated citizens from leaving. African professionals often move to Western countries. In 1983, the International Organization of Migration created a campaign to encourage these professionals to return home.

3. What campaign did the International Organization start, and why?

_____

_____

Name _____ Date _____

Health Care

BEFORE YOU READ

In the last section, you read about economic development in Africa.

In this section, you will learn about the efforts to combat the diseases that threaten Africa's people and culture.

AS YOU READ

Use this chart to help you take notes on this section.

	Causes	Effects
Issue 2: Health Care		

PLACES & TERMS

AIDS Acquired immune deficiency syndrome, a fatal disease that originated in Africa

cholera Treatable infection that is often fatal

malaria Disease carried by mosquitoes

tuberculosis Respiratory infection spread by human contact

UNAIDS UN group that monitors the world's AIDS epidemic

Disease and Despair (pages 465–466)

Where did HIV originate?

African nations are struggling to deal with many diseases. One of them is the fatal disease known as acquired immune deficiency syndrome, or **AIDS**. Human immunodeficiency virus (HIV), the virus that causes AIDS, originated in Central Africa. Controlling the spread of AIDS and other diseases is essential if the people of Africa are to improve the quality of their lives.

Lack of adequate sanitation and a clean water supply can lead to cholera. **Cholera** is a treatable infection that is often fatal. In 2001, widespread flooding caused an outbreak of cholera in Mozambique.

Mosquitoes carrying the disease **malaria** are common in Africa. Because so many mosquitoes carry this disease, it has become *resistant* to standard drug treatment.

AIDS and HIV create the most severe problems. Seventy percent of the world's AIDS cases are in Africa. There, AIDS is often accompanied by tuberculosis. **Tuberculosis** is a respiratory infection spread by human contact.

1. Why is malaria in Africa resistant to standard drug treatment?

_____

_____

AIDS Stalks the Continent (page 466)

How many have died of AIDS?

In the year 2000, AIDS killed three million people worldwide. Of these people, 2.4 million lived in Africa. In 2001, nearly 26 million people in Africa were living with either HIV or AIDS.

In the country of Swaziland, three out of every four deaths were *attributed* to AIDS. From 1992 to 2000, life expectancy in Swaziland fell 13 years. Now, the average life expectancy there is just 47 years.

Widespread disease has economic *consequences*. People who are sick work less. They earn less, and are pushed further into poverty. Economists *project* that by the year 2010, the GDP of South Africa will be 17 percent lower than it would have been without AIDS. Furthermore, **UNAIDS**, the UN program that studies the world's AIDS problem, estimates that $4.63 billion will be needed to fight the disease in Africa.

2. What is the economic impact of widespread disease?

_____

_____

Nations Respond (pages 466–467)

***How** is Brazil helping?*

Response to these epidemics comes from African nations and from countries around the world.

To fight malaria and other diseases carried by insects, African nations have instituted spraying programs. These programs will reduce the number of insects. In 2000, the Global Fund for Children's Vaccines gave more than 150 million dollars for immunization programs in Africa, Asia, and Latin America.

Some African countries are fighting disease by improving their own health care systems. Gabon, for example, has used oil revenues to improve its health care system. In addition, the African Development Fund approved a loan of nearly 13 million dollars to Mozambique. This will enable Mozambique to upgrade its public health facilities.

Fighting and preventing AIDS is being done at many levels. In December 2000, South Africa and Brazil reached an agreement to work together on AIDS prevention and care. Brazil has developed public health policies to combat AIDS and other diseases. Their policies are considered a model for fighting disease in developing countries.

Uganda and Senegal are two countries that have had success in preventing the spread of HIV. Uganda's success is the result of a high-level political commitment. Education programs have also been created. Same-day HIV tests and self-treatment kits are available. On the other hand, Senegal has controlled the spread of the disease from the beginning. They have an intensive education program. Infection rates in Senegal have remained below two percent since the mid-1980s.

UNAIDS says that HIV infections in 2000 in Africa dropped by 200,000 cases compared to 1999. The director of UNAIDS notes that this drop could be because so many people have died of AIDS. However, Africa is taking action. With these efforts, the continent can build an effective health care system. Then, they will be able to conquer the epidemics that threaten its people and cultures.

3. How has Senegal kept its infection rates low?

_____

_____

Effects of Colonialism

BEFORE YOU READ

In the last section, you read about efforts to improve health care in Africa.

In this case study, you will learn about efforts to bring peace and prosperity to Africa, despite a colonial past.

AS YOU READ

Use this chart to help you take notes about this case study.

	Causes	Effects
Case Study: Effects of Colonialism		

PLACES & TERMS

colonize To establish permanent settlements in a new territory

preside Sit in authority; exercise control

coup Short for "coup d'etat" (French for "strike at the state")—the violent overthrow of an existing government by a small group

intervention Stepping into a situation in order to maintain or alter the situation

ambivalence Not caring about something or someone

Colonizing Africa (page 468)

Why did European nations colonize Africa?

During the 1400s, Portuguese ships were looking for trade routes to Asia. They began landing on the coast of Africa. Soon other European countries were sending explorers to Africa. Coastal stations and forts dotted Africa's coast. These coastal trading stations would be the forerunners of a massive European colonial invasion.

By the mid-1800s, Europeans knew of Africa's rich natural resources. They wanted these raw materials for their industries. They also wanted markets where they could sell or trade goods. As a result, European nations began to colonize Africa. To **colonize** means to establish permanent settlements (colonies) in a new territory.

1. What did the Europeans want in Africa?

_____

_____

Challenges of Independence (pages 468–469)

What did Europeans not understand?

The European colonial powers began to leave Africa during the late 1950s. They left the new countries without stable governments. For the next 40 years, many of the newly born African nations and their peoples suffered through dictatorships and civil wars.

Europeans did not understand the incredible ethnic diversity of Africa. Many postcolonial African governments had difficulty getting different ethnic groups to cooperate. Dictators took advantage of these problems. These dictators exploited the people and resources of their own nations for personal gain. In addition, many Africans had no experience living in a democracy. They had lived in stateless societies.

But there is cause for hope. In the past decade, some African nations have been making progress. In 1994, the white minority government of South Africa finally yielded power to the black majority.

This ended decades of racial discrimination and social injustice.

In 2001, Ghana swore in a new president in a peaceful transfer of power. This was a change from the <u>coups</u> and assassinations that had occurred in previous changes of government. These are promising signs in a continent that is hoping for radical progress in the 21st century.

2. What problems did dictators take advantage of in Africa?

_____

_____

Problems Then and Now (pages 470–471)

How *was rubber collected in the Congo?*

Eyewitness Account: In 1899, a British official related an example of the brutality encouraged by the Belgian King Leopold. This official had been told by an eyewitness that canoes would arrive in a village, and soldiers would capture the women. They would then keep the women until villagers brought rubber from the forests.

Political Cartoon: A cartoonist illustrates the fact that the International Community doesn't always know what to do with Africa. The picture shows Zaire (the former name of the Democratic Republic of the Congo) in the middle of a circle. Around the circle marches the international community, going through stages identified as <u>Intervention</u>, Neglect, Apathy, and <u>Ambivalence</u>.

3. How does the political cartoonist characterize the international community's reaction to the Democratic Republic of the Congo (Zaire)?

_____

_____

Signs of Progress (pages 470–471)

Who *is Kwame Nkrumah?*

Editorial Commentary: In the first two decades of independence, Ghana was a political disaster. But now, Ghana is an example of legitimate democracy and successful economic reform. John Kufuor, a lawyer and businessman trained at Oxford in England, has been sworn in as president. The former military president, who dominated Ghana for nearly 20 years, stepped down peacefully when he lost the election.

Statement of Principle: Kwame Nkrumah was leader of postcolonial Ghana until he was overthrown in 1966. He writes that, though colonialism hurt Africa badly, African people must bury the past. It is time to look to the future. Africans must find an African solution to the problems. He believes that a united Africa could become one of the greatest forces for good in the world.

News Analysis: The United States is considering a law that will promote economic growth and reduce poverty in Africa. One journalist reacts to this by writing that Africa's leaders, in accepting help, are in effect begging to be recolonized. Africa's human and material resources have contributed to the development of Europe and America. But Africa is plagued by poverty, hunger, disease, corruption, and dept. Africans are turning to the former slave-masters and colonizers for a "bail-out."

4. What positive changes have occurred in Ghana?

_____

_____

Name _____ Date _____

Glossary/After You Read

attributed Described as being caused by

consequence Something that is the direct result of an action or circumstances.

integration Act of creating a whole; a uniting with something else

neglected Gave little attention; left undone

project To think about what might happen in the future, usually based on current trends

regard Consideration; esteem

resistant Able to resist; not defeated by

striving Devoting serious effort or energy

Places & Terms

A. If the statement is true, write "true" on the line. If it is false, write the word or words that would replace the underlined words to make it true.

_____ 1. HIV is believed to be the virus that causes <u>polio</u>.

_____ 2. Lack of adequate sanitation and clean water can lead to <u>cholera</u>.

_____ 3. The value of a commodity varies from day to day, which makes the economy of a <u>diversified country</u> unstable.

_____ 4. In Africa, AIDS is often accompanied by <u>tuberculosis</u>.

_____ 5. Economists believe that African nations must <u>diversify</u> their economies.

B. Write the letter of the place or term next to the description that explains it best.

a. diversify   d. AIDS

b. "one-commodity" country   e. tuberculosis

c. commodity

_____ 1. nation with an economy based almost entirely on one principle export

_____ 2. a fatal disease that originated in Africa

_____ 3. respiratory infection spread by human contact

_____ 4. an agricultural or mining product that can be sold

_____ 5. increase economic variety by promoting manufacturing and developing other industries

Main Ideas

1. Why have Africa's natural resources not yet widely benefited Africans?

   _____

   _____

2. What are some of the barriers to African development?

   _____

   _____

3. Why do African nations need to diversify?

   _____

   _____

4. What impact has AIDS had on Africa?

   _____

   _____

5. What are some of the steps being taken to combat the AIDS epidemic in Africa?

   _____

   _____

Thinking Critically

Answer the following questions on a separate sheet of paper.

1. Why would building regional cooperation help Africa with its economic development?

2. Why do you think education is having such a great impact on the spread of AIDS?

Name _____ Date _____

SOUTHWEST ASIA
Landforms and Resources

BEFORE YOU READ

In the last chapter, you read about economic development and health care in Africa.

In this section, you will learn about the physical features and resources of Southwest Asia.

AS YOU READ

Use this chart to take notes about the landforms and resources of Southwest Asia.

Landforms	
Resources	

PLACES & TERMS

wadi riverbed that remains dry except during the rainy season

Golan Heights a hilly plateau overlooking the Jordan River

Tigris River an important river that, along with the Euphrates, supported several ancient civilizations

Euphrates River an important river that, along with the Tigris, supported several ancient civilizations

Jordan River a river that flows from the mountains of Lebanon

Dead Sea a landlocked lake that is so salty that almost nothing can live in its waters

Landforms Divide the Region

(pages 487–489)

Why *is the Dead Sea dead?*

Southwest Asia forms a land bridge that connects Asia, Africa, and Europe. The region sits on a huge, shifting tectonic plate.

The most distinctive landform of Southwest Asia is the Arabian Peninsula. This peninsula is separated from the continent of Africa by the Red Sea on the southwest and the Persian Gulf on the east.

Another important landform in the region is the Anatolian Peninsula. The country of Turkey occupies this peninsula. It marks the beginning of the Asian continent.

Both of these peninsulas border on *strategic* waterways. The Red Sea, on the southwest side of the Arabian Peninsula, has a strategic opening to the Mediterranean Sea. This is the Suez Canal. Goods from southern and eastern Asia flow through this canal to ports in Europe and North Africa.

The Anatolian Peninsula is located between the Black Sea and the Mediterranean Sea. Two narrow waterways, or straits, are situated at the west end of the peninsula. These are the Bosporus Strait and the Dardenelles Strait. Controlling the straits means controlling trade and transportation to Russia and the interior of Asia.

Much of the Arabian Peninsula is covered by plains. The area is dry, sandy, and windy. Most of the land is barren, so little use is made of it. The plains are broken in places by low hills, ridges, and wadis. A **wadi** is a riverbed that remains dry except during the rainy season. On the southwestern corner of the peninsula, a range of mountains pokes out of the land. These are the Hejaz Mountains.

There is a small plateau in southwestern Syria called the **Golan Heights**. Also called Al Jawlan, this hilly plateau overlooks the Jordan River and the Sea of Galilee. This landform's strategic location has made it the site of conflict in Southwest Asia for decades.

The heart of Iran is a plateau surrounded by mountains. Isolated and high, the land is a stony, salty, and sandy desert. The foothills surrounding the plateau are able to produce some crops.

Much of the Anatolian Peninsula is also a plateau. Some areas are productive for agriculture. Other areas support flocks of sheep and goats. The Northern Plain of Afghanistan is a well-watered agricultural area. It is surrounded by high mountains that isolate it from other parts of the region.

The Hindu Kush Mountains of Afghanistan are linked with other ranges of mountains. These mountains frame southern Asia. Afghanistan is landlocked and mountainous, so contact with the outside world is difficult.

Southwest Asia is almost completely surrounded by bodies of water. This water provides avenues for trade. It also offers access to other parts of the region and to the rest of the world. However, the climate is arid. Because of this, few rivers flow the entire year.

Two of the region's most important rivers—the **Tigris** and **Euphrates**—supported several ancient river valley civilizations. Today, the Tigris and Euphrates flow through parts of Turkey, Syria, and Iraq. The valleys of these rivers are fertile and good for agriculture.

The **Jordan River** tumbles down from the mountains of Lebanon near Mount Hermon. Farther south, the river serves as a natural boundary between Israel and Jordan. The Jordan River flows into the Dead Sea. The **Dead Sea** is a landlocked salt lake. It is so salty that almost nothing can live in its waters. The Dead Sea is 1,349 feet below sea level— the lowest place on the exposed crust of the earth.

1. What feature makes trade and travel easier?

_____

_____

Resources for a Modern World
(pages 489–490)

How much of the world's oil is here?

Oil is the region's most abundant resource. Major oil fields are located in the Arabian Peninsula, Iran, and Iraq. Natural gas fields are also in the area. These *fossil fuels* run cars, trucks, factories, and power plants all over the world. Because of that, they provide a major portion of income for nations with petroleum reserves.

Today, about two-thirds of the world's oil reserves are found in Southwest Asia. It is found along the Persian Gulf and at offshore drilling sites. These reserves make the region important. Many countries, including the United States, depend on the region's oil.

Water is the most valuable resource in parts of Southwest Asia. In mountainous lands, such as Turkey, Iran, Lebanon, and Afghanistan, water is plentiful compared with the rest of the region. The water here can be used for hydroelectric power.

Elsewhere, water is a scarce resource. It must constantly be guarded and careful used. Efforts to conserve water are important. These efforts have been part of the culture of the people in this region for thousands of years.

Southwest Asia has other resources. There are deposits of coal, copper, potash, and phosphates. The deposits are scattered and not large. However, Iran and Turkey have good-sized deposits of coal.

In addition, around the Dead Sea, there are significant reserves of calcium chloride. These salts are used in manufacturing and chemical processes. For the most part, these deposits have not been heavily developed.

2. In which lands are water plentiful?

_____

_____

Chapter 21 → Section 2 (pages 491–493)

SOUTHWEST ASIA
Climate and Vegetation

BEFORE YOU READ
In the last section you read about the landforms and resources of Southwest Asia.

In this section, you will learn how climate and vegetation affect life in this region.

AS YOU READ
Use this chart to take notes about the climate and vegetation of Southwest Asia.

Climate	
Vegetation	

PLACES & TERMS
Rub al-Khali the most famous desert in the region, also known as the Empty Quarter

oasis an area in the desert where vegetation is found because water is available

salt flat an area where moisture has evaporated, leaving behind only chemical salt

Variety in Arid Lands (page 491)

***What** has transformed some deserts?*

Southwest Asia is extremely arid. Most areas receive less than 18 inches of *precipitation* a year. A huge portion of the region's land area is covered by rough, dry terrain. It varies from huge tracts of sand dunes to great salt flats.

Because the region is so dry, the region's rivers do not flow year round. The vegetation and animals can survive on little water and in extreme temperatures. In many areas of Southwest Asia, irrigation has transformed the deserts into productive farmland.

In other parts of the region, a Mediterranean climate prevails. This makes the land green and lush for at least part of each year. The land in Southwest Asia is broken up by ranges of mountains and plateaus. As a result, highland climates are found in many parts of the region.

1. Why don't the area's rivers flow year round?

_____

_____

Deserts Limit Movement (pages 491–492)

***What** is a salt flat?*

Deserts spread across the region. They reduce travel and limit most human-environment interaction. The surfaces of a desert may be covered with sand, salt, or rocks.

The most famous desert in the region is the <u>Rub al-Khali</u>. It is also known as the Empty Quarter. A local name for the desert is the "place where no one comes out." It is a vast desert. It is approximately the size of Texas. It is on the Arabian Peninsula. It covers about 250,000 square miles with sand ridges and dunes. The dunes reach as high as 800 feet. It is the one of the largest sandy deserts in the world. During the summer, the temperature on the surface of the sand often exceeds 186° F. As many as 25 years may pass without rainfall.

Next to the Rub al-Khali is the An-Nafud Desert. An occasional **oasis** interrupts the reddish dunes of this desert. An oasis is an area in the desert where vegetation is found because water is available. The water usually comes from underground springs. Severe sandstorms and brutal heat make this desert a barrier to travel across the Arabian Peninsula.

Extending north from the An-Nafud is the Syrian Desert. It separates the coastal regions of Lebanon, Israel, and Syria from the Tigris and Euphrates valleys.

The desert area that occupies parts of Israel is the Negev Desert. Unlike some deserts, this one produces crops through extensive irrigation.

In Iran, high mountains block rain, and dry winds increase evaporation. Winds evaporate the moisture in the salty soil. As a result, chemical salts remain, creating a salt flat. In Iran, there are two **salt flat** deserts. These are the Dasht-e Kavir in central Iran and the Dasht-e Lut in eastern Iran. The lands are salt crusted, surrounded by quicksand-like salt marshes. These rugged lands are almost uninhabited. They are barriers to movement across Iran.

2. What is the local name for the Rub al-Khali?

_____

_____

Semiarid Lands (page 493)

What *kind of goats do they raise in this area?*

On the fringes of the deserts are regions with a semiarid climate. Such lands are sometimes called steppes. These semiarid areas have warm to hot summers. There is enough rainfall to support grass and some low-growing shrubs.

Both cotton and wheat can be grown in this climate. The lands have good pastures for grazing animals. In Turkey, large herds of mohair goats graze in these lands. The hair from these goats, and the mohair fabrics made from it, are among Turkey's exports. Afghanistan also has areas of steppe land that are heavily cultivated.

3. What grows well in this area?

_____

_____

Well-Watered Coast Lands (page 493)

How *are dams helping?*

Some areas of Southwest Asia have adequate rainfall. There are hot summers and rainy winters along the Mediterranean coast and across most of Turkey. The weather is like that of southern California. This is a good climate for growing citrus fruits, olives, and vegetables.

Mild temperatures in the winter and irrigation in the dry summer make it possible to grow crops year round. The Mediterranean climate is a comfortable one in which to live. So these areas are heavily populated.

For thousands of years, the valleys of the Tigris and Euphrates rivers have been intensively farmed. Both Turkey and Iraq have constructed dams on the rivers to provide water all year long.

4. Why is this area heavily populated?

_____

_____

SOUTHWEST ASIA
Human-Environment Interaction

BEFORE YOU READ
In the last section you read about the climate and vegetation of Southwest Asia.

In this section, you will learn about the impact humans have had on the environment in this region.

AS YOU READ
Use this graphic to take notes about the human-environment interaction in Southwest Asia.

Human-Environment Interaction

PLACES & TERMS
drip irrigation practice of using small pipes that slowly drip water just above ground

desalinization the removal of salt from ocean water

fossil water water that has been in an aquifer for long periods of time

crude oil petroleum that has not been processed

refinery place where crude oil is converted into useful products

Providing Precious Water
(pages 495–496)

How *do arid countries get the water they need?*

In this dry region, water is the most critical resource. Ancient civilizations faced the problem of finding and storing water. Today, the same challenge exists for modern nations.

Nations today use both ancient and modern practices to find water supplies. Ancient practices for providing water include wells and animal-powered waterwheels. However, these are not *efficient* methods for large-scale farming.

To meet the needs of large farms and large populations, countries must construct dams and irrigation systems. Turkey is building a series of dams and a man-made lake on the upper Euphrates River. These will provide water and hydroelectricity. But the project is controversial. Countries downstream from the dam will lose the use of the water.

Israel has created the National Water Carrier project. This project uses a pipeline to carry water from the north of the country to sites in the center and south of the nation. The water comes from mountain areas, including the Golan Heights. It also comes from the Jordan River and Lake Kinneret (Sea of Galilee). Some of the water is used for agricultural in the Negev Desert. Some is used for drinking water. However, this project is a source of international conflict. The water sources flow through several countries, but access to the water is restricted.

Several countries in the region use **drip irrigation**. This is the practice of using small pipes that slowly drip water just above ground. The water drips just at the root zone. Evaporation is reduced, and water is conserved.

Other nations are developing ways to use ocean water. **Desalinization** is the removal of salt from ocean water. It is done at technically *sophisticated* water treatment plants. However, the water is too salty to use for irrigation. It is only used in sewage systems. Also, they cannot provide enough water to

Harsh and Arid Lands **185**

meet all the needs of people in Southwest Asia. Another source of water is the treatment of waste water—especially for agriculture.

Water pumped from aquifers is called **fossil water**, because it has been in the aquifer for a long period of time. Fossil water has little chance of being replaced. This is because the region has too little rainfall to refill the aquifers. It is estimated that the water in the aquifers will only last about 25–30 years.

1. How does drip irrigation conserve water?

_____

_____

Oil From the Sand (pages 497–499)

***Why** is this region economically important?*

The oil fields in Southwest Asia contain about two-thirds of the world's *petroleum* reserves. Petroleum is the source of gasoline and heating oil. It is also used to make everything from fertilizers to plastics. Petroleum products are an important part of the world economy. Having huge oil resources makes Southwest Asia an economically important region.

Millions of years ago, an ancient sea covered this region. Microscopic plants and animals lived and died in the waters. Their remains sank and became mixed with sand and mud on the sea bottom. Over time, pressure and heat turned these remains into hydrocarbons. Hydrocarbons form the chemical basis of oil and natural gas.

Oil and natural gas do not exist in underground pools. The oil is trapped in the microscopic *pores* of the rock. The more *porous* the rock, the more oil it can store. A barrier of nonporous rock above the petroleum deposits prevents the gas or oil from moving to the surface. Engineers use sophisticated equipment to remove the oil.

It takes technical skill and special equipment to find deposits of oil. For this reason, oil was not discovered in some parts of the region until the 1920s and 1930s.

Industrialization and automobiles made petroleum a valuable resource. Beginning in the late 1800s, oil companies searched the world for oil resources. The first Southwest Asian oil discovery

was in 1908, in Persia (now known as Iran). In 1938, oil companies found more oil fields in the Arabian Peninsula and Persian Gulf. World War II stopped further exploration until the war ended.

In 1948, oil companies discovered portions of one of the world's largest oil fields at *al-Ghawar*. It is on the eastern edge of the Rub al-Khali. It contains more than one-fourth of all Saudi Arabia's oil reserves.

Petroleum that has not been processed is called **crude oil**. Crude oil pumped from the ground must be moved to a **refinery**. A refinery converts the crude oil into useful products.

Pipelines transport crude oil either to refineries or to seaports. Tankers can move oil to other places for processing. Placement of pipelines depends on the location of existing seaports. From these ports, tankers carry the petroleum to markets in the rest of the world. In some places, refineries process the crude oil near the ports.

Moving oil from one place to another involves the risk of oil spills. The largest oil spill ever recorded was in January 1991, during the Persian Gulf War. Several tankers and oil storage terminals in Kuwait were blown up by Iraq. More than 240 million gallons of crude oil were spilled.

Buried pipelines help reduce the danger of above-ground accidents. However, oil spills on land do happen. Because oil is such a valuable commodity, the pipelines are carefully monitored. A drop in pressure might signal a leak. Leaks are quickly repaired.

Ocean-going tankers transporting oil are at a higher risk for causing pollution. Many tankers operate in shallow and narrow waterways. There is danger of oil spills due to collisions or running aground. Most modern tankers have double hulls, so that minor accidents will not result in oil spills.

2. What risks are involved in transporting oil by sea?

_____

_____

Name _____ Date _____

Glossary/After You Read

efficient most effective and least wasteful means of producing the desired results

fossil fuel fuels extracted from the earth, produced over a long period of time from plant or animal matter

petroleum a complex, oily, flammable liquid related to tar; also often called *crude oil* or *oil*

pores in rocks, pores are small holes that allow absorption of liquids

porous full of pores

precipitation deposit on earth of any form of moisture from the atmosphere; hail, rain, snow, mist, or sleet

sophisticated for technology: complex, refined, and advanced

strategic important or necessary

Places & Terms

A. Write the name or term in each blank that best completes the meaning of the paragraph.

drip irrigation   desalinization   fossil water

crude oil   wadis   refinery

Water is not always available in this arid region. In fact, some of the rivers are dry much of

the year. The dry riverbeds, which hold water only during the rainy season, are called

(1) _____. Because water is so precious, people try to conserve it.

They use (2)_____ to water their plants to avoid rapid evaporation.

Many methods for obtaining water have been attempted. Removing salt from ocean water,

called (3)_____, has supplied water that can only be used in sewage

systems. They pump (4)_____ out of the aquifers, but there is so little

rain that this water is not being replaced. However, though the region offers little water, it

offers wealth in the form of fossil fuels, particularly (5)_____ and

natural gas.

B. Write the letter of the place or term next to the description that explains it best.

a. Jordan River   c. Rub al-Khali   e. salt flat

b. Dead Sea   d. oasis

_____ 1. so salty that almost nothing can live in its waters and, at 1,349 feet below
           sea level, the lowest place on the exposed crust of the earth

_____ 2. known as the Empty Quarter or the "place where no one comes out"

_____ 3. an area in the desert where vegetation is found because water is available

_____ 4. in Iran, land that is salt crusted, hot, and dry

_____ 5. a river that flows south from the mountains of Lebanon, serving along part of
           its length as a natural boundary between Israel and Jordan

Main Ideas

1. How have people, goods, and ideas moved throughout this region in spite of high mountains and harsh deserts?

_____

_____

2. What are the area's two most valuable resources, and why are they valuable?

_____

_____

3. What variety exists in the region's arid lands?

_____

_____

4. What crops and animals are raised, and where?

_____

_____

5. Why are some of the water usage programs, such as dams and irrigation systems, creating controversy?

_____

_____

Thinking Critically

Answer the following questions on a separate sheet of paper.

1. Why are so many of this region's waterways considered strategic?

2. What might happen to the countries in this region if gasoline-burning engines in cars are replaced with electric engines, as some people predict?

The Arabian Peninsula

BEFORE YOU READ

In the last section, you read about human-environment interaction in Southwest Asia.

In this section, you will learn about the history and culture of the Arabian Peninsula.

AS YOU READ

Use this graphic organizer to take notes about what you discover in this section.

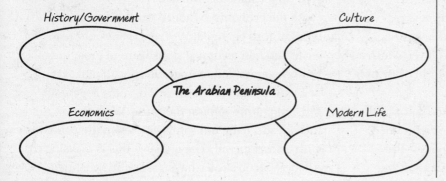

PLACES & TERMS

Islam a monotheistic religion based on the teachings of its founder, the Prophet Muhammad

Mecca holiest city of Islam

Muhammad founder of Islam

mosque Islamic place of worship

theocratic government controlled by religious leaders

OPEC Organization of Petroleum Exporting Countries, a group of oil-producing countries that helps members control oil prices

Islam Changes Desert Culture

(pages 503–504)

How did the Bedouins spread Islam?

The modern nations of the Arabian Peninsula are Bahrain, Kuwait, Oman, Saudi Arabia, Qatar, United Arab *Emirates,* and Yemen.

In the past, some towns in this subregion were trade centers for desert caravans. Others were ports where goods were exchanged. Goods came from many places. They came from East Asia along the Silk Road, from South Asia across the Indian Ocean, and from Europe across the Mediterranean Sea. Still, other towns were near desert oases or situated in fertile lands along major rivers.

Nomadic desert dwellers called Bedouins moved across the peninsula from oasis to oasis. Their fighting skills would eventually help them to spread a new religion that developed in the region—Islam.

Islam is a monotheistic religion based on the teachings of its founder, the *Prophet* Muhammad. Muhammad lived part of his life in the city of

Mecca. **Mecca** is the holiest city of Islam.

Islam united the people of the Arabian Peninsula. Certain religious duties are required of all Muslims (followers of Islam). These duties are called the Five Pillars. By following these duties, all Muslims shared a similar culture. The Five Pillars are (1) Faith—in Allah; (2) Prayer—five times a day, facing Mecca; (3) Charity—they must support the less fortunate; (4) Fasting—Muslims may not eat or drink anything between sunrise and sunset during Ramadan, the Islamic holy month; and (5) Pilgrimage—all able Muslims are expected to make a pilgrimage (hajj) to Mecca at least once. Prayer or worship may take place in a **mosque**, which is an Islamic place of worship.

Armies of Bedouin fighters moved across the desert. They conquered lands and put Muslim leaders in control. Arabic language and Islamic teachings and culture spread across Southwest Asia. It continued across three continents—Asia, Africa, and Europe.

1. What are the Five Pillars?

_____

_____

Governments Change Hands
(pages 504–505)

Who *was Abdul al-Aziz Ibn Saud?*

The governments of lands controlled by Muslims were **theocratic**. This means religious leaders controlled the government. Rulers relied on religious law for running the country. Some modern nations in the region, such as Iran, are still ruled by religious leaders.

Toward the end of the 1700s, the leaders of Muslim nations weakened. At the same time, European countries were growing in power. Much of Southwest Asia came under the control of Britain and France.

However, only part of the region was colonized. On the Arabian Peninsula, a daring leader named Abdul al-Aziz Ibn Saud was gaining power. Ibn Saud consolidated power over large areas of the Arabian Peninsula in the name of the Saud family. By the end of the 1920s, only small countries on the Arabian Gulf and parts of Yemen remained free of his control. In 1932, the whole area became known as Saudi Arabia. Descendants of Ibn Saud still rule Saudi Arabia today.

2. How did Saudi Arabia get its name?

_____

_____

Oil Dominates the Economy (page 505)

What *nations are part of OPEC?*

The principal resource in the economy of the Arabian Peninsula is oil. Arabian Peninsula nations make almost all of their export money from oil.

In 1960, a group of oil-producing nations formed the Organization of Petroleum Exporting Countries, also known as **OPEC**. The purpose of OPEC is to help members control worldwide oil prices. Saudi Arabia, Kuwait, Qatar, Iran, Iraq, and the United Arab Emirates are members of OPEC.

3. Why was OPEC formed?

_____

_____

Modern Arabic Life (pages 505–507)

What *is Ramadan?*

During the 20th century, the Arabian Peninsula began to modernize. Western technology and machines are changing lifestyles there. Trucks, automobiles, and motorcycles have begun to replace camels. The traditional open-air markets, called bazaars, or *souks,* are being replaced by Western-style supermarkets or malls.

As the economy switched to oil production, the types of jobs changed. Workers who could read and write and had technical skills were in great demand. Nations scrambled to upgrade educational systems.

Despite rapid modernization, some aspects of Muslim culture remain the same. Women cover their heads, hair, and sometimes even their faces with a scarf or veil. They believe this is pleasing to Allah. Women's roles have gradually expanded during the 20th century. More Arabic women are becoming educated.

Faithful Muslims stop their activities to pray at the prescribed times. In some countries, traffic stops during prayer times. If a person is not near a mosque, he or she may unroll a prayer rug on which to pray. On Fridays, the Muslim holy day, Muslims assemble for prayers at a mosque.

Fasting during the month of Ramadan is another duty that shapes Muslims' lives. A festival, Id Al-Fitr, marks the end of Ramadan.

4. What are two ways religious duties shape lives?

_____

_____

The Eastern Mediterranean

BEFORE YOU READ

In the last section, you read about the religion and economy of the Arabian Peninsula.

In this section, you will learn about the history, culture, and life of the Eastern Mediterranean.

AS YOU READ

Use this graphic organizer to take notes about what you discover in this section.

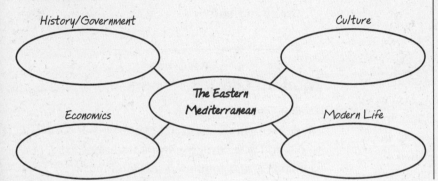

PLACES & TERMS

Western Wall only remaining piece of the Jewish temple in Jerusalem, also known as the Wailing Wall

Dome of the Rock shrine where Muslims believe the Prophet Muhammad rose into heaven

Zionism movement that supported the creation of a Jewish homeland

Palestine Liberation Organization (PLO) political group formed to regain Israeli land for Palestinian Arabs

Religious Holy Places (pages 510–511)

Why is Jerusalem so important?

Judaism, Christianity, and Islam are monotheistic religions. All three were founded in Southwest Asia. All three consider Jerusalem to be a holy city.

Jerusalem is the capital of Israel. For Jews, it is the center of their modern and ancient homeland. Located in the old part of the city is the Temple Mount. There, King Solomon built the First Temple. The Second Temple was constructed in 538 B.C. A portion of the Second Temple still stands. It is known as the <u>Western Wall</u>. Modern Jews pray at this holy site. It is all that remains of the Second Temple, which was destroyed in A.D. 70 by the Romans.

For Christians, Jerusalem is the sacred location of the final suffering and *crucifixion* of Jesus. Every year, thousands of Christians visit. Jerusalem was under Muslim control during the Middle Ages. During this time, Christians started the Crusades to liberate these lands. Eventually, the lands returned to the control of Muslims. The lands remained that

way until the nation of Israel was established in 1948.

To Muslims, Jerusalem is the third most holy city, after Mecca and Medinah. There is a *shrine* there called the <u>Dome of the Rock</u>. It is where Muslims believe the Prophet Muhammad rose into heaven. This shrine and a nearby mosque, Al-Aqsa, are located on the Temple Mount next to the Western Wall. These holy sites are close together. As a result, they have been the site of clashes between Jews and Muslims.

1. What holy sites are at the Temple Mount?

_____

A History of Unrest (pages 511–513)

What is Zionism?

The Ottoman Empire was a Muslim government based in Turkey. It controlled the Eastern Mediterranean lands from 1520 to 1922. In World War I, the Ottoman Empire sided with Germany.

Religion, Politics, and Oil **191**

When the empire collapsed, Britain and France received the lands of this subregion as part of the war settlement.

The land controlled by Britain was known as Palestine. In the 1800s, a movement called **Zionism** had begun. Its goal was to create and support a Jewish homeland in Palestine. Jewish settlers started buying land and settling there.

After World War I, Jewish immigration continued. However, Britain halted immigration in 1939, because Arabs rejected the idea of Jews having a homeland. To relieve tensions, Britain divided the area into two sections—Palestine and Transjordan. An Arab and British government ruled Transjordan. Palestine was governed by a the British, Arabs, and Jews.

At the end of World War II, thousands of Jewish survivors of the Holocaust wanted to settle in Palestine. Palestine was considered the Jewish homeland. World opinion supported the creation of a Jewish nation-state. The United Nations developed a plan to divide Palestine into two states, one for Arabs and one for Jews. The Arabs did not approve. However, the nation of Israel was established on May 14, 1948. Immediately, the surrounding Arab nations of Egypt, Syria, Lebanon, Jordan, Iraq, Saudi Arabia, and Yemen invaded Israel to prevent the *establishment* of the state. Jewish troops fought back and, by the 1950s, Israel was firmly established.

Caught in the middle were Palestinian Arabs and Christians. They either fled or were forced into UN-sponsored refugee camps. The land designated for the Palestinians is under Israeli control. In the 1960s, the **Palestine Liberation Organization (PLO)** was formed to regain the land for Palestinian Arabs.

2. Who attacked Israel in 1948, and why?

Modernizing Economics (page 513)

How *did war hurt Lebanon and Cyprus?*

The nations in this region are relatively young. Political divisions, refugees, lack of water, and a weak infrastructure make it difficult for these nations to develop healthy economies.

The creation of Israel produced a large number of Palestinian refugees. These refugees and their descendents have moved to many countries in this region. Some still live in UN-sponsored camps.

Civil wars in Lebanon and Cyprus have also caused disruptions in the economies of those nations. Roads and other infrastructure destroyed in the war must be rebuilt for economies to move forward.

All the nations of the Eastern Mediterranean have great potential for development. They have good climates. There are many places tourists could visit. They are well located for connecting to international markets. However, only Israel has been able to develop sophisticated industries such as computer software development.

3. What has caused economic development to be difficult?

Modern Life (pages 514–515)

What is traditional dining like?

Modern life in the Eastern Mediterranean is a blend of old and new. Strong cultural traditions exist, but cell phones and computers are common.

One aspect of life that remains traditional is dining. Most meals are eaten in the home. Traditional foods are served. The host may not eat with the guests. He is expected to attend to their needs during the meal.

Muslim Arabs make up the majority of people who live in the Eastern Mediterranean. However, in Lebanon and Israel there is a variety of cultures.

Since the 600s, Lebanon has been a refuge for both Muslims and Christians. A small group of Druze also live in Lebanon. This tightly knit group is very secretive about its religious practices. The cultural and religious variety in Lebanon makes it difficult to build the unity of the country.

Israel has a great variety of immigrants. The majority of immigrants are Jewish, but they come from the United States, Eastern Europe, the Mediterranean, Russia, and Ethiopia. The focus of Jewish culture helps to draw this diverse group together.

4. What makes building unity difficult in Lebanon?

The Northeast

BEFORE YOU READ

In the last section, you read about the history and development of the Eastern Mediterranean.

In this section, you will learn about the culture, economics, and life of the Northeast region.

AS YOU READ

Use this graphic organizer to take notes about what you discover in this section.

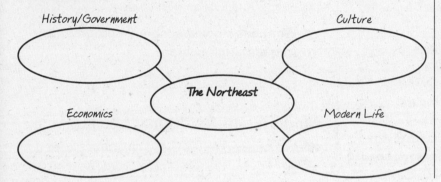

History/Government

Culture

Economics

The Northeast

Modern Life

PLACES & TERMS

Mesopotamia land between the Tigris and Euphrates rivers, where several ancient empires arose

Kurds an ethnic group in Southwestern Asia

Sunni larger of the two main branches of Islam; about 83 percent of Muslims are Sunni

Shi'ite smaller of the two main branches of Islam

Taliban extremist Muslim group in Afghanistan

A Blend of Cultures (page 516)

What *is "the land between the rivers"?*

The nations in this subregion include Turkey, Iran, Iraq, and Afghanistan. They are predominantly Muslim in religion. Only Iraq is Arabic in its cultural life.

Several of the ancient world's great civilizations were based in this subregion. Part of the cultural hearth known as the Fertile Crescent is located here. Some of the earliest civilizations developed in the area that is now Iraq. They grew up along the Tigris and Euphrates rivers. Sumer, Babylon, Assyria, and Chaldea all built empires in **Mesopotamia**, the "land between the rivers."

The people who live in this subregion claim membership in such ethnic groups as **Kurds**, Turks, Persians, and Assyrians. They speak languages such as Turkish and Farsi.

Some tensions exist between different ethnic groups, even though all follow the principles of Islam. After the death of the Prophet Muhammad, Muslims divided into two main branches—the **Sunni** and the **Shi'ite**. About 83 percent of all Muslims are Sunni. Most Iranians are Shi'ite.

1. What are the two main branches of Islam?

_____

Clashes Over Land; Clashes Over Leadership (pages 517–518)

What *caused clashes over land and leadership in the Northeast?*

The Kurds have been called a stateless nation. At the end of World War I, they were promised a homeland, but never received it. The land became part of Turkey, Iran, and Iraq. In March 1988, Iraq dropped poisonous gas on the Kurdish town of Halabja. An estimated 5,000 Kurds died. Clashes between the Kurds and the governments of Turkey, Iran, and Iraq continue. This conflict prevents the creation of a homeland for the Kurds.

Because of its location, Iran has become home to many refugees. In fact, Iran has the largest refugee population of any nation in the world. Shi'ite Iraqis were *persecuted* by the Iraqi government. They sought refuge with fellow Shi'ites in Iran. Refugees have also come from Afghanistan.

Access to the oil rich regions on the Persian Gulf is important to all nations that import oil. In 1990–1991, Iraq invaded Kuwait. This ignited the Persian Gulf War. The United States and 32 other nations fought to drive the Iraqis out of Kuwait. In addition to helping Kuwait, this also kept access to Kuwait's oil fields open.

President George W. Bush declared war on terrorism after the attacks of September 11, 2001. This led to clashes over leadership in the Northeast region. A very strict Muslim group called the <u>Taliban</u> was in power in Afghanistan. The Taliban was protecting Osama bin Laden and his al-Qaeda terrorist network. U.S.-led coalition forces removed the Taliban from power. The United States also overthrew Saddam Hussein, the dictator of Iraq. The United States feared that Hussein was developing weapons of mass destruction and helping terrorists.

2. Why were some leaders in the Northeast region overthrown?

Reforming Economies (pages 518–519)

What *steps have countries in the subregion taken to reform their economies?*

Turkey is developing its water resources. Hydroelectric plants supply energy. Irrigation boosts production of agricultural products. Turkey is the only nation in this subregion that produces significant amounts of steel. Turkey straddles two continents—Europe and Asia. Because of this, it is ideally located for trade.

Changes in Iran's government have had a major impact on the country's economic progress. The current government is supporting economic growth. Oil money fuels plans for developing a diversified economy.

After the Persian Gulf War, the United Nations placed Iraq under economic restrictions. This limited Iraq's foreign trade. It also reduced the amount of money available for food and medical supplies.

Afghanistan is one of the poorest nations on Earth. Most of the population is engaged in agriculture and animal herding. The war against the Taliban interrupted efforts to bring progress to the area. The new government has taken steps toward improving Afghanistan's economy.

3. What has slowed economic progress in Iraq and Afghanistan?

Modern and Traditional Life (page 519)

Why *do nations in the Northeast struggle over ways of life?*

Each of the nations in this subregion faces struggles over ways of life. Some people want to modernize. But others wish to preserve traditional ways.

Nowhere was this more obvious than in Afghanistan. There, the Taliban imposed rigid rules on society. After the regime was toppled, the new government began restoring civil liberties. In Turkey, Iran, and Iraq, similar groups exist but have not gained control of the governments.

4. What groups in the subregion oppose modernization?

Name _____ Date _____

Glossary/After You Read

crucifixion the act of putting to death by nailing hands and feet to a cross

emirate a region ruled by an emir; an emir is a nobleman or independent chieftain, especially in Arabia and Africa

establishment an act of bringing into existence

nomadic wandering from place to place, with no fixed residence

persecute to cause to suffer because of belief

prophet one who is said to be divinely inspired; one with more than ordinary spiritual or moral insight

shrine place in which devotion is paid to a saint or deity

Places & Terms

A. Write the letter of the place or term next to the description that explains it best.

a. PLO   d. Sunni

b. OPEC   e. theocratic

c. Zionism

_____ 1. movement that supported the creation of a Jewish homeland

_____ 2. political group formed to regain Israeli land for Palestinian Arabs

_____ 3. larger of the two main branches of Islam

_____ 4. a group of oil-producing countries that helps members control oil prices

_____ 5. government controlled by religious leaders

B. Circle the place or term that best completes each sentence.

1. _____ is the land between the Tigris and Euphrates rivers, where several ancient empires arose.

   Mecca   Mesopotamia   Muhammad

2. One ethnic group in Southwest Asia that is considered a stateless nation is the _____.

   Shi'ites   Sunnis   Kurds

3. In Jerusalem, the only part of the Second Temple that remains is the _____.

   Western Wall   Dome of the Rock   Mosque

4. A strict Muslim group called the _____ once controlled Afghanistan.

   Palestinian Liberation Organization   Kurds   Taliban

5. The holiest city of Islam is _____.

   Muhammad   Mecca   Mesopotamia

Main Ideas

1. How was Islam spread throughout the Arabian Peninsula?

   _____

   _____

2. What do most of the oil-producing countries do with money received for oil?

   _____

   _____

3. Which three religions have holy sites in the Eastern Mediterranean?

   _____

   _____

4. Why did the Arab nations invade Israel immediately after it was founded in 1948?

   _____

   _____

5. What, in addition to Islam, has influenced cultures in the Northeast region?

   _____

   _____

Thinking Critically

Answer the following questions on a separate sheet of paper.

1. Imagine that you met someone who was against modernization. What arguments might you use to convince that person that progress and economic development are good? What arguments do you think they might use to show that clinging to traditions are best?

2. The Jews in Israel came from highly developed countries, particularly in Europe. How do you think these factors contributed to the success of Israel?

Population Relocation

BEFORE YOU READ

In the last section, you read about the culture and development of Southwest Asia's Northeast region.

In this section, you will learn about the problems of relocated popluations in Southwest Asia.

AS YOU READ

Use this chart to help you take notes about this section.

	Causes	Effects
Issue 1: Population Relocation		

PLACES & TERMS

guest workers largely unskilled laborers recruited from south and east Asia

stateless nation a nation of people without a land to legally occupy

Palestinians Arabs who lived or still live in the area formerly called Palestine and now called Israel

West Bank strip of land on the west side of the Jordan River

Gaza Strip territory along the Mediterranean Sea just northeast of the Sinai Peninsula

New Industry Requires More Workers

(pages 525–526)

Why *were guest workers recruited?*

Life in Southwest Asia in 1900 seemed only slightly different from life there in 1100. Some people lived in villages are cities, while others herded livestock.

Then, in the early 1900s, everything changed. Geologists discovered huge deposits of petroleum and natural gas beneath the region's sand and seas. Western oil companies *leased* land in the region. They supplied the technology and workers to pump the fuel from the ground.

Many countries in Southwest Asia grew enormously wealthy from oil profits. The oil *boom* set off a century of rapid urbanization. Extensive road construction made cities and towns more accessible. Thousands of people migrated to the cities in search of jobs. They wanted a chance to share in the region's newfound riches.

Companies recruited people to fill the many job openings. The people they recruited came mostly from south and east Asia. These "**guest workers**" are largely unskilled labor. They filled jobs that the region's native peoples find culturally or economically unacceptable. In parts of the Arabian Peninsula, the immigrant workers actually outnumber the native workers.

The presence of so many guest workers has led to problems. There are cultural differences between the guest workers and their employers. Misunderstandings over certain customs may result in severe penalties. For example, a Filipino man was given six months in jail and expelled from the United Arab Emirates for brushing past a woman on a bus. Arabs viewed his behavior as insulting to the woman.

Sometimes the workers must live in special districts. This keeps them isolated from the Arab population. Others receive no wages for months at a time. Many immigrants find themselves unemployed and without money to get back home.

The large number of foreign workers is a concern to the governments of Southwest Asia. Some worry that depending on these workers will prevent the nation's own workers from developing their skills. Some fear that the immigrants could weaken a country's sense of national identity. Solving the cultural and economic issues over guest workers will be a challenge to the governments of the region.

1. What creates problems between Arabs and guests workers?

_____

_____

Political Refugees Face Challenges
(pages 526–527)

How *did the Kurds become a stateless nation?*

The ethnic group known as the Kurds has struggled to establish a nation for itself since World War I. In 1920, the *Allies* recommended creating a national state for the group after the Ottoman Empire broke up. But instead, this land became part of Turkey, Iraq, and Syria. The Kurds became a stateless nation—a nation of people without a land to legally occupy.

Turkey, Iraq, and Syria tried to absorb the Kurds into their populations. They did not succeed. The Kurds resisted control. Governments forcibly moved thousands of Kurds in an attempt to control them.

In Iraq, this forced migration ruined Kurdish homes, settlements, and farms. The Iraqi government used deadly chemical weapons on settlements of Kurds to kill them or force them to leave the area. In 2000, as many as 70,000 Kurds had been displaced from areas they called home. Many of the Kurds are forced to live in crowded relocation camps.

Another group of people in this region who have been displaced are the Palestinians. **Palestinians** are Arabs who lived or still live in the area formerly called Palestine. This area is now called Israel. Many Palestinians live in relocation camps in Israel. Others have moved to other parts of the region and throughout the world. They consider themselves to be a stateless nation.

Arabs did not believe Israel should exist, so they invaded following the creation of Israel in 1948. Arabs in Palestine had been promised homelands. However, Israel occupied some of these lands during the 1948–49 war. Between 520,000 and 1,000,000 Palestinian Arabs fled Israel.

Fifty-two refugee camps for Arab Palestinians were established in Lebanon, Jordan, Syria, the West Bank, and the Gaza Strip. The **West Bank** is a strip of land on the west side of the Jordan River. Jordan originally controlled the land. However, it lost control of the land in a war in 1967. The **Gaza Strip** is a territory along the Mediterranean Sea, just northeast of the Sinai Peninsula. Israel occupied it in the 1967 war.

The refugees have not been able to return to the areas of Israel that they claim are theirs. It is estimated that by 2005 there will be 8.2 million Palestinians worldwide. Their presence and their demand to return to Palestine are at the heart of the conflicts in the region.

2. How many Palestinian Arabs fled Israel when the Arab invasion failed in 1948–49?

_____

_____

Oil Wealth Fuels Change

BEFORE YOU READ

In the last section, you read about problems affecting Southwest Asia's population.

In this section, you will learn how wealth created by oil affects the region.

AS YOU READ

Use this chart to help you take notes about this section.

	Causes	Effects
Issue 2: Economic Development		

PLACES & TERMS

strategic commodity a resource so important that nations will go to war to ensure its steady supply

human resources the skills and talents of the people

Meeting the Global Demand (page 529)

Why *is steady economic growth difficult?*

At the start of the 21st century, oil fueled the world's industries and transportation. It also fueled the world's economies. Oil, sometimes called "black gold," was so vital that it became a <u>strategic commodity</u>. A strategic commodity is a resource so important that nations will go to war to ensure its steady supply.

Southwest Asia contains much of the world's supply of oil. About 64 percent of the world's proven oil deposits and 34 percent of its reserves of natural gas are found in this region. By 2020, exports from Southwest Asia will probably provide about 55.5 million barrels of oil per day. That is about 50 percent of world demand.

But these oil reserves have not always been of great benefit. One problem is that the world's oil prices rise and fall unpredictably. As a result, Southwest Asian countries cannot always plan on the amount of oil revenue. Unpredictable oil prices have also made it difficult for the region's nations to have steady economic growth. For example, when

oil prices were low in 1996 and 1997, Southwest Asia's economy grew slowly. Because of this experience, the nations of this region are realizing that they cannot base their economies on oil alone.

1. How much of the world's oil is found in this region?

_____

_____

Using Oil Wealth to Diversify
(pages 530–531)

What *resources are being developed?*

To promote economic growth, the oil-rich nations of Southwest Asia must used oil *profits* wisely. They need to modernize the region's infrastructure. They also need to develop their resources and improve education for their people.

The region has improved its infrastructure. Saudi Arabia, for example, has built new roads in rural areas. The country has built irrigation networks and facilities to store agricultural products. It has also built desalinization plants to remove salt from sea water. This will help provide water for cities and industrial use.

Other nations have constructed airports, shopping malls, and port facilities. These efforts are not always well coordinated, however. Some years ago, the United Arab Emirates built four international airports. The airports serve an area about the size of the state of Maine.

Toward the end of the 1900s, nations in the region began putting together information technology systems to serve businesses. Dubai launched a plan in 2000 called Internet City. The plan made it possible for its government to conduct business online.

Nations in the area are working to develop resources other than oil. One of the greatest needs is to develop agriculture. The region's arid conditions mean that the area is not able to produce great quantities of food. To trap much needed water, governments have built dams. They have also dug deep wells to tap water in underground *reservoirs*.

Saudi Arabia can boast several economic success stories. By 1985, improvements in agriculture allowed Saudis to meet the nation's demand for dairy, red meat, poultry, and eggs. The biggest Saudi success story, however, was wheat production. The Saudis wanted to reduce their dependence on imported wheat. They improved water supplies so that grain production could be expanded. By 1992, they were producing more than four million tons of grain. This was enough to meet their needs. They even had wheat left to export.

Other nations are making efforts to develop mineral resources other than oil. Oman revived its copper industry. It also reopened its chromium mines. Chromium is used in steel production for jet aircraft. Expanding these industries allowed the Omani economy to reduce its dependence on oil profits.

People are a valuable resource in any nation. Southwest Asian nations are developing their **human resources**—the skills and talents of the people. Many of these nations also realize that they must invest in all their people—including women.

Providing education and technology training are critical. Nations are expanding the opportunities for their citizens to gain an education. For example, Kuwait has established free education for all children through university level. For students who wish to study outside the country, the government pays their fees and provides money to cover their living expenses.

Many societies in Southwest Asia have strict rules concerning women's roles in society. Often, it is difficult for women to get an education and find employment. However, the shortage of workers in the region has opened economic opportunities for women.

2. How has the labor shortage helped women?

_____

_____

Name _____ Date _____

Religious Conflict Over Land

BEFORE YOU READ
In the last section, you read about the effects of wealth on oil-producing nations.

In this case study, you will examine the issues surrounding the control of Jerusalem.

AS YOU READ
Use this chart to help you take notes about this case study.

	Causes	Effects
Case Study: Religious Conflict		

PLACES & TERMS
Jerusalem capital of Israel, both now and in ancient times; ironically, the name means "City of Peace"

Arab-Israeli war ongoing series of attacks and invasion attempts against Israel, with the most notable conflicts occurring in 1948, 1967, and 1973

Six-Day War the Arab-Israeli war of 1967; a heavily built-up, Soviet-backed Egyptian army threatened to destroy Israel; called Six-Day War because Israel defeated the Egyptian army in only six days of fighting

Haram ash-Sharif Arabic name for the Temple Mount, site of the Dome of the Rock and Al-Aqsa mosque, both sacred to Muslims

Temple Mount Mount Zion, the site in ancient times of the Jewish temple

Control of Jerusalem (page 532)

Who *controls* Haram ash-Sharif?

The city of <u>Jerusalem</u> is sacred to Jews, Christians, and Muslims. Control of Jerusalem is a deeply emotional issue that affects the region's politics and population.

After World War II, the United Nations recommended that the city of Jerusalem become an international city. It would be under the control of an international governing group. It would not be controlled only by Arabs or Jews. But by the end of the <u>Arab-Israeli war</u> in 1948, Jerusalem was divided between Arabs and Israelis. Arabs took the Old City and East Jerusalem, located in the West Bank sector. The Israelis took control of West Jerusalem. During the <u>Six-Day War</u> of 1967, the Israelis captured the rest of Jerusalem.

Control of the holy sites within the Old City also became an issue. Although the Israelis captured the city, the Muslims retained control of their holy site, <u>*Haram ash-Sharif,*</u> called the <u>Temple Mount</u> by Jews.

As the Israelis gained control of the entire city of Jerusalem, they began adding Arab lands to the city. They placed Jewish settlements on those lands. Palestinian Arabs fled or were forced to leave the settlement lands. The Palestinians in Jerusalem and elsewhere have said that they should have the "right of return." That is, all Palestinians could return to the lands they once owned in Israel.

1. When did Israelis capture the rest of Jerusalem?

_____

_____

Proposed Solutions to the Conflict
(page 533)

What *suggestions have been made?*

The emotional and political issues of who should control Jerusalem makes it a difficult diplomatic problem to solve. Both the Israelis and Palestinians claim Jerusalem as the capital of their nation. Neither is willing to give it up to the other group. The following solutions have been proposed for the control of Jerusalem.

- Palestinians gain control of certain parts of East Jerusalem. Israel annexes several Jewish settlements near Jerusalem. This would enlarge Israeli territory in the area.
- Israel gains control of West Jerusalem and the Jewish Quarter of the Old City. Palestinians control the Old City and East Jerusalem. This is basically how the city is controlled today.
- Palestinians control the Temple Mount but give up the right of return to Israel. The sheer numbers of returning Palestinians would overwhelm the Israeli government.
- Give control of all holy sites to an international agency.

2. Why would "right of return" create problems?

_____

_____

International Involvement
(pages 534–535)

Why is interest in this area so widespread?

United Nations Resolution: UN Resolution 181, adopted in 1947, states that the city of Jerusalem should be maintained as an international city. A Trusteeship Council would be designated to administer the city on behalf of the UN. One objective was to protect and preserve the unique spiritual and religious interests located in the city, and to ensure peace. Another was to foster cooperation among the inhabitants of the city.

Editorial Commentary: For billions of believers who may never see it, Jerusalem is a city central to their sacred geography. This is why the future of this city is not just another Middle Eastern conflict. Both Israel and Palestine have real roots in the Holy Land. The United Nations, supported by the Vatican, wants to have Jerusalem under international control. The issue is not just political. No solution will work if it does not respect the

attachments to the city formed by each faith. The city has gained special meaning over 3,000 years of wars, conquest, and prophecy. This must be respected.

3. What objectives does the UN have for wanting to control Jerusalem?

_____

_____

Problems Remain (pages 534–535)

What stands in the way of problem resolution?

Political Cartoon: A dove with an olive branch, the symbol of peace, is pictured as a large puzzle. A Palestinian stands on one side of the puzzle, an Israeli on the other. Each has a puzzle piece marked "Jerusalem." However, the puzzle only has a space open for one piece.

Personal Observation: Yossi Sarid, an Israeli who advocates peace in the region, expressed his opinion on the peace process. He observed that there was only one issue that could make the Clinton peace proposal fail. That would be the right of return. He relates that Palestinian right of return would be the suicide of Israel. Israel was created out of the dreams of millions of Jewish refugees. Opening the gates to hundreds of thousands of Palestinians means that Israel would be bankrupt.

Official Statement: The Palestinian cabinet opposed President Clinton's plans, and issued a statement that said that they would never back off from their demands. They are committed to the full right of all Palestinians to return to this land. They will not yield one inch of Jerusalem or of their Islamic and Christian holy sites.

4. What seems to be the main point of disagreement in finding a resolution to the conflict?

_____

_____

Chapter 23 Today's Issues in Southwest Asia

Glossary/After You Read

Allies nations united against the Central European powers in World War I or those united against Hitler and the Axis powers in World War II

boom rapid widespread growth of economic activity

lease renting a piece of land

profits the amount left after expenses are subtracted from money earned

reservoir an extra supply, reserve

revenue money from all sources of income (such as taxes or investments) that a political unit (such as a nation or state) collects and puts into the treasury for public use

Places & Terms

A. If the statement is true, write "true" on the line. If it is false, write the word or words that would replace the underlined words to make it true.

_____ 1. The <u>Gaza Strip</u> is a territory along the Mediterranean Sea just northeast of the Sinai Peninsula that was occupied by Israel in the 1967 war.

_____ 2. The Kurds have no land that they can legally occupy, so this nation of people is called a <u>mobile population</u>.

_____ 3. Arabs who lived or still live in the land now called Israel are called <u>Asian Arabs</u>.

_____ 4. The people recruited from foreign countries to fill the many job openings are called "<u>guest workers</u>."

_____ 5. Oil is so vital to the industries and economies of the world that it has become a <u>national resource</u>.

B. Write the letter of the place or term next to the description that explains it best.

a. Palestinians   d. human resources

b. stateless nation   e. West Bank

c. strategic commodity

_____ 1. the skills and talents of the people

_____ 2. strip of land on the west side of the Jordan River

_____ 3. a resource so important that nations will go to war to ensure its steady supply

_____ 4. Arabs who lived or still live in the area formerly called Palestine and now called Israel

_____ 5. a nation of people without a land to legally occupy

Main Ideas

1. Why was it necessary to bring so many foreign workers to this region?

_____

_____

2. What actions by governments in the region have displaced the Kurds?

_____

_____

3. Why is oil considered a strategic commodity?

_____

_____

4. Why is it important for this region to diversify economically?

_____

_____

5. How can the nations of the region promote more economic growth?

_____

_____

Thinking Critically

Answer the following questions on a separate sheet of paper.

1. Why do you think the issue of guest workers is such as large problem in Southwest Asia?

2. How might expanded economic opportunities for women affect the economy of the region?

Name _____   Date _____

SOUTH ASIA
Landforms and Resources

BEFORE YOU READ

In the last chapter, you read about population problems and oil resources in Southwest Asia.

In this section, you will learn about the physical features and resources of South Asia, and how they shape life in the region.

AS YOU READ

Use this chart to take notes about the landforms and resources of South Asia.

Landforms	
Resources	

PLACES & TERMS

Himalaya Mountains the world's tallest mountains

subcontinent a landmass that is like a continent, only smaller

alluvial plain plain where soil is deposited by flooding rivers

archipelago island group

atoll island that is the low-lying top of a submerged volcano surrounded by coral reefs and shallow lagoons

Mountains and Plateaus (pages 551–552)

What *keeps rain from reaching the Deccan Plateau?*

South Asia includes seven countries—India, Pakistan, Bangladesh, Bhutan, Nepal, Sri Lanka, and the Maldives.

South Asia is sometimes called a subcontinent. A **subcontinent** is a landmass that is like a continent, only smaller. South Asia has more than one billion *inhabitants*.

South Asia was formed around 60 millions years ago. At that time, the great continent of Gondwana broke apart, and a large piece drifted northward. That piece collided with Central Asia. The violent collision of the two tectonic plates forced the land upward into a chain of mountain ranges. These mountains are still growing. They form the northern edge of the South Asian subcontinent.

The Hindu Kush lie at the western end of this mountain chain. These mountains separate Pakistan from Afghanistan. For centuries, the Hindu Kush stood in the way of Central Asian tribes that tried to invade India.

Even more magnificent are the **Himalaya Mountains**. These are the tallest mountains in the world. The Himalayas form a barrier between India and China. Mount Everest, the world's tallest peak, sits at the heart of this range. High up in these mountains lie the remote kingdoms of Nepal and Bhutan.

The collision of tectonic plates that pushed up the Himalayas created a smaller mountain range in central India. This is the Vindhya Mountains. Beyond the Ganges Plain lies the Deccan Plateau. This large plateau covers much of southern India. Mountain ranges stand on either side of the plateau. These are the Western Ghats and the Eastern Ghats. These mountains separate the plateau from the coast. They also block the moist winds and keep rain from reaching the interior.

1. What event created the Himalaya Mountains?

_____

_____

The Land Where Continents Collided **205**

Rivers, Deltas, and Plains
(pages 552–553)

Why is the Northern Indian Plain heavily populated?

The Northern Indian Plain lies between the Deccan Plateau and the northern mountains. This large lowland region stretches from Pakistan in the west to Bangladesh in the east.

The three great rivers of India are the Indus, the Ganges, and the Brahmaputra. The Indus flows through Pakistan to the Arabian Sea. The Ganges flows eastward across northern India. The Brahmaputra winds through Bangladesh. The Ganges and Brahmaputra eventually meet to form one huge river delta. Then they flow into the Bay of Bengal.

These rivers play a key role in supporting life in South Asia. Their waters provide irrigation for agriculture. They also carry rich, *alluvial* soil down from the mountains. When the rivers overflow their banks and flood the surrounding plains, they leave a layer of alluvial soil. These plains are called **alluvial plains**. The alluvial soil enriches the land.

This plain is the most heavily populated part of South Asia. The area contains about three-fifths of India's population. Many of South Asia's largest cities are located there. Population densities at the eastern end of the plain are especially high. This is the area of the Ganges-Brahmaputra delta.

2. What are the three great rivers of India?

_____

_____

Offshore Islands (page 553)

Where is Sri Lanka?

Two island groups are also part of South Asia. These are Sri Lanka and the Maldives. Sri Lanka is located in the Indian Ocean just off India's southeastern tip. The Maldives are located farther off the Indian coast to the southwest.

Sri Lanka is a large, tear-shaped island country. It is lush and tropical. In the center of the island is a range of rugged mountains. Many small rivers flow from these mountains to the lowlands below. The northern side of the island consists of low hills and

farmland. Circling the island is a coastal plain that includes long beaches with palm trees.

The Maldives is an **archipelago**, or island group. It is made up of more than 1,200 small islands. Only about 200 islands are inhabited. The islands are the low-lying tops of submerged volcanoes. They are surrounded by coral reefs and shallow *lagoons.* This type of island is called an **atoll**.

3. What is an atoll?

_____

_____

Natural Resources (pages 554–555)

How does the region use its rivers?

South Asia relies on its soil and water resources. The river systems enrich the farmland with alluvial soil. They also bring the water needed to grow crops. Many types of fish are found in South Asian rivers and coastal waters. These waters also provide transportation and power.

Most energy in South Asia is generated from mineral resources. India has abundant coal and petroleum. India, Pakistan, and Bangladesh have natural gas resources. Uranium deposits in India provide fuel for nuclear energy.

South Asia also has large iron-ore deposits. India exports iron ore and also uses it in its steel industry. India supplies most of the world's mica, a mineral used in making electrical equipment. This is one reason that India has a growing computer industry.

4. What minerals provide energy in South Asia?

_____

_____

SOUTH ASIA
Climate and Vegetation

Before You Read

In the last section you read about the landforms and resources of South Asia.

In this section, you will learn about the climate and vegetation of this region.

As You Read

Use this chart to take notes about the climate and vegetation of South Asia.

Climate	
Vegetation	

PLACES & TERMS

monsoon seasonal winds

cyclone violent storm with fierce winds and heavy rain

Climate—Wet and Dry, Hot and Cold

(pages 556–558)

What are South Asia's main climate zone?

South Asia has six main climate zones. The highland zone has the coldest climate. This is the area of the high Himalayas and other northern mountains. There, snow exists year round.

The lower elevations are much warmer. They include the lush foothills and valleys of Nepal, Bhutan, and northern India. They are in the humid subtropical zone that stretches across much of South Asia. The Northern Indian Plain occupies much of this region.

The semiarid zone is found at the western end of the plain and in parts of the Deccan Plateau. There, the temperatures are high and rainfall is light.

The desert zone covers much of the lower Indus Valley. This valley is in the borderlands of western India and southern Pakistan. The driest part of this area is the Thar Desert. It gets very little rain— about ten inches a year.

The tropical wet zone is found along the western and eastern coasts of India and Bangladesh. Temperatures are high there, and rainfall is heavy. In fact, Cherrapunji, a village in northeast India, holds the world's record for monthly rainfall—366 inches.

Southern Sri Lanka also has a tropical wet climate. However, northern Sri Lanka has a tropical wet and dry climate.

Although climate varies in South Asia, the region as a whole is greatly affected by monsoons. **Monsoons** are seasonal winds. From October through February, dry winds blow across South Asia from the northeast. Then, from June through September, the winds blow in from the southwest. These winds bring moist ocean air. Heavy rains fall, especially in the southern and eastern portions of South Asia. This rainfall is *crucial* to life on the subcontinent. However, the monsoons can cause severe hardship for millions. Those living in the lowlands of India and Bangladesh often experience flooding. The monsoons are also highly unpredictable. Some areas may get too little rain, while others get too much. The monsoons are an essential but difficult feature of life in South Asia.

The most extreme weather pattern of South Asia is the cyclone. A <u>cyclone</u> is a violent storm with fierce winds and heavy rain. Cyclones are most destructive in Bangladesh. Bangladesh is a low-lying coastal region where high waves can swamp large parts of the country. A severe cyclone can cause widespread damage and kill thousands of people.

1. How do monsoons both help and hurt the region?

_____

_____

Vegetation: Desert to Rain Forest
(page 558)

What *trees are found in the tropical wet zone?*

Plant life in South Asia varies according to climate and altitude. Vegetation ranges from desert shrub and temperate grasslands to dense forests in the wettest areas.

The most heavily forested parts of South Asia lie within the tropical wet zone. This is especially true of the western coast of India and southern Bangladesh. Lush rain forests of exotic woods, such as teak and ebony are found here. There is also bamboo. Mangroves grow in the delta areas.

The highland zone in the north has forests of pine, fir, and other evergreens. The river valleys and foothills of the humid subtropical zone have forests of sal, oak, chestnut, and various plants.

Deforestation is a problem in all these zones. For example, less than one-fifth of India's original forests remain. Cutting down forests has caused soil erosion, flooding, climate changes, and lost wildlife habitats.

The semiarid areas of South Asia have less vegetation. This includes the Deccan Plateau and the Pakistan-India border. The main plant life here is desert shrub. There is a mixture of low trees and grasses.

The driest areas, such as the Thar Desert, have little plant life. As a result, these areas also have few people. The tropical wet and dry climate of northern Sri Lanka produces both grasses and trees.

2. What serious problems have occurred because of deforestation?

_____

_____

Name _____ Date _____

SOUTH ASIA
Human-Environment Interaction

Before You Read

In the last section you read about the climate and vegetation of South Asia.

In this section, you will learn about the impact humans have had on the environment in this region.

As You Read

Use this graphic to take notes about the human-environment interaction in South Asia.

Human-Environment Interaction

PLACES & TERMS

Ganges River important South Asian river, considered sacred by Hindus

Hinduism the religion of most Indians

storm surge high waters brought by cyclones

estuary an arm of the sea at the lower end of a river

Living Along the Ganges (pages 560–561)

***Why** is the Ganges in trouble?*

The <u>Ganges River</u> is the most famous of all South Asian rivers. It flows more than 1,500 miles from Himalayas to the Bay of Bengal. It drains an area nearly twice the size of France. The area drained by the Ganges is home to more than 350 million people.

The religion of most of the people in India is <u>Hinduism</u>. For Hindus, the Ganges is a sacred river. It provides water for drinking, farming, and transport. But to Hindus, the river's spiritual aspect is just as important.

The Ganges is known in India as *Gangamai*, which means "Mother Ganges." The Hindus worship the river as a goddess. They believe its waters have healing powers.

Many temples and sacred sites line the banks of the Ganges. In some places, wide stone steps lead down to the water. Pilgrims come from all parts of India to drink and bathe in the river's waters. They also come to scatter the ashes of *deceased* family members on the river.

In the city of Varanasi, there is one of the most sacred sites on the Ganges River. Every day, thousands of people gather there. As the sun rises, Hindu *pilgrims* enter the river for purification and prayer. They float baskets of flowers and burn candles on the water. It is a daily celebration of the Hindu faith in the Ganges.

Unfortunately for the people of India, the Ganges is in trouble. There have been many centuries of intense human use. The Ganges has become one of the most polluted rivers in the world. Millions of gallons of raw sewage and industrial waste flow into the river every day. The bodies of dead animals float on the water. Even human corpses are thrown into the water. As a result, the water is poisoned with toxic chemicals and deadly bacteria.

The Land Where Continents Collided **209**

Thousands of people who bathe in the river or drink the water become ill.

Since 1986, the government of India has tried to restore the health of the river. Plans have called for a network of sewage treatment plants to clean the water. They also call for tougher regulations on industrial polluters. So far, progress has been slow.

Pollution in the Ganges will also require a change in the way people view the river. Many Hindus believe the Ganges is too holy to be harmed by pollution. They believe that "Mother Ganges" will fix any problems.

1. What do Hindus think of the Ganges River?

_____

_____

Controlling the Feni River
(pages 562–563)

***Why** did the Feni need to be closed?*

In Bangladesh, the most important river is the Brahmaputra. Bangladesh also has many other rivers. One of the rivers is the Feni.

The Feni River flows through a low-lying coastal plain before it reaches the sea. This area borders the Bay of Bengal. This flat, marshy area is subject to flooding during the wet season. During the wet season, monsoon rains swell the rivers. The rivers often overflow their banks.

Cyclones are also a problem here. They sweep across the Bay of Bengal. Cyclones bring high waters—called **storm surges**—that swamp low-lying areas.

Over the years, storm surges at the mouth of the Feni River have caused great hardship. Sea water surges up the river and onto the coastal flatlands. Villages and fields are flooded. There is great destruction. On smaller streams, villages sometimes build earthen dikes. This blocks the water and protects their farms. But such structures are not effective against flooding of large rivers.

In the 1980s, engineers in Bangladesh proposed building a dam. The plan faced many difficulties. The mouth of the river is nearly a mile wide.

Bangladesh has a large population. The country's human resources became the key to the project. There were plenty of unskilled workers available for construction work. To help plan the job, Bangladesh hired engineers from the Netherlands.

The project began in 1984. The project emphasized the use of cheap materials and low-tech procedures. The first step was to lay down heavy mats. The mats were made of bamboo, reeds, and boulders. This was done to prevent erosion of the river bottom. Workers piled more boulders on top of the mats. They then covered the boulders with clay-filled bags. After six months of work, they had built a partial closure across the mouth of the Feni.

At that point, gaps in the wall still allowed water to flow in and out. Engineers had chosen February 28, 1985, as the day to close the river. This was the day of the lowest tide. When the tide went out, 15,000 workers rushed to fill in the gaps with clay bags. In a seven-hour period, they laid down 600,000 bags. When the tide came back, the dam was closed.

After that, dump trucks and earthmovers added more clay to raise the dam to a height of 30 feet. Then, workers placed concrete and brick over the sides of the dam. Finally, they built a road on top. Bangladesh now had the largest estuary dam in South Asia. An **estuary** is an arm of the sea at the lower end of a river.

Everyone wondered if the dam would hold in a storm. Three months later, a cyclone swept across the Bay of Bengal. A storm surge hit the dam, but the dam held. The Feni River closure offers hope for similar solutions in other low-lying areas.

2. What made planning the dam difficult?

_____

_____

Name _____   Date _____

Glossary/After You Read

alluvial relating to or composed of material—such as clay, silt, or sand—that is deposited by running water

crucial the determining factor in a situation

deceased dead

inhabitants permanent residents of a place

lagoon shallow area of water, such as a channel or pond, that is near or connects with a larger body of water

pilgrim one who travels to a shrine or holy place as a religious duty

---

Places & Terms

A. Write the name or term in each blank that best completes the meaning of the paragraph.

monsoons   cyclones

storm surges   alluvial plain

estuary

Water is important in South Asia, but it can be both a friend and an enemy. When the rivers overflow their banks, they deposit rich soil on the (1)_____.
This flooding most often comes during the wet season, when seasonal winds called (2)_____ bring heavy rains. Sometimes the monsoons bring too much rain, and sometimes the region experiences (3)_____, violent storms with fierce winds and heavy rains. When these storms hit, they can bring high waters, called (4)_____, which swamp low-lying areas. To protect the land from this high water, Bangladesh built a large dam across the part of the Feni River where the sea meets the river's waters (called an (5)_____).

B. Write the letter of the place or term next to the description that explains it best.

a. Hinduism   d. atoll

b. Ganges   e. subcontinent

c. archipelago

_____ 1. one of the most polluted rivers in the world

_____ 2. a landmass that is like a continent, only smaller

_____ 3. the religion of most of India's inhabitants

_____ 4. an island that is the low-lying top of a submerged volcano surrounded by coral reefs and shallow lagoons

_____ 5. an island group, such as the Maldives

Main Ideas

1. Why is South Asia sometimes called a subcontinent, and why is it sometimes called the Indian subcontinent?

   _____

   _____

2. What are three or more resources that help sustain life and the economy in this region?

   _____

   _____

3. What are three or more of the six climate zones in South Asia?

   _____

   _____

4. What are the seasonal weather patterns like that affect much of this region?

   _____

   _____

5. Why is the Ganges River so important to India?

   _____

   _____

Thinking Critically

Answer the following questions on a separate sheet of paper.

1. Based on what you know of the creation of the subcontinent of South Asia, why do you think the mountains to the north are still growing?

2. How would you explain the problems of the Ganges to someone who lived along the river?

Chapter 25 Section 1 (pages 567–572)

India

BEFORE YOU READ

In the last chapter you, read about the physical geography of South Asia.

In this section, you will learn about the history and culture of India.

AS YOU READ

Use this graphic organizer to take notes about what you discover in this section.

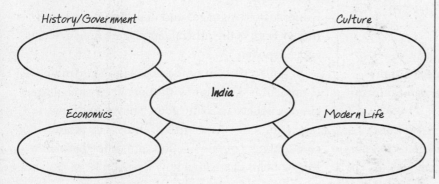

PLACES & TERMS

Mughal Empire empire established by Muslim invaders in the early 1500s

raj Hindi word for *reign,* used to identify the period of British rule over India

nonviolent resistance form of protest used by Mohandas Gandhi, which employs any means of protest except violence

land reform a more balanced distribution of land among farmers

Green Revolution name given to results of plant research by American plant breeder, Norman Borlaug, who won the Nobel Prize for averting famine in India

caste system Hindu system of social classes

Invasions, Empires, and Independence (pages 567–568)

***What** is nonviolent resistance?*

Indian civilization began in the Indus Valley around 2500 B.C. A thousand years later, Aryan invaders crossed the mountains into India. Aryans were from the plains north of Iran. The Aryans established small kingdoms on the Ganges Plain. They pushed the Dravidians toward the south.

Beginning in 321 B.C., the Mauryan Empire united most of India. Centuries later, the Gupta Empire came to power. It ruled over northern India.

Muslims conquered the Indus Valley, and occupied the Ganges Plain. By the early 1500s, they had established the **Mughal Empire** over much of India.

In the 1500s, European traders came to India. They established trade relations with India's rulers. French, Dutch, and Portuguese traders set up trading colonies. It was the British who won out.

The British East India Company was a business and political organization. Through it, Britain gained control over India's trade in 1757. In 1857,

there was a revolt. Britain put down the revolt and established direct rule over India. The period of British rule, called the **raj**, lasted for 90 years.

British rule brought benefits to India, but most Indians resented it. The Indian leader Mohandas Gandhi began an *opposition* movement. He used **nonviolent resistance**, a form of protest that never used violence. In 1947, India became independent.

1. What empire was established in the 1500s?

_____

_____

Governing the World's Largest Democracy (pages 568–569)

***How** is India's government like Britain's?*

Under Prime Minister Nehru, India adopted a constitution. India became a democratic republic. Like the United States, India is a *federation* of states. It is held together by a strong central government. Like Britain, India's top official is a prime minister.

Ethnic, cultural, and religious factors influence Indian politics. Muslims, Sikhs, and Tamils are minorities whose interests must be taken into account. There are about 150 millions Muslims in India.

In 1984, Sikhs were angered by Indian police. They killed Prime Minister Indira Gandhi, daughter of Nehru. Seven years later, Tamil extremists killed Indira Gandhi's son, Prime Minister Rajiv Gandhi.

2. What factors influence Indian politics?

_____

Economic Challenges (pages 569–570)

What *industry dominates in Bangalore?*

Most Indians work on farms. The majority of farms are small. <u>Land reform</u> would mean a more balanced distribution of land. However, land reform has not made much progress.

One change has made a difference. American scientists developed grains that yielded more food. They also introduced new farming techniques to improve production. These developments came to be called the <u>Green Revolution</u>. These discoveries were used to avert famine in India.

Industry is important, too. Cotton textiles have long been a major product. Now, India is a major producer of iron, steel, chemicals, machinery, and food products.

The city of Bangalore is home to hundreds of computer companies. They are taking advantage of India's low wages and highly skilled workers.

3. What are some of India's major products?

_____

Life in Modern India (pages 570–571)

What *is "Bollywood"?*

Marriage and family remain at the center of Indian life. Most Indians follow the custom of arranged marriages. That is, their *spouses* are chosen for them by their families. Sometimes, wealthier urban couples choose their own spouses. Indian families are large. Often, many relatives live under one roof.

Many Indians eat a vegetarian diet. Meat eating is limited by Muslim and Hindu religious practices.

Indians enjoy sports, music, and movies. There is an enormous Indian film industry based in Mumbai (Bombay). It is known as "Bollywood."

Most Indians still work on farms. Education will become more important as the economy changes.

4. What is an arranged marriage?

_____

Indian Culture (pages 571–572)

How *many languages are spoken in India?*

Hundreds of languages and dialects are spoken in India. Hindi is the official language. English, too, is widely spoken.

About 80 percent of the population is Hindu. Hinduism is a religion with roots in Aryan culture. Hindus believe in many gods. They also believe in reincarnation—the rebirth of souls. The moral consequences of one's actions are called karma. Karma helps determine how a person is reincarnated.

The <u>caste system</u> is an important part of Hinduism. It is a system of social classes. Four castes made up the original system. The Brahmans were priests and scholars. The Kshatriyas were rulers and warriors. The Vaisyas were farmers and merchants. The Sudras were artisans and laborers.

5. What is the caste system?

_____

Name _____   Date _____

Pakistan and Bangladesh

BEFORE YOU READ

In the last section, you read about the history and development of India.

In this section, you will learn about the culture, economics, and life of Pakistan and Bangladesh.

AS YOU READ

Use this graphic organizer to take notes about what you discover in this section.

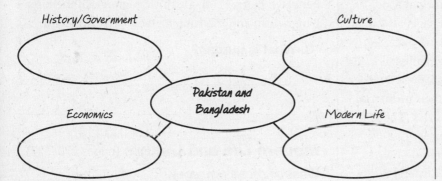

PLACES & TERMS

Indus Valley civilization the largest of the world's first civilizations

partition the separation of East and West Pakistan from India in 1947

Kashmir territory bordering India and Pakistan

microcredit small loans available to poor entrepreneurs

entrepreneur person who starts and builds a business

Ramadan month-long period of fasting for Muslims

New Countries, Ancient Lands
(pages 573–574)

What was the result of partition?

The <u>Indus Valley civilization</u> was the largest of the world's first civilizations. It arose around 2500 B.C. in what is now Pakistan. It was a highly developed, urban civilization. This civilization fell around 1500 B.C. The Aryans invaded soon after. As you read in the section on India, the Mauryan, Gupta, and Mughal empires ruled this area at various times. This was followed by British rule.

The end of British rule in 1947 brought the partition of India. This <u>partition</u> was the separation from India of the new Muslim country of West and East Pakistan. This was a period of violence between Muslims and Hindus. About one million people died.

West and East Pakistan shared a religious bond. However, ethnic differences and the 1,100-mile distance between the two halves eventually drove them apart. The people of East Pakistan began to

call for their own state. The government of West Pakistan opposed such a move. Civil war broke out in 1971. That year, with Indian aid, East Pakistan won its independence. It became the country of Bangladesh.

Both Bangladesh and Pakistan have struggled to establish democracy since gaining independence. Pakistan has fought several destructive wars with <u>Kashmir</u>, a nearby territory that borders Pakistan and India.

1. How did Bangladesh become a country?

_____

_____

Struggling Economies (pages 574–575)

How does microcredit help small businesses?

Pakistan and Bangladesh have large, rapidly growing populations. In fact, Bangladesh is the eighth most populous country in the world. Both have economies that depend primarily on agriculture.

Most farmers in Pakistan and Bangladesh work small plots of land. They struggle to grow enough to feed their families. The government has tried to modernize farming methods, but many farmers follow traditional ways. Climate also hinders crop yields. Large areas of Pakistan are arid. Bangladesh is affected by seasonal monsoons and cyclones.

The most productive farming areas of Pakistan are the irrigated portions of the Indus Valley. Here, farmers grow enough cotton and rice to allow for export. They also produce wheat for *domestic* use. The moist delta lands of Bangladesh are ideal for growing rice. Rice is the country's principal food crop. Fishing, mainly for freshwater fish, is also vital to the economy of Bangladesh.

Neither Pakistan nor Bangladesh is highly industrialized. Most factories are small. Even so, both countries are trying to increase their industrial base. They have growing *textile* industries. They provide an important source of revenue and employment. Both countries export cotton garments. Pakistan also exports wool carpets and leather goods.

An important economic development has been the creation of <u>microcredit</u>—small loans available to poor entrepreneurs. <u>Entrepreneurs</u> are people who start and build businesses. Under this program, businesses too small to get loans from banks can join forces and apply for microcredit.

2. What do these countries export?

_____

_____

One Religion, Many Peoples (page 576)

What *language did Pakistan adopt?*

Most people in Pakistan and Bangladesh are Muslims. The faithful observe typical Muslim customs. These include daily prayer and participation in <u>Ramadan</u>, a month-long period of fasting.

In general, Pakistan is stricter in imposing Islamic law on its citizens. Many follow the custom of purdah, the seclusion of women. Women are prevented from having contact with men who are not relatives. When they appear in public, they wear veils. In Bangladesh, purdah is less common. Women do not have to wear veils. Religious practices are more relaxed.

Pakistan is ethnically diverse. There are five main ethnic groups—Punjabis, Sindhis, Pathans, Mujahirs, and Balocks. Each group has its own language. Each group has regional origins within the country except the Mujahirs. They migrated from India in 1947. To avoid favoring one region over another, the government chose Urdu—the language of the Mujahirs—as the national language.

In contrast, the people of Bangladesh are mainly Bengalis. Bengal is the historic region that includes Bangladesh and the Indian state of West Bengal.

3. What is purdah?

_____

_____

Modern Life and Culture (pages 576–577)

What *do people here enjoy?*

Life in Pakistan and Bangladesh revolves around the family. Most people live in small villages. They have simple homes made of such materials as sun-baked mud, bamboo, or wood. However, there are also large, crowded cities.

Poetry is a special interest in Pakistan and Bangladesh. The tradition of oral literature is strong. The greatest literary figure in Bangladesh is the poet Rabindranath Tagore. He won the Nobel Prize for literature in 1913.

Music and dance are also important forms of expression. Both countries share music traditions similar to those of India.

4. Who is Rabindranath Tagore?

_____

_____

Nepal and Bhutan

BEFORE YOU READ

In the last section, you read about the history and development of Pakistan and Bangladesh.

In this section, you will learn about the culture, economics, and life of Nepal and Bhutan.

AS YOU READ

Use this graphic organizer to take notes about what you discover in this section.

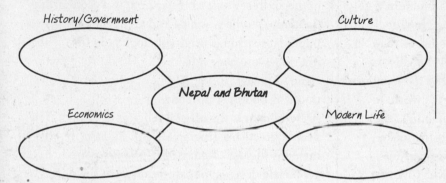

PLACES & TERMS

constitutional monarchy kingdom in which the ruler's powers are limited by a constitution

Sherpa traditional mountain guide of the Everest region, of Tibetan ancestry

Siddhartha Gautama also known as Buddha, founder of Buddhism

mandala geometric designs that are symbols of the universe

Mountain Kingdoms (pages 580–581)

How are these countries governed?

Nepal and Bhutan are located in the Himalayas. The main geographic feature of both countries is their mountainous landscapes. The towering, snow-capped Himalayas run along the northern border with China.

The rugged landscape of Nepal and Bhutan has isolated the two countries throughout their histories. Both countries are landlocked. The mountainous terrain and landlocked location have made them hard to reach. They were also difficult to conquer and settle. China controlled Bhutan briefly in the 1700s. Great Britain invaded both countries during the 1800s. Great Britain had some influence on these countries because of its control of neighboring India. But Nepal and Bhutan generally remained independent and isolated.

For much of their history, Bhutan and Nepal were split into small religious kingdoms or ruling states. Hindu kings ruled Nepal. Buddhist priests

controlled Bhutan. In time, unified kingdoms emerged in both countries. The kingdoms were led by *hereditary* monarchs who passed the throne to their *heirs*.

Today, the governments of both Nepal and Bhutan are **constitutional monarchies**. They are kingdoms in which the ruler's powers are limited by a constitution. In Bhutan, the king is still the supreme ruler. In Nepal, the king shares power with an elected parliament.

1. What aspects of the countries kept them isolated?

_____

_____

Developing Economies (pages 581–582)

What crops and animals are raised here?

Both Bhutan and Nepal are poor countries. Their economies are based mainly on agriculture. Because

A Region of Contrasts **217**

of the mountainous terrain, neither country has much land fit for cultivation. Most farm plots are small, soils are poor, and erosion is a problem. Farmers create terraces. This is an ancient technique of cutting steplike fields for growing crops on hillsides or mountain slopes. It increases the amount of farmland and helps limit soil loss.

Common farm products include rice, corn, potatoes, and wheat. Common livestock are cattle, sheep, and yaks. Yaks are long-haired animals related to cows. In Bhutan, the government has promoted the growing of fruit for export. It has also tried to improve farming practices.

The timber industry is important to both countries. However, deforestation is a problem. The manufacturing part of the economy is growing. It includes wood products, food processing, cement production, and other goods.

One of the fastest-growing industries in Nepal is tourism. Tourists come from around the world to visit the valley of Kathmandu. Kathmandu is the capital of Nepal. From here, tourists often make trips into the Himalayas. Hotels and restaurants, transportation, and other services have grown to meet the needs of the tourist industry. But tourism is a mixed blessing. It has damaged the environment. Increased trash and pollution are most noticeable in rural areas.

Bhutan, has taken a different approach to tourism. Bhutan is concerned about the impact of tourists on national life. The country regulates the tourist business. It allows only limited numbers of visitors and keeps some areas of the country off limits.

2. What impact is tourism having?

_____

_____

Rich Cultural Traditions (pages 582–583)

***What** is the official religion of Bhutan?*

Various ethnic groups inhabit the Himalayan region. In Nepal, the majority of the people are Indo-Nepalese Hindus. Their ancestors came from India many centuries ago. Nepal also has a number of groups of Tibetan ancestry. Among them are the Sherpas. **Sherpas** are the traditional guides of the Everest region.

The main ethnic group of Bhutan is the Bhote. They trace their origins to Tibet. Most Bhotes live in three-story houses made of wood and stone. The families live on the second floor. The first floor is for livestock. Bhutan also has a sizable Nepalese minority in the southern lowlands.

Religion is a powerful force in both Nepal and Bhutan. Although the great majority of Nepalese are Hindus, Buddhism also has deep roots in Nepal. The founder of Buddhism was born in southern Nepal in the sixth century B.C. His name was **Siddhartha Gautama**, but he was also known as the Buddha. Buddhist teachings originally took hold in Nepal. But they were later replaced by Hindu rulers who came to power. Today, Hindu practices still shows traces of Buddhist influence.

Buddhism is the official religion of Bhutan. The people practice a Tibetan style of Buddhism. This includes the use of *mandalas*. **Mandalas** are geometric designs that are symbols of the universe. They aid in meditation. Early communities in Bhutan were organized around large fortress-like monasteries. These are still found in many parts of the country.

Folk arts and festivals are an important part of Himalayan culture. During festivals in Nepal and Bhutan, musicians play traditional songs on flutes, drums, and long brass horns. Colorfully costumed dancers perform dances based on religious stories.

3. How did Hinduism come to Nepal?

_____

_____

Sri Lanka and the Maldives

BEFORE YOU READ

In the last section, you read about the history and development of Nepal and Bhutan.

In this section, you will learn about the culture, economics, and life of Sri Lanka and the Maldives.

AS YOU READ

Use this graphic organizer to take notes about what you discover in this section.

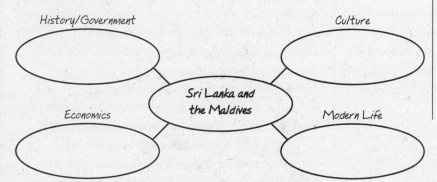

PLACES & TERMS

Sinhalese the Indo-Aryan people who settled Sri Lanka in the sixth century B.C.

Tamils Dravidian Hindus from southern India who arrived in Sri Lanka in the fourth century A.D.

sultan Muslim ruler

History of the Islands (pages 584–585)

How *did the Maldives become Muslim?*

In the sixth century B.C., Indo-Aryans crossed the narrow *strait* separating India from Sri Lanka. These people came to be known as the <u>Sinhalese</u>. They absorbed the island's native inhabitants. They adopted Buddhism. The Sinhalese created an advanced civilization on Sri Lanka. They built sophisticated irrigation systems that allowed farming on arid land.

In the fourth century A.D., another group of Indians began to arrive in Sri Lanka. These were the <u>Tamils</u>. They were Dravidian Hindus from southern India. They brought a different culture and language to Sri Lanka. The Tamils settled in the northern end of the island. The Sinhalese moved farther south.

Europeans began to colonize Sri Lanka in the 1500s. First came the Portuguese, then the Dutch. The British took control of the island in 1796. They called it Ceylon. Ceylon gained independence in

1948. In 1972, it adopted a new constitution and renamed itself the Republic of Sri Lanka.

After independence, tensions grew between the Sinhalese and Tamil populations. The Tamils were in the minority. They claimed that the Sinhalese discriminated against them. They called for their own independent state. In the 1980s, civil war broke out. Violence has claimed many lives since then and continues to disrupt Sri Lankan life.

The Maldives were settled by Buddhists and Hindus from Sri Lanka and India. This occurred some time before 500 B.C. Arab traders later made frequent visits. By the 12th century A.D., the population had converted to Islam. Six dynasties of Muslim rulers, or <u>sultans</u>, governed the Maldives after that. In 1968, the Maldives declared itself a republic. It is now headed by an elected president.

1. What caused civil war in Sri Lanka?

_____

_____

Life in the Islands (pages 585–586)

What is the national dance of Sri Lanka?

In Sri Lanka, Sinhalese Buddhists make up nearly 75 percent of the population. Tamil Hindus are about 18 percent. Around 7 percent of the people are Muslims. They are descended from early Arab traders. There is also a small community of mixed-race European Christians. They are known as Burghers.

Most Sinhalese live in the southern, western, and central parts of the country. The Tamils are concentrated in the northern Jaffna Peninsula. Much fighting has taken place there. Another group of Tamils lives in the central highlands. These people are the descendants of Indian migrants who came to work on British plantations in the 1800s. Muslims are found mainly in the eastern lowlands. The capital city, Colombo, is a busy urban center. But most Sri Lankans continue to live in smaller towns and villages.

In the Maldives, most of the people are descended from the early Sinhalese and Dravidian inhabitants. They mixed with Arab, Southeast Asian, and Chinese traders over the centuries. The official language, Divehi, is unique to the Maldives.

Religion plays a key role in the culture of Sri Lanka. Buddhist and Hindu temples, Muslim mosques, and Christian churches dot the landscape. Art and literature are strongly influenced by these religious traditions. Folk dancing is a notable cultural tradition on the island.

Muslim customs have a strong influence in the Maldives. Islam is the state religion. No other religions are allowed. One of the highlights of Maldivian culture is bodu beru, or "big drum." This is a popular tradition of music and dance based on drumming.

2. Why is there only one religion in the Maldives?

Economic Activity in the Islands
(pages 586–587)

What has disrupted Sri Lanka's economy?

The Maldives and Sri Lanka face economic tough economic challenges. However, each country has made good use of its assets to promote economic growth. Today, the Maldives and Sri Lanka have the highest per capita incomes in South Asia.

Sri Lanka's economy is based on agriculture—mainly rice farming. Sri Lanka also has large areas devoted to plantation agriculture. These large farms produce crops such as tea, rubber, and coconuts for export. Sri Lanka is one of the world's leading tea-producing countries. Manufacturing is increasing. But other sectors of the economy are less important. Deforestation has damaged the timber industry. The fishing and mining industries are relatively small. The one exception is gem mining. Sri Lanka is famous for sapphires, rubies, and topaz.

In the Maldives, farming is limited by a lack of land. Most food has to be imported. Fishing for tuna, mackerel, and sharks was long the main economic activity. However, tourism is now the main economic activity. The islands' beautiful beaches, coral reefs, and marine life draw visitors from around the world.

Until the 1980s, tourism was also growing in Sri Lanka. Then the civil war began. The tourist industry collapsed. Warfare has disrupted other economic activities. It has also damaged the countries infrastructure—its roads, bridges, power systems, and other services. Until peace returns to Sri Lanka, the economy is likely to struggle.

While the Maldives is at peace, it faces a different challenge. The islands lie low in the water. If global warming melts the polar ice caps, the islands could be flooded completely.

3. What used to be the main economic activity in the Maldives?

Name _____   Date _____

Glossary/After You Read

domestic relating and limited to one's own country

federation a union of organizations; an alliance

heir one who inherits a title or office

hereditary received through inheritance; passed from parents to children

opposition hostile or contrary action; something that opposes

reign sovereignty; royal authority

spouse husband or wife; married person

strait narrow stretch of water connecting two large bodies of water

textile cloth, especially a woven or knit cloth

Places & Terms

A. Write the letter of the place or term next to the description that explains it best.

a. Mughal Empire

b. Indus Valley civilization

c. Siddhartha Gautama

d. constitutional monarchy

e. raj

_____ 1. kingdom in which the ruler's powers are limited by a constitution

_____ 2. term used to identify the period of British rule over India

_____ 3. founder of Buddhism, also known as the Buddha

_____ 4. empire established by Muslim invaders in the early 1500s

_____ 5. the largest of the world's first civilizations

B. Circle the place or term that best completes each sentence.

1. Plant research that helped save India from famine was called the

   _____.

   Land Reform   Nonviolent Resistance   Green Revolution

2. The _____ is the Hindu system of social classes.

   microcredit   caste system   partition

3. The month-long period of fasting for Muslims is called _____.

   Ramadan   Tamil   Mandala

4. _____ are the traditional mountain guides of the Everest region.

   Sinhalese   Sherpas   Sultans

5. In Bangladesh, an important development that has helped small businesses grow is the creation of small loans called _____.

   caste system   entrepreneur   microcredit

Main Ideas

1. How is the government of India like that of the United States, and how is it like Britain's?

   _____

   _____

2. What effect did the presence of both Muslims and Hindus have when India gained independence?

   _____

   _____

3. How do Islamic practices differ between Pakistan and Bangladesh?

   _____

   _____

4. Why are tourists interested in Nepal and Bhutan?

   _____

   _____

5. What effect has civil war had on Sri Lanka?

   _____

   _____

Thinking Critically

Answer the following questions on a separate sheet of paper.

1. What do you think is the biggest problem currently facing the countries in South Asia? Explain.

2. Knowing that industrialization can create problems such as rapid urbanization and pollution, why are these countries so eager to industrialize?

Population Explosion

BEFORE YOU READ

In the last section, you read about the culture and development of Sri Lanka and the Maldives.

In this section, you will learn about population growth in South Asia.

AS YOU READ

Use this chart to help you take notes about this section.

	Causes	Effects
Issue 1: Population Explosion		

PLACES & TERMS

basic necessities food, clothing, and shelter

illiteracy the inability to read or write

Growing Pains (pages 593–594)

What *problems have been created by growth?*

On May 11, 2000, the population of India officially hit one billion. That *milestone* was a mixed blessing. The Indian population is growing so quickly that many of its citizens lack life's basic necessities. The **basic necessities** are food, clothing, and shelter. The question for India is how to manage the population so that economic development can continue. In fact, this is the question for all of South Asia.

When India gained its independence from Britain in 1947, the population was 300 million. By 2000, the population had more than tripled. India's population is so large that an annual growth rate of less than two percent is too much. It would represent a population explosion. The growth rate needs to slow down. If it doesn't, India will be home to 1.5 billion people in another 40 years. These people will be living in a land about one-third the size of the United States. India will be the most populous country in the world. It will be more populous than China.

India is not alone in its sky-rocketing population. In 1998, India, Pakistan, and Bangladesh were among the ten most populous countries in the world. South Asia is home to 22 percent of the world's population. But these people live on less than three percent of the world's land area.

South Asia's increased population has created problems. Regional governments have found it difficult to meet the needs of their people. Poverty and illiteracy are widespread. **Illiteracy** is the inability to read or write. Poverty and illiteracy have left millions without hope that their lives will improve. Poor sanitation and the lack of health education have caused outbreaks of disease.

Officials have made estimates of what it would take just to keep pace with population growth. These estimates are based on continued growth at the current rate. Every year, India would have to build 127,000 village schools, hire nearly 400,000 new teachers, construct 2.5 million new homes, create 4 million new jobs, and produce an additional 6 tons of food.

1. At the present rate of growth, what would India's population be in 2040?

_____

_____

Managing Population Growth

(pages 594–595)

Why do people continue to have big families?

South Asia has struggled for decades to find solutions to its population explosion.

India has an annual health-care budget of nearly $1 billion. It spends much of it on encouraging Indians to have smaller families. "Let's have small families for a stronger India" is one slogan from their *campaign*.

For many reasons, these programs have had only limited success. Indian women usually marry before age 18 and start having babies early. For the poor, children are a source of income. They can beg for money on the streets as early as their third birthday. They can work in the fields not too many years later.

For many Indians, children represent security in old age. If a family has lots of children, there will probably be someone around to take care of the parents when they are old. Also, the infant *mortality* rate is high in South Asia. Almost 75 babies die per 1,000 babies born. In the United States, that rate is 7 babies die per 1,000 babies born. Indians try to have many children to ensure that some will reach adulthood.

Many factors that affect population growth can be changed through education. However, education funds are limited. For example, India spends less than $16 per pupil annually for primary and secondary education. Only a small fraction of this amount is spent on educating girls. By contrast, the annual per pupil spending in the United States is $6,320. That's about 400 times as much.

Education is essential for breaking the cycle of poverty. Education can provide South Asians with the means to raise their standard of living. It can also help improve the status of females by giving them job opportunities outside the home. Better health education can reduce the need for large families by ensuring that more babies reach adulthood. The future development of South Asia depends on the success of such efforts to control population growth.

2. How can education help in this situation?

_____

_____

Living With Extreme Weather

BEFORE YOU READ

In the last section, you read about South Asia's population explosion.

In this section, you will learn about how this region copes with seasonal weather extremes.

AS YOU READ

Use this chart to help you take notes about this section.

	Causes	Effects
Issue 2: Extreme Weather		

PLACES & TERMS

summer monsoon a wet wind that blows June through September from the southwest across the Indian Ocean toward South Asia

winter monsoon a dry wind that blows October through February, from the northeast across the Himalayas toward the sea

The Monsoon Seasons (page 597)

When *does the summer monsoon blow?*

South Asia is home to an annual cycle of powerful, destructive weather. The monsoon is part of this cycle. *Contrary* to popular belief, the monsoon is a wind system, not a rainstorm. There are two monsoon seasons. One is the moist summer monsoon. The other is the dry, cool winter monsoon.

The **summer monsoon** winds blow from the southwest across the Indian Ocean toward South Asia. They blow from June through September. The winds stir up powerful storms. These storms release vast amounts of rain and cause *severe* flooding.

The **winter monsoon** winds blow from the northeast across the Himalayas toward the sea. They blow from October through February. Unlike the summer monsoon, the winter winds carry little moisture. A drought can result if the summer monsoon fails to bring normal levels of moisture. From March through May, there are no strong *prevailing* wind patterns.

1. What is the direction of the winter monsoon.

_____

_____

Impact of the Monsoons (pages 597–599)

How *does the weather affect politics in the region?*

The monsoon winds shape the rhythms of life—and death—for people in South Asia. They also affect relations between countries.

The rains that come with the summer monsoons are important to the agriculture of South Asia. They help nourish the rain forests. They irrigate crops. And they produce the floodwaters that deposit layers of rich sediment on the soil. However, heavy flooding can also damage crops.

The summer monsoons can cause tremendous damage. Cyclones commonly come with the summer monsoons. (Cyclones are called hurricanes in the United States.) They can be deadly.

Cyclones destroy farmland, wipe out villages, and cause massive flooding. The 1970 cyclone that struck Bangladesh killed more than 300,000 people.

It left hundreds of thousands homeless. In fact, because of the monsoons, Bangladesh was the site of some of the worst natural disasters of the 20th century.

The droughts that come with the dry winter monsoon bring other problems. Lush landscapes can become arid wastelands. This can happen almost overnight. This cycle of storms, floods, and drought have made lives and economies in South Asia difficult and complicated.

The climate of South Asia makes agriculture difficult. Crops often disappear under summer floodwaters or wither in the drought-parched soil. With so many mouths to feed, the countries of South Asia must buy what they cannot grow. The threat of famine is ever present. But the people suffer from more than just crop failures. They may also lose their homes and families to weather-related *catastrophes*. Most people are too poor to rebuild their homes and lives. Governments often lack the resources to provide much help.

When possible, steps have been taken to lessen the damage. These steps include building houses on stilts, erecting concrete cyclone shelters, and building dams to control floodwaters.

The region also receives international aid. Other governments and international agencies have loaned billions of dollars to South Asian nations. But the frequency of South Asia's seasonal disasters stretches the aid thin. Also, when the aid is a loan, it burdens these countries with debt.

Weather in South Asia has caused more than natural disasters. It has also caused political disputes. For example, India shares the Ganges River with Bangladesh. When India wanted to bring water to Kolkata, India constructed the Farakka Dam across the Ganges River. The dam was built at a point just before the river enters Bangladesh. That left little water for drinking and irrigation in southern Bangladesh. Bangladeshi farmers lost farmland. Many of them illegally fled their country for India.

The two countries finally settled the dispute in 1997. They signed a treaty giving each specific water rights to the Ganges. Still, the dispute is an example of the role weather plays in both the politics and economics of the region.

2. What good things happen when the summer monsoon rains come?

_____

_____

Chapter 26   Case Study (pages 600–604)   *Reading Study Guide*

Territorial Dispute

BEFORE YOU READ

In the last section, you read about South Asia's seasonal weather extremes.

In this case study, you will examine the dispute between India and Pakistan over Kashmir.

AS YOU READ

Use this chart to help you take notes about this case study.

	Causes	Effects
Case Study: Territorial Dispute		

PLACES & TERMS

Kashmir territory located at the foot of the Himalayas, surrounded by India, Pakistan, and China.

maharajah a Hindu prince

A Controversy over Territory

(pages 600–601)

What *difficult decision faced Kashmir's maharajah?*

In 1947, the British government formally ended its colonial rule over the Indian subcontinent. Britain helped with the transition, which included the dividing of India. Indian Muslims proposed that Muslims have their own country. Each Indian state could decide if it wanted to be part of Muslim Pakistan, part of Hindu India, or remain independent. Generally, the choice was made on religious grounds. But Kashmir had a unique problem.

<u>Kashmir</u> is a territory located at the foot of the Himalayas. It is surrounded by India, Pakistan, and China. The population in 1947 was largely Muslim. However, Kashmir's leader, the <u>maharajah</u> of Kashmir, was Hindu. The maharajah tried to keep Kashmir independent. But the plan failed. The maharajah then tried to join India. But Pakistani soldiers invaded Kashmir. After a year's fighting, India still controlled much of Kashmir. Since 1948, India and Pakistan have fought two more wars. But

the situation remains unresolved.

India and Pakistan each control part of Kashmir. Even China controls part. China captured a remote northern mountain area of Kashmir in 1962.

There is more to the conflict than politics and religion. The Indus River flows through Kashmir. Many of the river's tributaries originate in Kashmir. The Indus is a vital source of drinking and irrigation water for Pakistan. So, the Pakistanis are unwilling to let India control such a vital resource. Kashmir has become a strategic prize that neither country will give up.

1. Why is Pakistan worried about control of Kashmir?

_____

_____

_____

A Nuclear Nightmare (page 601)

Why did nuclear testing horrify the world?

In 1998, India and Pakistan both tested nuclear weapons. After tests, both nations promised to seek a political solution to the problem. But the possibility of nuclear war has made the dispute more dangerous.

Despite frequent cease-fires, the border clashes continue. Also, Pakistan is supporting Muslims in Kashmir who have been fighting Indian rule since the late 1980s.

Both India and Pakistan have large populations and widespread poverty. A great deal of money has been spent on troops, weapons, and nuclear programs. This money might have been used to educate millions of children. It might have been used to address social problems.

Resolving the status of Kashmir would benefit India, Pakistan, and Kashmir. It would offer the people of these countries the peace they need to begin improving the quality of their lives. It would also reduce political tensions in the region.

2. How might stopping the dispute help people?

_____

_____

The Positions (page 602)

What is Pakistan's position?

Government Document: The Ministry of Foreign Affairs in Pakistan published a policy stating that said that they welcomed the involvement of the international community in the peace process. However, they were also clear that they were going to safeguard their interests in the territory. They also said that they would continue to offer full support to those within Kashmir who were continuing to fight.

Government Policy Declaration: Indian President Kocheril Raman Narayanan said that statements about how dangerous the region is worried him. He felt that such comments encouraged violence. He said that the only danger is from those who have not sworn to commit to peace. He stated that India will never threaten another country and would never use nuclear weapons first. However, India will insure the country's security.

3. Which country sounds more interested in peace?

_____

_____

The Impact on People (page 603)

What is it like to live in this region?

Political Cartoon: A cartoon shows two poor men, one from India and one from Pakistan. Each of the two men is carrying a missile on his back. They are bent over and straining beneath their heavy loads. Nearby, a man with a stop watch and starter's gun looks like he is ready to start a race.

Political Speech: Mehbooba Mufti, a leader of the nationalist Jammu and Kashmir People's Democratic Party, hopes that the conflict will be resolved. She says that everything has changed. The schools, colleges, roads, bridges, and buildings they had 50 years ago have all been destroyed. There was a good education system with good teachers, but it is gone. She thinks Kashmir must become a bridge between Pakistan and India. She does not know when this will happen.

Personal Story: Mohammed Aziz, a Kashmiri native, says that no one sleeps well in his town. They never know when the shells will come. There used to be hotels and tourism. Now, everything is closed. Education has stopped. There is no medication and no one to care for the ill.

4. Who seems to bear most of the burden of this dispute?

_____

_____

Name _____   Date _____

Glossary/After You Read

campaign a connected series of plans or events designed to bring about a particular result

catastrophe tragic event; extreme misfortune; ruin

contrary opposite

milestone a significant point in development

mortality proportion of deaths to the population

prevailing most frequent, predominant

severe harsh; inflicting physical discomfort or hardship

Places & Terms

A. Fill in the blanks with the correct place or term. Each term is used only once.

illiteracy   summer monsoons

Kashmir   winter monsoons

basic necessities

1. The population is growing too quickly. There is a great deal of poverty in this region, and

   many people lack the _____.

2. The weather adds to the hardship. There may be drought and crops may die during the

   _____.

3. Cyclones are dangerous and frequent companions of the _____.

4. India and Pakistan have fought over _____ since 1947.

5. Schools have been destroyed, so the amount of _____ has increased.

B. Write the letter of the place or term next to the description that explains it best.

   a. illiteracy   d. summer monsoon

   b. basic necessities   e. maharajah

   c. winter monsoon

   _____ 1. wet winds that blow from the southwest across the Indian Ocean toward
                South Asia

   _____ 2. cool, dry winds that blow from the northeast across the Himalayas toward
                the sea

   _____ 3. inability to read or write

   _____ 4. Hindu prince

   _____ 5. food, clothing, and shelter

Main Ideas

1. How does the population explosion hurt the quality of people's lives in South Asia?

_____

_____

2. Why is it difficult to convince people in this region to have smaller families?

_____

_____

3. How can education help break the cycle of poverty?

_____

_____

4. The summer monsoons often bring storms and floods, what can happen if they do not bring enough rain?

_____

_____

5. How has improving the availability of water in some places caused political tension?

_____

_____

Thinking Critically

Answer the following questions on a separate sheet of paper.

1. If you were to create an education program to help with the problems in South Asia, what would you want to teach them first?

2. How do the population explosion and the weather extremes each contribute to making the other problem worse?

Name _____   Date _____

Chapter 27 Section 1 (pages 619–623)   *Reading Study Guide*

EAST ASIA
Landforms and Resources

BEFORE YOU READ

In the last chapter, you read about the challenges faced by South Asia.

In this section, you will learn about the physical features and resources of East Asia, and how they shape life in the region.

AS YOU READ

Use this chart to take notes about the landforms and resources of East Asia.

Landforms	
Resources	

PLACES & TERMS

Kunlun Mountains mountains, located in the west of China, which are the source of two of China's great rivers

Qinling Shandi Mountains mountains that divide the northern part of China from the southern part

Huang He river in northern China; also called the Yellow River

Chang Jiang longest river in Asia; also known as the Yangtze River

Xi Jiang river in the south of China; also called the West River

Landforms: Mountains and Plateaus
(pages 619–620)

***Where** is the Gobi Desert?*

The countries in East Asia include China, Japan, Mongolia, Taiwan, North Korea, and South Korea. In East Asia, the rugged *terrain* acted as a barrier.

The worlds highest mountains are located on the western edge of East Asia. As you read in Unit 8, the Himalayas, the world's tallest mountains, lie along the border separating China from India. North of the Himalayas are the **Kunlun Mountains** in western China. They are the source of two of China's great rivers, the Huang He and Chang Jiang.

The **Qinling Shandi Mountains** are in southeastern and east central China. These mountains divide the northern part of China from the southern part.

There are few flat surfaces in this mountainous land. However, the region has some low basins and barren deserts. The Plateau of Tibet (also known as the Xizang Plateau) is one of these flat areas. Also in western China are the Tarim Basin and the Taklimakan Desert. The Gobi Desert stretches from

northwest China into Mongolia. It is one of the largest deserts in the world.

1. Which two rivers start in the Kunlun Mountains?

_____

_____

Peninsulas and Islands (pages 620–621)

***Which** parts of China were once European colonies?*

The eastern coast of China features several peninsulas. These include the Shandong Peninsula, the Leizhou Peninsula, and the Macao Peninsula. Macao was owned by Portugal until 1999. Because of its peninsulas China has a long coastline.

Bordering China on the east is the Korean Peninsula. This peninsula contains the two independent nations of North Korea and South Korea.

The islands off China include Hainan and part of Hong Kong. Hong Kong used to be a British colony. In 1997, Hong Kong reverted to the authority of

A Rugged Terrain **231**

mainland China. Hong Kong was long one of the most important harbors in the world. The smaller nations of East Asia are located on islands and peninsulas.

2. What did China's many peninsulas allow?

_____

_____

River Systems (pages 621–622)

What *does Chang Jiang mean?*

China has three great rivers. The <u>Huang He</u> (Yellow River) of northern China starts in the Kunlun Mountains in the west. The river winds east for about 3,000 miles. It empties into the Yellow Sea. The river and the sea get their names from the yellow silt that the river carries to its delta. Another name for the river is "China's sorrow," because of its flooding.

The <u>Chang Jiang</u> (Yangtze River) is the longest river in Asia. It flows 3,450 miles from Xizang (Tibet) to the East China Sea. The river has been a major trade route since ancient times.

The <u>Xi Jiang</u> (West River) flows eastward through southeast China. It joins up with the Pearl River (Zhu Jiang) to flow into the South China Sea. Important mineral resources are located in this river's valley.

The Yalu River is another important river of the region. The Yalu is about 500 miles long. It forms the border between North Korea and China. In 1950, Chinese troops entered the Korean War by crossing the river and attacking United Nations forces.

3. Why is the Huang He called "China's Sorrow"?

_____

_____

Resources of East Asia (page 622–623)

How *do the rivers and seas benefit this region?*

The mountains in East Asia limit the amount of land available for agriculture. For this reason, China's population is concentrated in the east, where river basins are located to irrigate fields.

Forests are abundant in the region. China, Japan, Taiwan, North Korea, and South Korea have forest resources. Japan has kept most of its forests in reserve by buying timber from other countries.

China has abundant reserves of petroleum, coal, and natural gas. Korea has some coal reserves. Japan has deposits of coal. China's resources have enabled it to be mostly self-sufficient. Japan's shortage of resources has forced it to trade for what it needs.

China's mineral resources include iron ore, lead, zinc, copper, and other minerals. Mongolia, North Korea, and South Korea have important mineral reserves. Japan has some minerals reserves, too.

China's river systems provide crop irrigation, electric power, and transportation. To control flooding on the Chang Jiang and produce electricity, China is building the Three Gorges Dam.

People in East Asia look to the sea for food. In fact, Japan has developed one of the largest fishing industries in the world. Japanese factory ships process huge amounts of seafood.

4. Why is China's population concentrated in the east?

_____

_____

Name _____   Date _____

EAST ASIA
Climate and Vegetation

Before You Read

In the last section you read about the landforms and resources of East Asia.

In this section, you will learn how climate and vegetation affect life in the region.

As You Read

Use this chart to take notes about the climate and vegetation of East Asia.

Climate	
Vegetation	

PLACES & TERMS

typhoon tropical storm that occurs in the western Pacific

Taklimakan Desert desert located in western China

Gobi Desert desert located in northern China and southeast Mongolia

High Latitude Climate Zones (page 625)

Where *do mosses and lichens grow?*

Typhoons occur in parts of East Asia. A **typhoon** is a tropical storm that occurs in the western Pacific. But aside from typhoons, the weather in East Asia is similar to that of the United States. Both are at the same latitude. Both have similar climate zones.

There are subarctic climate zones along Mongolia's and China's northern borders with Russia. The summers in these areas range from cool to cold. The winters are brutally cold. They test the survival skills of the inhabitants. The climate is generally dry.

The typical vegetation in this area is northern evergreen forest. Varieties of mosses and lichens also grow in the subarctic zone. They grow on rocks and tree trunks.

Highland climates are found mostly in western China. The temperature in the highland zones varies. The farther north the latitude and the higher the elevation, the colder the climate. The western highlands are sparsely populated. This is due to the

severe climate and topography.

The vegetation in the highlands also varies with elevation. Forest and *alpine* tundra are the typical vegetation regions. Tundras have no trees. The soil a few feet below the surface is permanently frozen. In this environment, only mosses, lichens, and shrubs can grow. Because of the cold and the difficulty of growing crops, few people live here.

1. Where are highland climates found?

_____

_____

Mid-latitude Zones (page 626)

What *are the temperate grasslands good for?*

Mid-latitude zones are more comfortable to live in. They have moderate climates. The land is productive. The rainfall is sufficient for agriculture. An important resource of these zones is their forests.

Northeastern China, North Korea, northern South Korea, and northern Japan have humid continental climates. The forests in this climate zone are mainly coniferous. Over the years, agriculture has *transformed* the landscape. Farms have replaced many of the forests. Temperate grasslands are also found in this region. The grasslands are ideal for grazing.

Southeastern China, southern South Korea, southern Japan, and northern Taiwan are in a humid subtropical zone. The forests in humid subtropical zones are both deciduous and coniferous. The broad-leafed deciduous trees are usually found in the north. The coniferous forests are mainly found in areas of the south with sand soil. Loggers and farmers have greatly reduced the forests in the southeast.

2. What has happened to forests in each of these climate zones?

_____

_____

Dry Zones (pages 626–627)

Which is the best area for finding dinosaur fossils?

Dry zones of the region include both steppes and deserts. There is relatively little vegetation. These zones are not good for agriculture. Because of this, they have not been settled much by people. Instead, nomads have used the semiarid areas to graze livestock.

Parts of the Mongolian Plateau make up the semiarid zones of the region. The vegetation of semiarid zones consists mainly of short grasses. These grasses provide food for grazing animals and livestock.

Most of the deserts in the region are found in the west central area of the mainland. The **Taklimakan Desert** is located in western China. It lies between the Tian Shan and Kunlun mountains. The **Gobi Desert** is located in northern China and southeast Mongolia. The Gobi is a prime area for finding dinosaur fossils. Thousands of dinosaurs roamed through the region millions of years ago.

3. Why are these zones thinly populated?

_____

_____

Tropical Zones (page 627)

What areas are tropical?

The tropical zones of East Asia contain mainly wet climates. The primary vegetation region is rain forest.

The tropical climate zone in East Asia is fairly small. It includes a small strip of land along China's southeastern shore, the island of Hainan, and the southern tip of Taiwan. These areas have high temperatures, heavy rainfall, and high humidity every month of the year. The tropical rain forest in these places is made up of tall broadleaf trees. The trees grow densely in the rain forests.

4. What is the climate like in this zone?

_____

_____

Name _____ Date _____

EAST ASIA
Human-Environment Interaction

BEFORE YOU READ
In the last section you read about the climate and vegetation of East Asia.

In this section, you will learn about the impact humans have had on the environment in the region.

AS YOU READ
Use this graphic to take notes about the human-environment interaction in East Asia.

Human-Environment Interaction

PLACES & TERMS
Three Gorges Dam dam being built across the Chang Jiang (Yangtze River)

PCBs industrial compounds that contributed to Japanese pollution

landfill method of solid waste disposal in which refuse is buried between layers of dirt to fill in or reclaim low-lying ground

The Three Gorges Dam (pages 628–630)

What *negative effects will the dam have?*

China's Chang Jiang is the third longest river in the world, after the Nile and the Amazon. The **Three Gorges Dam** is being built on the Chang Jiang.

The Three Gorges Dam is China's largest construction project. It will be the world's largest dam. When completed, the dam will be more than 600 feet high. It will *span* a valley more than one mile wide. This dam will create a reservoir nearly 400 miles long. At least 1,000 towns and villages will disappear under the waters of the reservoir when the dam is completed.

Work began on the dam in 1993. The building of the Three Gorges Dam is a complicated issue. The dam will have both positive and negative effects. Experts disagree about whether or not the dam should be built. But the Chinese government argues that the dam will have three positive effects.

First, the dam will help control the frequent

flooding. Second, the dam will generate huge amounts of electrical power. The third benefit of the dam will be to make it easier for ships to reach China's interior.

Most observers agree that the Three Gorges Dam will also have negative effects. The question is whether the negative effects are greater than the positive effects.

First, the human costs will be high. Huge numbers of people will be displaced. Second, the dam is likely to cost more money than was first estimated. Third, many are concerned about the impact on the environment.

The Three Gorges Dam is scheduled to be completed in 2009. However, the Chinese government has been haphazard in protecting the environment. Some international groups are reluctant to invest in the project because of environmental concerns. This may delay the dam's completion.

1. What positive effects will the dam have?

_____

_____

Use of Space in Urban Japan
(pages 630–631)

What *contributed to pollution in the cities?*

Japan faces geographic challenges that are different from those facing China. One of the most important challenges is that Japan is made up of a series of mountainous islands. Most of the cities are on the coasts of these islands. Because of the nearby mountains, many of these cities cannot expand to absorb any more of the Japanese population. The population of Japan is about 127 million people.

Tokyo offers an example of the problems facing Japan's cities. It is one of the world's largest cities. It holds more than 25 million people. However, there is no more land for the city to grow.

More than 60 percent of the Japanese people live on only about 3 percent of the land. The population is clustered along the narrow, flat coastal plains.

These plains are among the most densely populated areas in the world. The largest cities in Japan are Tokyo, Yokohama, Osaka, Nagoya, and Sapporo. Close to 80 percent of the people in Japan live in cities.

Partly because of their large populations, some Japanese cities have become very polluted. For example, in the 1950s and 1960s, a number of Japanese cities experienced poisoning from mercury and **PCBs**. PCBs are industrial compounds that build up in animal tissue and can cause disease and birth defects. PCBs were banned in 1977. Cars and factories still cause massive levels of air and noise pollution.

The Japanese have shown great ingenuity in adapting to limited space. Because of the cost of land, houses are small by American standards. The rooms are separated by sliding screens and are *sparsely* furnished. People sleep on thin mattresses called futons. Futons can be rolled up and stored during the day.

Many people live in apartments. This is especially true in the biggest cities. It is not uncommon for a family of four to live in a one-bedroom apartment. Some Japanese attempt to escape the overcrowding by moving away from the city to distant suburbs. However, this often results in commutes to work of two or three hours.

One of the solutions to the shortage of space is landfill. **Landfill** is a method of solid waste disposal. Refuse is buried between layers of dirt to fill in or reclaim low-lying ground. The Japanese have used landfill to reclaim land for most of its major cities along the coast. Tokyo, for example, has built factories and refineries on landfill. Coastal *reclamation* has enlarged the port areas. These ports are designed to handle the great number of ships that sail in and out.

2. Why can't Japan's cities expand farther?

_____

_____

Glossary/After You Read

alpine of, relating to, or growing on elevated slopes above the timberline

reclamation a recovering or reclaiming of something

span to reach or extend across

sparsely characterized by few and scattered elements

terrain geographical area, a piece of earth, ground

transform to change in character or condition

Places & Terms

A. Write the name or term in each blank that best completes the meaning of the paragraph.

typhoons   Kunlun Mountains

Huang He   Three Gorges Dam

Chang Jiang

The _____, or Yellow River, is sometimes called "China's Sorrow,"

because of the terrible floods it has caused. China's longest river is the

_____, or Yangtze. To control the flooding on this river, and to

create more electricity, China is building the _____. Both of these

important rivers originate in the _____ in western China. Of course,

flooding is not the only problem in this region. There are tropical storms called

_____ that also cause damage.

B. Write the letter of the place or term next to the description that explains it best.

a. landfill   d. Xi Jiang

b. Qinling Shandi Mountains   e. PCBs

c. Gobi Desert

_____ 1. desert located in northern China and southeast Mongolia; one of the largest deserts in the world

_____ 2. industrial compounds that contributed to Japanese pollution

_____ 3. method of solid waste disposal in which refuse is buried between layers of dirt to fill in or reclaim low-lying ground

_____ 4. river in the south of China; also called the West River

_____ 5. mountains that divide the northern part of China from the southern part

Main Ideas

1. What physical features in China limited people's movement and increased isolation?

_____

_____

2. Why is western China more sparsely populated than eastern China?

_____

_____

3. What has happened to the forests in mid-latitude zones in East Asia?

_____

_____

4. What are the reasons China is building the Three Gorges Dam?

_____

_____

5. How is Japan using landfill to help it solve one of its biggest problems?

_____

_____

Thinking Critically

Answer the following questions on a separate sheet of paper.

1. What factors contribute to Japan's dependence on trade and fishing?

2. What are at least three questions would you want to have answered if you were in charge of deciding whether or not to complete the Three Gorges Dam?

Chapter 28   Section 1 (pages 635–639)   *Reading Study Guide*

China

BEFORE YOU READ
In the last chapter you, read about the physical geography of East Asia.

In this section, you will learn about the history and culture of China.

AS YOU READ
Use this graphic organizer to take notes about what you discover in this section.

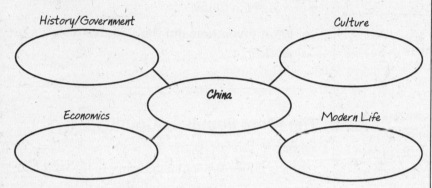

PLACES & TERMS
dynasty series of rulers from the same family

sphere of influence area of China where a European country could control trade without interference from other Western nations

Boxer Rebellion reaction by Chinese against foreign control

Mao Zedong leader of China's Communist Party from 1949 to 1976

Confucianism Chinese ethical tradition based on the teachings of the Chinese philosopher Confucius

Taoism Chinese religion based on the teaching of Lao Tzu

Buddhism religion that came into China from India

China's Early History (page 635)

What *did Shi Huangdi achieve?*

China has been a settled society for more than 4,000 years. At one time, China was made up of a number of smaller states. China has been ruled by dynasties. A **dynasty** is a series of rulers from the same family.

The first Chinese dynasty was the Shang, which arose during the 1700s B.C. It ruled central China for 600 years. It was overthrown by the Zhou Dynasty.

The next important dynasty was the Qin. In 221 B.C., Qin emperor Shi Huangdi united small states under a strong central government.

Another important dynasty was that of the Han. These rulers pushed the empire into central Asia. The area had been controlled by nomadic warriors.

In 1644, the Manchu people of Manchuria invaded China. They established the Qing Dynasty. In 1911, the Manchus were overthrown by revolutionaries. This ended the dynasties and the Chinese empire.

1. What were some important early dynasties?

_____

China Opens Up to the World
(pages 636–637)

What *ended the Boxer Rebellion?*

China and Europe had few contacts until the 1800s. Then, European powers wanted access to Chinese markets and imposed treaties that granted them special privileges. Trade in China was divided into **spheres of influence**—areas where a country could control trade without interference from other nations. This outside control led to the **Boxer Rebellion** in 1900. Chinese militants attacked and killed Europeans in China. A force of 20,000 soldiers finally defeated the Boxers.

After the Boxer Rebellion, the Manchu rulers tried to reform the government. It was too late. In 1912, Sun Yat-sen and others founded the *Kuomintang,* or Nationalist Party. Sun Yat-sen died in 1925. General Chiang Kai-shek took over the Nationalist Party. Chiang's troops united most of the country in the 1920s.

During the 1920s and 1930s, the Communist Party became increasingly powerful. In 1949, the Nationalist Party was defeated by the Communists led by **Mao Zedong**. The Communists ruled mainland China from Beijing. They named the country the People's Republic of China. Chiang and the Nationalists fled to Taiwan.

2. What was the *Kuomintang* and who founded it?

_____

Rural and Industrial Economies
(pages 637–638)

Where *is China's industrial heartland?*

When the Communist Party came to power in 1949, it promised to modernize China. It planned to encourage the growth of industry. From the 1950s through the 1970s, the central government tried to do this by planning all economic activities. This approach failed. Since the 1980s, China has allowed the marketplace and the consumer to play a role in the economy.

China remains largely rural. About 60 percent of China's workers work on farms. Farming is possible on only about 13 percent of China's land because much of the west is made up of mountains and deserts.

China's industrial heartland is in the northeast. Here, there are resources important to manufacturing, such as coal, iron ore, and oil.

3. What prevented economic progress before the 1980s?

_____

A Rich and Complex Culture (page 638)

What *is Confucianism?*

China has developed architecture, literature, painting, sculpture, music, and theater. Pottery, bronze *vessels*, jade disks and other works of art have been found at burial sites. The Chinese

invented paper, printing, gunpowder, the compass, and cloth made from silk.

China has three major religions or ethical traditions. The beliefs of most Chinese people include all three. **Confucianism** is based on the teachings of the Chinese philosopher Confucius. Confucius lived in the 500s B.C.

Taoism got its name from a book called the *Tao Te Ching*. The book is said to be based on the teaching of Lao Tzu, who also lived in the 500s B.C.

Buddhism came into China from India. It had grown into an important religion by A.D. 300. Confucianism and Taoism influenced Buddhism as it developed in China.

4. What inventions did the Chinese give the world?

_____

The Most Populous Country (page 639)

What *are "barefoot doctors"?*

China is the most populous country in the world. The country's estimated population in the year 2000 was 1.3 billion. Seventy percent of the people live in 12 *provinces* located in the east of the country.

One of China's achievements since 1950 has been to provide health care for its people. The health-care system mixes old and new ideas. Traditional herbs are important. So is acupuncture. China also uses modern drugs and surgery. Most Chinese cities have hospitals. Villages have clinics with trained medical workers called "barefoot doctors."

5. On which types of medicine does China rely?

_____

Mongolia and Taiwan

BEFORE YOU READ

In the last section, you read about the history and development of China.

In this section, you will learn about the culture, economics, and life of Mongolia and Taiwan.

AS YOU READ

Use this graphic organizer to take notes about what you discover in the section.

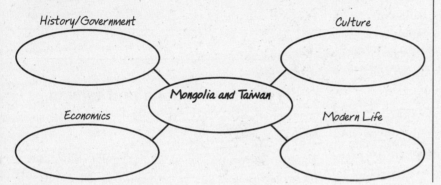

PLACES & TERMS

economic tiger country with rapid economic growth

Pacific Rim the countries surrounding the Pacific Ocean

A History of Nomads and Traders

(pages 642–643)

***What** was the extent of the Mongol Empire?*

The Mongols were nomadic herders for thousands of years. In 1206, Genghis Khan united the Mongol clans and led them in conquering Central Asia. In 1227, he was succeeded as Great Khan by his son, Ogadai. The empire extended from the Pacific coast of China westward into Europe.

The Mongol Empire broke up in the 1300s. In the 1600s, the Chinese gained control of Mongolia. In 1911, the Mongolians finally pushed the Chinese out. Under the influence of its powerful neighbor, Russia, Mongolia became the Mongolian People's Republic in 1924. Then, the Communists ruled Mongolia. However, after the fall of the Soviet Union in 1989, the Communist Party in Mongolia lost its power.

Over the centuries, many groups from China came to the island of Taiwan. As a result, there were large Chinese settlements on the island. The Qing Dynasty, from Manchuria, conquered Taiwan in 1683.

The Japanese seized Taiwan (then called Formosa) after winning a war with China in 1895. Japan kept the island until its defeat in World War II. Then Chinese Nationalists took control of the island. They were fighting the Communists for control of mainland China. When the Nationalists lost to the Communists in 1949, they moved their government to Taiwan. There they established the Republic of China. However, China's Communist government has never recognized Taiwan as a separate country.

1. How was Taiwan settled?

_____

_____

Cultures of Mongolia and Taiwan
(pages 643–644)

What are the Three Games of Man?

Kublai Khan was the Mongol emperor of China when Marco Polo visited in the 1200s. In the mid-1300s, the Chinese drove the Mongols out. In the 1600s, the Chinese conquered Mongolia. China ruled Mongolia for hundreds of years. The Mongols adopted many of the ways of Chinese culture.

The most important festival in Mongolia is the Three Games of Men. This festival dates back 2,300 years. It begins each year on July 11th. The three games are wrestling, archery, and horse racing.

The culture of Taiwan is Chinese. The capital city of Taipei has Buddhist temples and museums of Chinese art. The island has many universities and about 30 daily newspapers. Most people speak Mandarin, the official language of Northern China.

In Taiwan, about half of the people practice a blend of Buddhism, Confucianism, and Taoism. A large number practice Buddhism alone.

2. How was China able to influence Mongolian life?

_____

_____

Two Very Different Economies
(pages 644–645)

What is the Pacific Rim?

For centuries, the economy of Mongolia was based on nomadic herding. A large part of the population still herds and manages livestock. The animals Mongolians raise are sheep, goats, camels, horses, and cattle. Of the millions of animals in Mongolia, one-third are sheep.

Mongolia is developing its industry. Under Communism, the state owned and operated the factories. When the Soviet Union fell apart, Mongolia was one of the first Communist countries to shift to a market economy. Mongolia has large deposits of coal and petroleum. It also has deposits of copper, gold, and iron. These resources are used in manufacturing and construction industries.

Taiwan has one of the world's most successful economies. Taiwan's prosperity is based on its strong manufacturing industries and its trade with other nations. Among the most successful products of its factories are televisions, calculators, and computers.

Taiwan is considered one of the economic tigers of Asia, along with Singapore and South Korea. An **economic tiger** has rapid economic growth due to cheap labor, high technology, and aggressive exports. Taiwan is one of the prosperous, industrialized nations of the Pacific Rim. The **Pacific Rim** is made up of the countries surrounding the Pacific Ocean.

3. How is Mongolia's economy changing?

_____

_____

Daily Life in Mongolia and Taiwan
(pages 645–646)

What is Taiwan's top sport?

Today, many of the people of Mongolia still spend their days raising sheep, cattle, and goats. Some still follow the nomadic way of life. However, most people now care for livestock on farms and ranches.

Those who remain nomads guide their animals from grassland to grassland. The nomads live in tents called yurts. These are made of felt, covered with leather or canvas.

While Mongolia remains isolated, Taiwan has opened itself up to many Western influences. For example, baseball has become popular in Taiwan and many other Asian countries, especially Japan.

4. What is a yurt?

_____

_____

The Koreas: North and South

BEFORE YOU READ

In the last section, you read about the history and development of Mongolia and Taiwan.

In this section, you will learn about the culture, economics, and life of North and South Korea.

AS YOU READ

Use this graphic organizer to take notes about what you discover in the section.

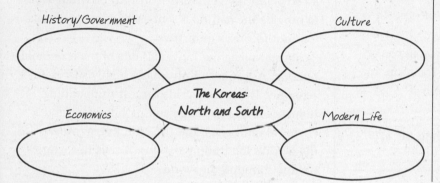

PLACES & TERMS

Three Kingdoms the kingdoms of Koguryo, Paekche, and Silla, which formed on the Korean Peninsula in the A.D. 300s.

Seoul capital of South Korea and the largest city in the region

Pyongyang the largest city in North Korea

A Divided Peninsula (pages 647–648)

***What** country conquered Korea in 1910?*

Korea is a peninsula. To the east lies the Sea of Japan. To the west lies the Yellow Sea. To the south lies the Korea Strait. To the north lie China and Russia.

The ancestors of today's Koreans came to the peninsula at least 5,000 years ago from Manchuria and North China. Over the centuries, different clans or tribes controlled different parts of the country. About 2000 B.C., the first state, called Choson, arose in Korea.

Around 100 B.C., China conquered the northern half of the peninsula. This began a history of conquests and invasions by China and Japan.

Korea was partially conquered by China. Koreans gradually won back their territory. By the late A.D. 300s, the **Three Kingdoms** had formed on the peninsula. Koguryo was the kingdom in the northeast. Paekche was in the southwest. Silla was in the southeast. In the 660s, Silla conquered the

other two and controlled the peninsula for hundreds of years.

In 1392, a general named Yi became ruler of Korea. He founded a dynasty that lasted for hundreds of years. The dynasty came to an end in 1910, when Japan took control of the peninsula. The Japanese ruled Korea until the end of World War II.

After Japan's defeat in World War II, the northern part of Korea came under the influence of the Soviet Union. The southern half came under the influence of the United States. In 1950, North Korean troops invaded South Korea. This started the Korean War. The war ended in 1953. A treaty was signed that divided the peninsula between the Communist state of North Korea and the capitalist country of South Korea. In 2000, the two nations began talking about reuniting.

1. What event started the Korean War?

_____

_____

Influences on Korean Culture
(pages 648–649)

What influence has China had on Korean culture?

In philosophy and religion, Korea has adapted many ideas from China. Confucianism is a system of teachings based on the beliefs of the Chinese scholar Confucius. His ideas about social order have influenced many Koreans. Buddhism came to Korea by way of China. It, too, has influenced many people in Korea. In addition, Confucianism and Buddhism shaped early forms of Korean art.

Since World War II, two major influences have had a *profound* effect on Korea. First, communism has molded the culture of North Korea. Non-Communist South Korea has been influenced by Western culture.

In North Korea, the government only allows art that glorifies communism or the folk tradition. In South Korea, artists have more freedom of expression.

2. What effect has communism had on art?

_____

_____

Moving Toward Unity (pages 649–650)

How large are the armies in this region?

After World War II, both North Korea and South Korea built up huge armies. The armed forces of South Korea number over 600,000 soldiers and sailors. The armed forces of North Korea are even larger, numbering well over one million. Recently there has been an attempt to *defuse* the situation.

In June 2000, the leaders of both Koreas declared their intention to reunite the two countries. The defense chiefs of the two Koreas agreed to reduce tensions along their border. Perhaps the most important development was that families in the North and South were allowed to visit each other.

3. What have Korea's leaders recently declared?

_____

_____

Economic and Human Resources (page 650)

How large is Seoul?

Before the Korean War, the economies of North and South Korea were agricultural. After the war, industry gained in importance in both countries.

If North and South Korea reunite, they will form an economic powerhouse. North Korea will be able to provide the natural resources and raw materials for South Korea's industries.

South Korea, like Taiwan, is one of the economic tigers of Asia. South Korea has a highly successful economy. It has the world's largest shipbuilding industry. It also has large automobile, steel, and chemical industries. Today, South Korea is one of the world's top trading nations. It sells its factories' products around the world.

Most of the people in Korea live on plains along the coast or in river valleys among the mountains of the peninsula. South Korea has 45 percent of the Korean Peninsula's land area. However, it has about 66 percent of its people. Of Korea's cities, <u>Seoul</u> is by far the largest. It has a population of more than ten million. The largest city in North Korea is <u>Pyongyang</u>. It has a population of more than 2.5 million.

4. How have the Korean economies changed since the Korean War?

_____

_____

Japan

BEFORE YOU READ

In the last section, you read about the history and development of North and South Korea.

In this section, you will learn about the culture, economics, and life of Japan.

AS YOU READ

Use this graphic organizer to take notes about what you discover in the section.

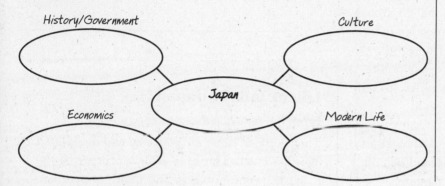

History/Government   Culture

Japan

Economics   Modern Life

PLACES & TERMS

samurai professional soldier who served the landowners or clan chiefs in ancient Japan

shogun general of the emperor's army, with the powers of a military dictator

Samurai and Shogun (pages 651–652)

What *was the job of the samurai?*

Japan lies east of China. In their earliest history, the Japanese were close enough to China to feel its civilizing effects. However, they were far enough away to be protected from invasion.

Some evidence suggests that the ancestors of today's Japanese came across Siberia to Japan. By about A.D. 500, most of Japan was actively growing food. Weapons and tools made of bronze and iron were introduced, as were textiles.

Until well into the A.D. 300s, Japan was not a unified country. By the A.D. 400s, the Yamato clan had become the ruling clan. By the A.D. 600s, the leaders of the Yamato clan called themselves emperors of Japan.

In 794, the rulers moved their capital to Heian (modern Kyoto). The era from 794 to 1185 is called the Heian period. Japan had a strong central government. However, in time, the great landowners and clan chiefs acted as independent rulers.

Professional soldiers called <u>samurai</u> served the landowners and clan chiefs as bodyguards and warriors. Samurai means "one who guards."

In 1192, after a struggle between two powerful clans, the Japanese emperor created the position of shogun. The <u>shogun</u> was the general of the emperor's army.

Rule by the shoguns lasted for about 700 years. During these years, the Japanese fought off Mongol invasion. They saw the arrival of Portuguese traders in the 1500s. In 1853, they received Commodore Matthew Perry from the United States. Perry's arrival ended Japan's isolation.

During the late 1800s, Japan's government began bringing Japan into the modern age. By the early 1900s, Japan had become a major power. In the first part of the 1900s, Japan expanded its empire.

On December 7, 1941, the Japanese made a surprise attack on the U.S. naval base at Pearl Harbor in Hawaii. The attack brought the United States into World War II. Japan surrendered in 1945.

After World War II, the United States introduced political and economic reforms into Japan. Eventually, Japan became a democracy—a constitutional monarchy with an emperor and a parliament.

1. What was the job of the daimyo?

_____

_____

An Economic Powerhouse
(pages 652–654)

What *caused the economic downturn of the 1990s?*

The population of Japan is about 126 million. About 75 percent of Japan's people live in cities. Japan has few minorities. Most of Japan's population and most of its industry and manufacturing are on the east coast of the main island of Honshu. Tokyo is in this area. Japan uses imported resources to manufacture products.

Business and government have worked together to create Japan's success during the second half of the 1900s. After the war, loans from Western nations helped Japan.

After four *decades* of rapid growth, Japan's economy began to slow down in the 1990s. Competition from other East Asian countries was one cause of the decline. Japanese investments in Southeast Asia suffered when the economies there had problems.

2. Where is most industry and manufacturing located?

_____

_____

Japanese Culture (page 654)

How *has the West influenced Japanese culture?*

In developing their culture, the Japanese borrowed from China. Japanese language, religion, art, music, and government were all influenced by the Chinese.

The city of Kyoto reflects the Japanese ideals of beauty. Gardens, palaces, and temples show a spare, elegant and refined style.

Traditional theater is still performed in Japan. Noh plays developed during the 1300s. They deal with subjects from history and legend. Performers wear masks. Kabuki plays developed in the 1600s. Kabuki uses an exaggerated acting style and vivid costumes.

Japanese painting was influenced by Chinese techniques and themes. Artistic works include long picture scrolls, ink paintings, and wood-block prints.

Contact with the west has influenced modern Japan. Sporting events such as baseball, golf, soccer, and tennis are popular. Western-style music is also popular, including jazz, classical, and rock.

3. What did the Japanese adapt from China?

_____

_____

Life in Today's Japan (page 655)

What *has contributed to Japan's prosperity?*

The people of Japan are educated and disciplined. This has enabled Japan to achieve prosperity.

Japan's education system is highly structured. Students often attend school six days a week. They have shorter summer vacations than American students. During high school, students often take additional classes at private schools, called juku. This is to help them get into good colleges.

The hardworking Japanese are now making some changes in the way their society is run. People are increasingly demanding an end to pollution and overcrowding. Also, the work force is making demands for shorter workdays and more vacation.

4. What changes are the Japanese trying to make?

_____

_____

Chapter 28   Shared Cultural Traditions   *Reading Study Guide*

Glossary/After You Read

decade a period of ten years
defuse to make harmless
profound extending far below the surface

province an administrative district or division of a country
vessel a utensil for holding something; for example, a bowl or bottle

Places & Terms

A. Write the letter of the place or term next to the description that explains it best.

a. Three Kingdoms   d. sphere of influence

b. Mao Zedong   e. economic tiger

c. Taoism

_____   1. country with rapid economic growth

_____   2. area of China where a European country could control trade without interference from other Western nations

_____   3. leader of China's Communist Party from 1949 to 1976

_____   4. Chinese religion based on the teaching of Lao Tzu

_____   5. Koguryo, Paekche, and Silla, which formed on the Korean Peninsula in the A.D. 300s.

B. Circle the place or term that best completes each sentence.

1. A series of rulers from the same family is a _____.

   dynasty   shogun   samurai

2. The reaction by Chinese against foreign control was called the _____.

   Sphere of Influence   Economic Tiger   Boxer Rebellion

3. _____ is the capital of South Korea and the largest city on the peninsula.

   Pyongyang   Seoul   Dynasty

4. A _____ was the general of the emperor's army, with the powers of a military dictator.

   samurai   shogun   economic tiger

5. The religion that came to China from India was _____.

   Taoism   Confucianism   Buddhism

Main Ideas

1. In what ways has Chinese influence been spread in the region?

_____

_____

_____

2. How do Mongolia and Taiwan differ in their relationship with China?

_____

_____

_____

3. Why is the Korean Peninsula divided in two?

_____

_____

_____

4. What role did the samurai play in ancient Japan?

_____

_____

_____

Thinking Critically

Answer the following questions on a separate sheet of paper.

1. How did the choice of capitalism over communism benefit Taiwan?

2. What issues will North and South Korea need to address if they are to be united?

The Ring of Fire

BEFORE YOU READ

In the last section, you read about the culture and development of Japan.

In this section, you will learn about the effect of earthquakes and volcanoes in East Asia.

AS YOU READ

Use this chart to help you take notes about the section.

	Causes	Effects
Issue 1: Ring of Fire		

PLACES & TERMS

Ring of Fire chain of volcanoes that outlines the Pacific Rim

Great Kanto earthquake destructive earthquake that struck Tokyo in 1923

tsunami huge wave caused by an underwater earthquake

Physical Forces in the Ring of Fire
(page 661)

***What** causes earthquakes?*

Many Japanese cities are threatened by earthquakes. This is because Japan is part of the Ring of Fire. The <u>Ring of Fire</u> is a chain of volcanoes that lines the Pacific Rim.

The outer crust of the earth is made up a of huge tectonic plates. These massive plates are slowly moving, continually bumping into or sliding past each other.

When a *dense* oceanic plate meets a less dense continental plate, the oceanic plate slides under the continental plate. This process is called subduction. The area where the oceanic crust is subducted is called a trench.

In East Asia, the Pacific oceanic plate encounters the Eurasian continental plate. When the oceanic plate moves under the continental plate, it crumples the continental crust. This builds mountains and volcanoes such as those that form the Ring of Fire.

At the same time, tremendous stress builds up along the edges of the plates. The stress keeps building until eventually the plates move suddenly and violently. The result is an earthquake.

1. What is subduction?

_____

_____

The Geology of Japan (page 662)

***What** is a tsunami?*

The Japanese islands exist because of subduction. The islands were formed by volcanoes created as the Pacific plate slid under the Eurasian plate.

Living along the Ring of Fire means living with volcanic activity. During the time historical records have been kept, at least 60 volcanoes have been active on the islands of Japan. In fact, the best-known landform in Japan, Mount Fuji, is a volcano.

Earthquakes are common in Japan. An average 1,000 quakes occur each year. Most are too mild to affect people's lives. Some, however, cause massive death and destruction. The <u>Great Kanto earthquake</u> struck in 1923. This earthquake and the fires it caused killed an estimated 140,000 people. It left the city of Tokyo in ruins. The quake partially or completely destroyed nearly 700,000 homes.

Another geological threat to Japan comes from the sea. When an earthquake occurs under the ocean floor, part of the floor moves. If the quake is strong enough, this shift may produce a tsunami. A <u>tsunami</u> is a huge wave with great destructive power. Underwater volcanic eruptions and coastal landslides also cause tsunamis. Some tsunamis have reached heights of over 100 feet.

2. How common are earthquakes in Japan?

_____

_____

Preparing for Disasters (page 663)

Why are older buildings not as safe as newer ones?
For thousands of years, people have tried to predict when natural disasters will occur. Today, they are still trying. Vulnerable nations, such as Japan, are working to improve their defenses against geological forces.

Many older buildings in Japan are not as likely to withstand earthquakes as newer buildings. There are other problems. For example, some buildings have been constructed on ground or landfill that is not stable. Underground gas lines are likely to rupture in the event of an earthquake and spread fires. Crowded blocks and narrow streets add to the problem. Fire spreads easily and rapidly. Rescue attempts are difficult.

Today, Japan has a strict building code. Whenever a quake rocks some area of the nation, engineers are quick to study the effects. They study how different types of buildings responded to the movement caused by the quake. The results of their studies affect the rules about construction materials and techniques. This has made newer buildings safer than older ones.

Because of the dangers, the Japanese people understand the importance of being prepared for disasters. Schoolchildren participate in yearly disaster drills with local fire fighters. Organizations offer courses on disaster preparedness and disaster management. These organizations include the Japanese Red Cross Society and the Asia Pacific Disaster Management Center.

Japan and the other countries along the Ring of Fire cannot change the geology that shapes their lives. They can, however, learn more about it. They can also prepare to deal with disaster when it strikes next.

3. How do people in Japan prepare for disaster?

_____

_____

Trade and Prosperity

BEFORE YOU READ

In the last section, you read about the earthquakes and volcanoes along the Ring of Fire.

In this section, you will learn about the benefits of global trade for this region.

AS YOU READ

Use this chart to help you take notes about the section.

	Causes	Effects
Issue 2: Trade		

PLACES & TERMS

UNICEF the United Nation's Children's Fund

global economy economic system in which nations are dependent on each other for goods and services

Jakota Triangle zone of prosperity that includes Japan, South Korea, and Taiwan

recession extended decline in general business activity.

sweatshop workplace where people work long hours under poor conditions, and are paid only pennies

Opening Doors (pages 665–666)

Why *did Europe want East Asia's isolation to end?*

At the beginning of the 1990s, the economies of East Asia were growing rapidly. But, in some parts of the region, there was a dark side to this growth. In 1995, <u>UNICEF</u> (the United Nations Children's Fund) reported that more than half a million children in East Asia were working in factories or begging on the streets.

The process by which East Asia became an economic powerhouse took centuries. Until the 1500s, the nations of East Asia had been fairly isolated from the rest of the world. As demand grew in the West for Asian products, European traders tried to end East Asia's isolation. They used a variety of means to do this, including force.

By the end of the 1800s, the nations of Europe had signed treaties with China. These treaties gave them distinct spheres of influence in the East. These spheres of influence were areas where they could control trade without interference from other Western nations.

In 1853, Commodore Matthew Perry set sail from the United States to Japan. His goal was to establish trade and diplomatic relations between Japan and the United States. His persuasion took the form of a display of power. This opened the doors to the East for the United States and Europe.

After World War II, the nations of East Asia began industrializing. They used cheap labor to produce goods for trade. Trade between East and West steadily increased.

At the same time, regional economies began to emerge. These *evolved* from national economies. Eventually, a global economy developed. In a <u>global economy</u>, nations became dependent on each other for goods and services. For example, Japan imported many natural resources from around the world. The Japanese then transformed these resources into manufactured goods. These goods were then sold around the globe. The nations of East Asia used their supplies of cheap labor to become manufacturing powerhouses.

1. What is a global economy?

_____

_____

Powerful Economies of East Asia

(pages 666–667)

***What** important lesson has the world learned about the global economy?*

During the 1980s and early 1990s, many Asian economies did very well. The most powerful of the Pacific Rim nations of East Asia—Japan, Taiwan, and South Korea—enjoyed record prosperity. These three countries formed part of a zone of prosperity. Some call this zone the <u>Jakota Triangle</u>, for **Ja**pan, **Ko**rea (South), and **Ta**iwan. By the 1990s, however, these economies were about to experience problems.

Some East Asian economies that looked healthy were actually mismanaged and burdened by debt. The Asian economic "miracle" had been based in part on efficiency and innovation. It also had been built partly on the sacrifices of very poor and very young workers. These workers were paid low wages. Then, some banks and other companies went bankrupt. This sparked panic among foreign investors. These investors began selling their Asian *stocks* and *currency*. In some countries, riots broke out. In Japan and South Korea, ruling politicians had to resign. Japan's economy entered a recession. A <u>recession</u> is an extended decline in general business activity. South Korea and Taiwan also had recessions.

Today, the economies of many nations are interconnected. Because of this, the crisis in Asia spread throughout the world. Uncertainty led to concern at the New York Stock Exchange and other national exchanges. The World Bank and the International *Monetary* Fund loaned money to East Asian countries that promised to *reform.* This began to reverse the downslide. However, the world had learned an important lesson. A global economy could threaten as well as improve prosperity.

The economic crisis led to an awareness in East Asia that serious reform was necessary. Reform would have to include increased wages for adult workers. It would also need to include a ban on child-labor and forced-labor practices. It would also mean an end to sweatshops. <u>Sweatshops</u> are workplaces where people work long hours under poor conditions. They are paid only pennies. Sweatshops are run to enrich manufacturers. At the beginning of the 21st century, reforms had begun. Asian economies were showing signs of renewed life.

2. What workplace reforms are needed in East Asia?

_____

_____

Chapter 29   Case Study (pages 668–671)   *Reading Study Guide*

Population and the Quality of Life

BEFORE YOU READ

In the last section, you read about benefits to East Asia of global trade.

In this case study, you will examine the pressures put on people and the environment by huge populations.

AS YOU READ

Use this chart to help you take notes on this case study.

	Causes	Effects
Case Study: Population		

PLACES & TERMS

life expectancy the length of time the average person in a group or nation is expected to live

literacy the ability to read and write

fertility rate the average number of children an average woman would have during her lifetime

Patterns of Population (page 668)

What *was East Asia like in the mid-1900s?*

Many countries in East Asia have been successful in dealing with the basic problem of feeding their people. Now they face other problems. Many of these problems are caused by expanding populations in the region.

In the middle of the 1900s, the nations of East Asia ranked among the least developed in the world. Widespread poverty was the norm. **Life expectancy** was short. **Fertility rates** were high, as were infant and maternal death rates. In 1950, East Asian women often married young and gave birth to six children on average. Most economies remained rural.

1. What were some of the problems facing the nations of East Asia around 1950?

_____

_____

Addressing Population Problems

(pages 668–669)

How *has the fertility rate changed in East Asia?*

Unrestricted population growth puts tremendous pressure on the region's environment. Food production on existing farmland is barely adequate. The absence of basic sanitation has fouled the region's water supplies. In some countries, such as China, the water tables are being drained to dangerously low levels. Fortunately, the governments of East Asia are moving quickly to reverse course.

Aggressive family planning programs were begun in the region. Fertility rates began leveling off and then dropping. By the year 2000, women were marrying much later and giving birth to an average 2.5 children. In China alone, the fertility rate dropped from 6.22 children per woman in 1950–1955 to just 1.82 in the year 2000.

This drop in fertility rates, combined with industrialization, led to fast economic growth. By the 1990s, the economies of East Asia were booming. The booming economies transformed social and economic conditions. In a generation, the region's quality of life has improved. Life expectancy and literacy rates are among the highest in the world.

2. How have women's lives changed?

_____

_____

The Quality of Life (page 669)

How has life expectancy changed in the region?

These changes in East Asia have been dramatic. However, they have not solved all of the region's problems. Some countries in the region (such as China and Japan) are among the most populous in the world.

The huge population of the region puts pressure on the environment. Even if China were to maintain a modest growth rate of 1 percent a year, it would add 13 million people to its population every year.

The growing populations are concentrated in the cities of the region. They must be provided with housing, sanitation, and transportation. Pollution, overcrowding, and flooding are all problems that are made worse by an expanding population.

However, not all such family planning programs were well received. Some citizens criticized China's one-child-per-family policy as harsh and an assault on their rights.

In spite of these difficulties, East Asia has shown the world that rapid social and economic progress are possible. This progress requires that people and their leaders work together. They also need to work with the world community.

3. What does an expanding population make worse?

_____

_____

Growth, the Environment, and the Economy (pages 670–671)

How do smaller families affect economics?

Bar Graph: U.S. Census Bureau shows population statistics from 2000 to 2050. Population is likely to grow by 152 percent in Africa and by 48 percent in Asia.

Policy Statement: In speaking to a Chinese audience about environmental issues, former president Bill Clinton pointed out that industrialization and overcrowding had led to serious problems in China. He said that polluted air and water would hinder China's progress. Smog is so bad that some cities disappear on satellite photographs. Respiratory illness is China's biggest health problem.

Fact Sheet: There has been a strong connection between population control and economic development. With fewer children, households placed more of their earnings in savings, and governments reduced public spending. Combined with advances in business and education, this could lead to a better-educated work force, higher wages, and more job opportunities.

4. What impact have overcrowding and industrialization had on China?

_____

_____

Considering Resources (page 671)

How does growth affect resources?

Political Cartoon: The artist illustrates the pressure on existing resources. He shows the natural environment being destroyed in order to make room for the expanding human population.

News Analysis: An article from Asiaweek.com reports that birth rates are still growing in some countries. It relates that the most important resource at risk is clean water. This is needed for drinking. It is also needed for food production and to control hygiene-related diseases.

5. Why is clean water needed?

_____

_____

Glossary/After You Read

currency paper money in circulation

dense having mass that is greater and more compacted together

evolved developed

monetary of or relating to currency

reform removal or correction of an abuse, a wrong, or errors

rupture a breaking apart

stocks shares bought in a business

Places & Terms

A. If the statement is true, write "true" on the line. If it is false, write the word or words that would replace the underlined words to make it true.

_____ 1. A <u>recession</u> sometimes reaches heights of over 100 feet.

_____ 2. People work long hours in poor conditions and for low wages in <u>manufacturing powerhouses</u>.

_____ 3. A <u>global economy</u> is an economic system in which nations are dependent on each other for goods and services.

_____ 4. Living along the <u>Ring of Fire</u> means living with volcanic activity.

_____ 5. An extended decline in general business activity is a <u>recovery</u>.

B. Write the letter of the place or term next to the description that explains it best.

a. Ring of Fire

b. Great Kanto earthquake

c. UNICEF

d. Jakota Triangle

e. tsunami

_____ 1. the United Nation's Children's Fund

_____ 2. destructive earthquake that struck Tokyo in 1923

_____ 3. huge wave caused by an underwater earthquake

_____ 4. chain of volcanoes that outlines the Pacific Rim

_____ 5. zone of prosperity that includes Japan, South Korea, and Taiwan

Main Ideas

1. How does living along the Ring of Fire affect Japan?

   _____

   _____

   _____

2. What happened to East Asian economies after World War II?

   _____

   _____

   _____

3. What led to the economic problems of the 1990s in East Asia?

   _____

   _____

   _____

4. What has the world learned is one effect of the global economy?

   _____

   _____

   _____

Thinking Critically

Answer the following questions on a separate sheet of paper.

1. How does Japan's location affect the way its cities are built?

2. Why do you think that some East Asian countries were willing and able to operate sweatshops and use child labor?

Name _____ Date _____

SOUTHEAST ASIA, OCEANIA, AND ANTARCTICA
Landforms and Resources

BEFORE YOU READ

In the last chapter, you learned about the challenges facing East Asia.

In this section, you will learn about the physical features and resources of Southeast Asia, Oceania, and Antarctica. You will also learn how physical geography shapes life in the region.

AS YOU READ

Use this chart to take notes about the landforms and resources of Southeast Asia, Oceania, and Antarctica.

Landforms	
Resources	

PLACES & TERMS

archipelago group of islands

Oceania the combined islands of the Pacific Ocean

high island an island created by a volcano

low island an island made of coral reefs

Great Barrier Reef a 1,250-mile-long chain of coral reefs off Australia's east coast

Southeast Asia: Mainland and Islands (pages 689–690)

What landforms are found in Southeast Asia?

Southeast Asia has two different subregions. One is the southeastern corner of the Asian mainland. The other subregion includes thousands of islands.

Mainland Southeast Asia lies on two peninsulas. The Indochinese Peninsula lies south of China. It has a rectangular shape. The Malay Peninsula is a narrow strip of land about 700 miles long. It stretches south from the mainland. Then it curves southeast. It serves as a bridge between the mainland and the islands.

Most of the islands of Southeast Asia are found in archipelagos. An **archipelago** is a group of islands. The Philippines and the islands of Indonesia are part of the Malay Archipelago.

The mainland has several mountain ranges. In general, they run north and south. One example is the Annamese Cordillera. These ranges fan out from a mountainous area to the north.

On the islands, most of the mountains were made by volcanoes. Southeast Asia is part of the Pacific Ring of Fire. Volcanic eruptions and earthquakes are common there.

The mainland has several large rivers. These run from the north through valleys between mountain ranges. One example is the Mekong River. It begins in China and crosses several Southeast Asian nations. Finally, it becomes a wide delta on the coast of Vietnam. Millions of people use the Mekong for farming and fishing.

Southeast Asia has a long, uneven coastline. This coastline has many ports. The ports allow Southeast Asians to travel and trade on the sea.

Fertile soil is a valuable resource in Southeast Asia. Both volcanic activity and flooding rivers add nutrients to the soil. The rivers and nearby sea have large numbers of fish. Southeast Asians rely on fishing. Parts of the region have mineral resources. These include petroleum, tin, and gems. Many industries use those resources.

1. What are Southeast Asia's two subregions?

_____

_____

Lands of the Pacific and Antarctica
(pages 690–692)

Why *is it difficult to know how many islands are in Oceania?*

No one knows how many islands are in the Pacific Ocean. Some geographers think there are more than 20,000. As a group, the Pacific Islands are called **Oceania**. (The Philippines, Indonesia, and other islands near the mainland are not part of Oceania.) In the southwestern Pacific lie New Zealand and Australia. These two countries are often seen as part of Oceania.

The number of islands in Oceania often changes. Erosion causes some islands to vanish. Other forces create new islands. Most Pacific islands fall into one of two categories: high islands or low islands. **High islands** are created by volcanoes. **Low islands** are made of coral reefs.

Oceania is not rich in resources. The low islands have poor soil. Most of the islands lack minerals. But a few islands do have resources. New Caledonia has nickel, chromium, and iron. New Guinea has copper, gold, and oil. Nauru has phosphate. Both Fiji and the Solomon Islands have gold. The scarcity of resources has made it hard to develop industry.

New Zealand has two main islands, North Island and South Island. South Island has dramatic scenery. Running down the center of this island is a 300-mile-long mountain range. This range is called the Southern Alps. It has 16 peaks over 10,000 feet high. It also has more than 360 glaciers.

North Island has hilly ranges and a volcanic plateau. It is less mountainous than South Island. North Island has fertile farmland. It also has forests that support the lumber industry. Its coastline has harbors that are used as seaports. Like South Island, North Island has many rivers that run to the sea.

New Zealand has few mineral resources. The people of New Zealand have built dams on its swift-flowing rivers. Those dams generate electricity. Also, North Island has a volcanic area with underground steam. Engineers use this steam to run generators.

Australia is the smallest continent. It is also the flattest. Near the eastern coast is a chain of highlands called the Great Dividing Range. This range runs roughly parallel to the coast. Unlike New Zealand's mountains, few of these peaks rise higher than 5,000 feet. None of the peaks are volcanic. To the west of this range stretches a vast expanse of plains and plateaus.

Australia and New Zealand are different in other ways. Australia has few rivers. The largest river is the Murray River, which flows into the Southern Ocean. Forestry is not a major industry in Australia, but the country is rich in minerals. It is the world's leading supplier of *bauxite*, diamonds, opals, lead, and coal.

Along Australia's northeast coast is the **Great Barrier Reef**. It is a 1,250-mile-long chain of reefs and islands. Some 400 species of coral are found there.

Antarctica is the fifth largest continent. It contains the South Pole. Antarctica is generally shaped like a circle. A thick ice sheet hides its surface. Under the ice lies a varied landscape. The Transantarctic Mountains divide the continent in two. West Antarctica is a group of separate islands linked by the ice sheet.

Antarctic's ice sheet is the largest supply of fresh water in the world. Geologists believe that resources may lie beneath the ice. Those resources might include coal, minerals, and perhaps petroleum. But in 1991, 26 nations agreed not to mine Antarctica for 50 years.

2. What minerals does Australia supply to the world?

_____

_____

SOUTHEAST ASIA, OCEANIA, AND ANTARCTICA
Climate and Vegetation

BEFORE YOU READ
In the last section you read about the landforms and resources of
Southeast Asia, Oceania, and Antarctica.

   In this section, you will learn how climate and vegetation affect life
in this region.

AS YOU READ
Use this chart to take notes about the climate and vegetation of
Southeast Asia, Oceania, and Antarctica.

Climate	
Vegetation	

PLACES & TERMS
outback sparsely populated, arid, inland region of Australia

Widespread Tropics (pages 694–695)

***Which** areas get monsoons?*

A tropical wet climate is found on the coasts of
Myanmar, Thailand, Vietnam, and Oceania. It is
also found in most of Malaysia, Indonesia, and the
Philippines. Temperatures are high. Most of
Southeast Asia has an average yearly temperature of
80° F. Parts of Southeast Asia receive over 100
inches of rain a year.

   Some places in this climate zone have different
conditions. *Elevation,* ocean breezes, and other
factors can create cooler temperatures. In Indonesia
some places are so high that they have glaciers.

   Bordering the tropical wet climate zone is the
tropical wet and dry climate zone. In this zone,
monsoons shape the weather. Monsoons are winds
that cause wet and dry seasons. This climate is
found in parts of Myanmar, Thailand, Laos,
Cambodia, and Vietnam. It generally occurs to the
north or inland of the wet climate zone.

   Temperatures stay hot in this zone. But rainfall
varies greatly during the year. Local conditions and
landforms can affect the amount of rain and snow.

For example, mountains create rain shadows.
Monsoons often cause disastrous weather. During
the wet season, typhoons can occur in Southeast
Asia and Oceania.

   Southeast Asia has an amazing variety of
vegetation. For example, there are many kinds of
trees. Near the equator, there are tropical evergreen
forests. Deciduous forests are more common in the
wet and dry climate zone. These deciduous forests
contain teak. Teak is a valuable tree that Asians cut
down to sell.

   In general, Oceania does not have diverse
vegetation. The low islands have poor soil and small
amounts of rain. As a result, plants don't grow well.
Some high islands have rich, volcanic soil and
plentiful rain.

**1. In which climate zone do Indonesia and
   the Philippines lie?**

_____

_____

Bands of Moderate Climate
(pages 695–696)

How do mountains affect Australia's climate?

Australia lies completely in the Southern Hemisphere. New Zealand is even farther south. Australia and New Zealand have generally moderate climates.

A mountain chain runs parallel to the east coast of Australia. The narrow strip between the mountains and ocean has mostly two climate zones. The northern half of this strip has a humid subtropical climate. This climate has hot summers, mild winters, and heavy rainfall. It is one of the wettest regions in Australia. It receives an average of 126 inches of rain a year. This climate is also found in northern Vietnam, Laos, Thailand, and Myanmar.

New Zealand and the southern part of Australia's east coast share a marine west coast climate. Ocean breezes warm the land in the winter and cool it in the summer. As a result, temperatures are mild. New Zealand's forests mostly contain evergreens and tree ferns. Those trees and plants do well in such a climate.

New Zealand receives rainfall year round. But the amount varies dramatically from one part of the country to the other. For example, the mountains of South Island cause rain to fall on their western slopes. Because of this, the eastern part of the island is dryer. Mountains change the climate in another way. The mountainous inland areas of New Zealand are cooler than the coasts.

Mountains affect Australia's climate, too. The Great Dividing Range forces winds carrying moisture to rise. As they rise, they shed their rain before moving inland. For that reason, the marine west coast climate and humid subtropical climates exist only on the east coast. That coast is Australia's most heavily populated region. The moist coastal areas are also the only parts of Australia where trees grow taller than 300 feet.

2. What trees and plants are in New Zealand's forests?

_____

_____

Hot and Cold Deserts (page 697)

Why is Australia's interior so dry?

One-third of Australia is desert. The desert area lies in an oval in the center of the continent. This region receives less than ten inches of rain a year. It is too dry for agriculture or for grazing. *Encircling* the desert is a band of semiarid climate. This area receives no more than 20 inches of rain a year. Crops can only be grown there by using irrigation.

Several things cause Australia's dryness. Because it lies in the tropics and subtropics, Australia is hot. Rain evaporates easily. And the mountains make the rain fall on the coasts instead of on the interior.

Few people live in the dry interior. Australians call the *sparsely* populated inland region the **outback**. The Royal Flying Doctor Service gives medical care to the people who live in the outback.

Antarctica is the earth's coldest, driest continent. Its lands are located around the South Pole. It has an ice cap climate. In the winter, the inland temperatures can fall to 70° F below zero or colder. Cold air doesn't hold moisture well. Because of this, Antarctica's air has only one-tenth the water vapor found in the air of warmer regions. As a result, Antarctica receives little precipitation. It is often called a polar desert. The snow that does fall rarely melts. So Antarctica has heavy snow and ice cover.

The plants of Antarctica have to survive severe cold and long periods of darkness. Lichens and mosses can grow there.

3. Why is Antarctica often called a polar desert?

_____

_____

SOUTHEAST ASIA, OCEANIA, AND ANTARCTICA
Human-Environment Interaction

Before You Read

In the last section you read about the climate and vegetation of Southeast Asia, Oceania, and Antarctica.

In this section, you will learn about the way humans have learned to live in this region. You will also learn about how humans have changed the environment.

As You Read

Use this graphic to take notes about the human-environment interaction in Southeast Asia, Oceania, and Antarctica.

Human-Environment Interaction

PLACES & TERMS

voyaging canoe double-hulled, ocean-going canoe developed by Pacific Islanders

outrigger canoe canoe with a frame and attached float that helps balance the canoe

atoll ringlike coral island or string of small islands surrounding a lagoon

Bikini Atoll at one time, the site of U.S. atomic-weapons testing

Traveling the Pacific (pages 698–699)

How did Pacific Islanders sail on the ocean?

Most scholars believe the people who settled the Pacific Islands came from Southeast Asia. They first moved to islands close to the mainland. They traveled on land bridges. They also sailed there in small rafts and canoes. In time, they sailed farther out into the Pacific Ocean. To do this, they needed methods of navigation.

Pacific Islanders steered by the stars. They also used charts made of sticks and shells. The sticks showed the patterns of waves found in a specific area of the ocean. The shells showed where islands were located. Pacific Islanders kept the secret of how to use these charts until the late 1800s.

To sail the vast ocean, Pacific Islanders built huge **voyaging canoes** with double *hulls*. Having two hulls made the canoe stable. It also enabled the

canoe to carry lots of weight. The canoes had sails to catch the winds. Cabins were built on the platform atop the hulls. Those cabins housed the voyagers and their supplies. Those supplies often included plants that the travelers hoped to grow in their new home.

The islands where Pacific Islanders settled often had lagoons. The large voyaging canoes were hard to use in the lagoons. In those places, they used the outrigger canoe. An **outrigger canoe** has a frame with an attached float. This frame extends from one side. The float helps balance the canoe.

1. What are the advantages of having two hulls in the voyaging canoe?

_____

_____

Invasion of the Rabbits (pages 699-700)

How did rabbits get introduced to Australia?

The people who settled the Pacific Islands carried familiar plants with them. So did the Europeans who built a colony in Australia. They also brought European animals, such as the rabbit. The rabbit is a small animal, but it nearly ruined the Australian landscape.

In Europe, many people hunt rabbits for food. In 1859, Thomas Austin released 24 rabbits into Australia so he could hunt them. The rabbit population grew faster than hunters could kill it. A single pair of rabbits can have up to 184 descendants in 18 months. Plus, rabbits have few natural enemies in Australia. By 1900, Australia had more than a billion rabbits.

Australia's arid climate produces few plants. Rabbits graze close to the ground. This kills or weakens the plants that do grow. Rabbits wiped out native plants and destroyed crops. They ruined pastures. This made it harder to feed herds of sheep.

Australians have tried to control the number of rabbits. They imported foxes to *prey* on rabbits. But the foxes were a danger to Australian wildlife. In the early 1900s, the government built a 2,000-mile fence to keep rabbits from spreading to the southwest. This fence worked for only a short time. The rabbits broke through to the new region.

In the 1950s, the government infected wild rabbits with a disease. More than 90 percent of wild rabbits died. The smaller number of rabbis ruined fewer pastures. Australians were able to raise more sheep. But rabbits became immune to the disease. Their numbers boomed again.

Now, Australians are trying many methods to reduce rabbit numbers. They are using poison and introducing new rabbit diseases. They are building fences. And they are destroying the places where rabbits have their nests.

2. How are Australians trying to control the number of rabbits?

_____

_____

Nuclear Testing (pages 700–701)

What led to the tests on Bikini Atoll?

Beginning in the 1940s, the United States and Soviet Union waged an arms race. They each tried to make more powerful nuclear weapons than the other. As part of its weapons program, the United States wanted to test nuclear bombs. In the 1940s and 1950s, the United States conducted 66 tests in the Pacific.

In the Marshall Islands of the central Pacific lies **Bikini Atoll**. An **atoll** is a ringlike coral island or string of small islands around a lagoon. Bikini Atoll was the site of U.S. atomic-weapons tests.

Bikini lay far away from regular shipping and air travel routes. So the U.S. government chose Bikini for testing. In 1946, the government moved 167 Bikini Islanders to another atoll. Then the government held two atomic-weapons tests. From 1951 to 1958, the U.S. government held about 60 more tests there. The most dramatic of these was the test of a hydrogen bomb code-named Bravo. That blast polluted Bikini Atoll with high levels of radiation. It polluted several other atolls and islands too. Many islanders were injured or made ill.

In the meantime, the Bikini Islanders could not return to their home. The first atoll where they moved could not support human life. In 1948, they moved to the island of Kili. It was impossible to grow enough food there. They could not fish there either.

In the late 1960s, the U.S. government said Bikini Atoll was safe for humans. Several islanders went back to their home. Then, in 1978, doctors discovered dangerous levels of radiation in the islanders' bodies. The islanders had to leave again. A cleanup began in 1988.

3. How did the tests affect Bikini islanders?

_____

_____

Name _____ Date _____

Glossary/After You Read

bauxite an ore that is the principal source of aluminum

elevation the height to which something is raised above the ground

encircling surrounding; forming a circle around

hull the frame or body of a ship

prey to catch and eat

sparsely characterized by few and scattered elements

Places & Terms

A. Write the name or term in each blank that best completes the meaning of the paragraph.

outrigger canoes   low islands

voyaging canoes   high islands

Oceania

Scattered across the Pacific Ocean are thousands of islands, which are collectively

known as (1) _____. Among these islands there are many

(2) _____, which were created by volcanoes. There are also

(3) _____, which were made of coral reefs. The people who settled the

islands of this region probably came from Southeast Asia. Pacific Islanders developed

huge, double-hulled (4) _____. For use in the lagoons where they

settled, the Pacific Islanders used (5) _____.

B. Write the letter of the place or term next to the description that explains it best.

a. Bikini Atoll   d. archipelago

b. outback   e. atoll

c. Great Barrier Reef

_____ 1. group of islands

_____ 2. 1,250-mile-long natural wonder off Australia's east coast

_____ 3. ringlike coral island or string of small islands surrounding a lagoon

_____ 4. at one time, the site of U.S. atomic-weapons testing

_____ 5. sparsely populated, arid, inland region of Australia

Main Ideas

1. Why are fishing, trade, and travel such a big part of life in Southeast Asia?

_____

_____

2. Why is it difficult for geographers to determine the number of islands in Oceania?

_____

_____

3. Why is the vegetation not diverse on the low islands?

_____

_____

4. What factors contribute to the dryness of Australia's interior?

_____

_____

5. How did Pacific Islanders use sticks and shells to navigate?

_____

_____

Thinking Critically

Answer the following questions on a separate sheet of paper.

1. What reasons might the Pacific Islanders had for exploring and colonizing the islands of Oceania?

2. The U.S. Department of Agriculture now has strict rules about bringing plants, fruit, and living things into the country from overseas. Why do you think they have these rules, and how would you convince someone to obey the rules? Use the case of rabbits in Australia as an example.

Southeast Asia

BEFORE YOU READ

In the last chapter you, read about the physical geography of Southeast Asia, Oceania, and Antarctica.

In this section, you will learn about the history and culture of Southeast Asia.

AS YOU READ

Use this graphic organizer to take notes about what you discover in this section.

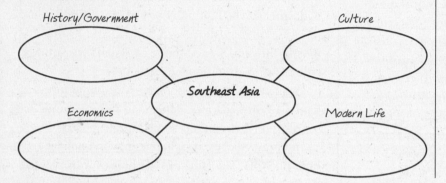

PLACES & TERMS

mandala a state organized as rings of power around a central court

Khmer Empire a powerful mandala that lasted from the 800s to the 1400s in what is now Cambodia

Indochina a French colony made up of Cambodia, Laos, and Vietnam

Vietnam War a conflict in which the United States tried to prevent the takeover of South Vietnam by Communist North Vietnam

ASEAN Association of Southeast Asian Nations

A Long History of Diversity
(pages 705–706)

How do mandalas differ from other states?

China and India had an influence on ancient Southeast Asia. China ruled northern Vietnam for more than a thousand years. Chinese art, technology, political ideas, and ethical beliefs shaped the culture of Vietnam. Hinduism and Buddhism spread from India. They shaped religion and art in much of Southeast Asia.

Early Southeast Asian states did not have set borders. Instead, they were mandalas. A **mandala** is a state set up as rings of power around a central court. This region of power changed in size over time. The **Khmer Empire** was a mandala. It lasted from the 800s to the 1400s in what is now Cambodia.

The years 1300 to 1800 were important in the history of Southeast Asia. Five powerful states arose. They existed where Myanmar, Vietnam, Thailand, Java, and the Malay Peninsula are now. There was much trade within the region. During

that period, people in the region began to see themselves as part of nations. Also, large cities began to develop.

1. How did India influence the region?

_____

Colonialism and its Aftermath
(pages 706–707)

When did Europeans begin to arrive in the region?

Southeast Asians traded with merchants from Arabia and India. Arab traders brought Islam to the region.

Starting in 1509, large numbers of Europeans came to Southeast Asia. At first, most Europeans did not want to set up colonies there. They just wanted to make money. Europeans took over much of the region's trade. Over time, the rulers of Southeast Asia lost power. By the 1900s, Europeans had made all of the region except Siam into colonies. (Siam is called Thailand now.)

Colonial rulers set up governments at a central place in each colony. The rulers forced the colonies to produce crops for Europe. Some crops were rubber, sugar, rice, tea, and coffee. These actions had the unplanned effect of sparking *nationalism.*

Japan took over the region during World War II. Southeast Asians soon realized that Japan was using the region to help itself. But the Japanese did put some Southeast Asians in leadership roles.

After the war, some Southeast Asian leaders wanted their nations to be free. Several nations gained freedom without a war. In contrast, Indonesia had to fight the Dutch for independence. <u>Indochina</u> was a French colony. It was made up of Cambodia, Laos, and Vietnam. The Vietnamese defeated the French in 1954. After that, the colony became four nations. They were Cambodia, Laos, North Vietnam, and South Vietnam. Communists ran North Vietnam. The United States tried to stop North Vietnam from taking over South Vietnam. This led to the <u>Vietnam War</u> (1957–1975). In 1973, the United States pulled out of Vietnam. In 1975, South Vietnam lost the war. Vietnam became a single country, which Communists ran.

2. Which two colonies had to fight for independence?

An Uneven Economy (pages 707–708)

What is the goal of ASEAN?

The people of Cambodia, Myanmar, Laos, and Vietnam are mostly farmers. Rice is the chief food crop. The lack of industry has many causes. The Vietnam War wiped out factories. Thousands of refugees fled. As a result, the countries had fewer workers. Political unrest has blocked growth. But Vietnam has built industry. It has also sought foreign trade.

In general, Brunei, Indonesia, Malaysia, the Philippines, Singapore, and Thailand are more wealthy. They have been growing industry. These six countries have members of ASEAN longer than the other four have. <u>ASEAN</u> is the Association of Southeast Asian Countries. It tries to help the region's economy grow. It also promotes peace.

In these six countries, the processing of farm products is the chief industry. Other industries make fabric, clothing, and electronic products. Service industries are important. So are energy sources and mining.

3. What caused a lack of industry in some countries?

A Rich Mosaic of Culture/Changing Lifestyles (pages 708–709)

What art forms exist in the region?

Southeast Asia has many religions. Buddhism is widespread. The Philippines is mostly Catholic (because of Spanish rule). Indonesia and Brunei are mostly Muslim. Some Southeast Asians are Hindus. Others follow traditional local beliefs.

Thailand and Indonesia have traditional forms of dance. In those dances, dancers in rich costumes act out stories. Vietnam has some famous poetry.

In many villages, people live in wood houses built on stilts. The stilts protect houses from floods. Roofs are usually made of *thatch.* Wealthy families may have a tin roof. Some villagers still wear traditional clothing. Yet modern inventions, such as radios, are slowly changing village life.

A growing number of people are moving to cities. In Southeast Asian cities, most people live in apartments. There is not enough housing for the people moving to cities. Many live in shacks in slums.

4. What problem is the migration to cities creating?

Oceania

BEFORE YOU READ

In the last section, you read about the history and development of Southeast Asia.

In this section, you will learn about the culture, economics, and life of Oceania.

AS YOU READ

Use this graphic organizer to take notes about what you discover in this section.

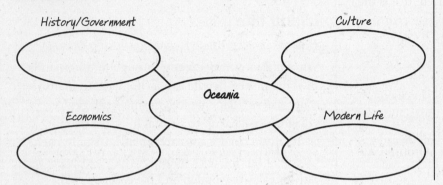

History/Government

Culture

Oceania

Economics

Modern Life

PLACES & TERMS

Micronesia region of Oceania, name means "tiny islands"

Melanesia region of Oceania, name means "black islands"

Polynesia region of Oceania, name means "many islands"

subsistence activities activities in which a family produce only the food, clothing, and shelter that they themselves need

copra dried meat of coconuts

taro plant with a starchy root, used for food

A History of the Islands (pages 712–714)

What *caused turmoil in the 1900s?*

All the nations of Oceania except Nauru are island groups. These nations are Fiji, Kiribati, Marshall Islands, Federated States of Micronesia, Palau, Papua New Guinea, Samoa, Solomon Islands, Tonga, Tuvalu, and Vanuatu.

Prehistoric people journeyed from Southeast Asia to nearby Pacific Islands. They used land bridges that have since disappeared. They also used small rafts or canoes. In time, they made large voyaging canoes that could sail longer distances. For thousands of years, their descendants continued to migrate. They went as far east as Hawaii. They also went as far south as New Zealand and as far west as Madagascar.

For centuries, the people of Oceania had little contact with the rest of the world. They developed their own ways of life. Oceania has three regions. They are Micronesia, Melanesia, and Polynesia. <u>Micronesia</u> means "tiny islands." <u>Melanesia</u> means "black islands." <u>Polynesia</u> means "many islands."

Beginning in the 1500s, many Europeans explored the Pacific. Perhaps the most famous was the British captain James Cook. He was the first European to visit many of the islands.

In the 1800s, European missionaries arrived. They tried to convert the people to Christianity. Traders came for products such as coconut oil. Sailors hunted whales. Settlers started plantations. They grew coconuts, coffee, pineapples, or sugar.

Island societies began to grow weak. Western ways often replaced island customs. Europe and the United States took over the islands.

The islands experienced turmoil in the 1900s. In World War II, both the Allies and the Japanese wanted to control the Pacific. They fought battles in Oceania. After the war, some islands were used as nuclear test sites. Over time, the people of many of islands began to want self-rule. Since 1962, 12 nations have gained independence. Foreign nations still rule many other islands.

1. What are the three regions of Oceania?

_____

_____

A Traditional Economy (page 714)

How is foreign investment helping the region?

Most of Oceania has an economy in which people do not work for wages. Instead, they work at **subsistence activities**. This means that a family produces only the food, clothing, and shelter they themselves need.

Many islands do not have fertile soil. But some high islands do have good soil. So agriculture is the region's main economic activity. The chief crops are bananas, sugar, cocoa, coffee, and copra. **Copra** is the dried meat of coconuts. Fishing is also a major source of food and income.

Since jet travel began, many tourists have come to Oceania. Tourists spend money in the islands. But they also need hotels, stores, roads, and vehicles. These threaten the islands' environment and ways of life.

A few islands besides Nauru have industries. For example, Papua New Guinea is developing a large copper mine. Large towns on other islands have factories that produce goods. Some of those goods are coconut oil and soap. More and more people in the Pacific Islands are moving to cities to find jobs.

2. What are the chief crops of the region?

_____

_____

Culture of the Islands (pages 714–715)

What arts and crafts are produced in the region?

Oceania has a great number of languages. Some 1,100 of the world's languages are spoken there. The people of Papua New Guinea alone speak some 823 languages. Many Pacific Islanders also speak European languages. English is the most common.

Christianity is the most widely spread religion. In addition, some Pacific Islanders still practice the traditional religions of their people.

Many Pacific Islanders produce arts and crafts. They weave baskets and mats from the leaves of palm trees or other plants. They carve masks and utensils from wood. Some islanders make their living selling such items to tourists.

3. How many languages are spoken in this region?

_____

_____

Island Life (page 715)

How is communication technology helping Oceania?

Ways of living vary greatly throughout the islands. In some places, people live as nomads. In many other places, islanders live in small villages. A village may have up to several hundred people. Generally, a chief leads each village. Usually, each extended family has a house or cluster of houses. The houses are wooden and have thatch roofs.

Village economies center on farming and fishing. Most villagers eat seafood, fresh fruit, and native plants. Many islanders grow **taro**, a plant with a starchy root. Taro can be eaten as a boiled vegetable. It is also made into breads, puddings, or a paste called poi.

Oceania has few cities. The cities that do exist have been growing. Rapid urban growth has created problems. These include sprawling *shantytowns,* a lack of sanitation, and a breakdown of family ties.

Modern communications systems are helping Oceania. They help central authorities to stay in touch with distant islands. They also link the Pacific Islands with the rest of the world.

4. What are traditional villages like?

_____

_____

Australia, New Zealand, and Antarctica

BEFORE YOU READ

In the last section, you read about the history and development of Oceania.

In this section, you will learn about the culture, economics, and life of Australia, New Zealand, and Antarctica.

AS YOU READ

Use this graphic organizer to take notes about what you discover in this section.

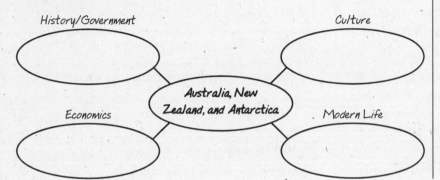

PLACES & TERMS

Aboriginal people native people of Australia

Maori early settlers of New Zealand

penal colony place to send prisoners

Treaty of Waitangi treaty between British and Maori that gave the British control of New Zealand

pakehas Maori term for white people

History: Distant European Outposts

(pages 718–719)

When was gold discovered in Australia?

The **Aboriginal people** moved to Australia from Asia about 40,000 years ago. When Europeans arrived in Australia, about 500 Aboriginal groups were there. The Aboriginal people had complex religious beliefs and social roles.

New Zealand was settled first by the **Maori**. The Maori sailed from Polynesia more than 1,000 years ago. They lived by fishing, hunting, and farming.

Captain James Cook of Britain was the first European to explore these two lands. He explored New Zealand in 1769. He explored Australia's east coast in 1770. Antarctica was discovered in 1820.

In 1788, Britain began to colonize Australia. They founded Sydney as a **penal colony**. That is a place to send prisoners. Hunters and whalers from Europe, America, and Australia came to New Zealand. No one settled Antarctica because of its cold climate.

In Australia, the colonists sometimes had violent

fights with the Aboriginal people. Many natives died. Also, natives died from European diseases.

In New Zealand, in 1840, the British and Maori signed the **Treaty of Waitangi**. It gave Britain control of New Zealand. The two groups disagreed about what the treaty really meant. Conflicts over who owned the land helped cause the Land Wars. They lasted from 1845 to 1847 and from 1860 to 1872. Many Maori died in the fighting.

Gold was found in Australia in 1951. It was found in New Zealand in 1861. Hundreds of thousands of people moved to the two countries. Few miners grew rich, but most stayed there.

1. How did the Maori live originally?

_____

_____

Migration and Conquest **269**

Modern Nations (page 720)

What *did a 1959 treaty determine for Antarctica?*

In 1901, the colonies in Australia joined into a single, independent nation. New Zealand became self-governing in 1907. Both Australia and New Zealand remained in the British Commonwealth.

In 1893, New Zealand became the first country to grant women the vote. It was one of the first countries to give old-age *pensions* to its citizens.

In both Australia and New Zealand, native people are usually less well off than other people. To improve their lives, the Aboriginal people and the Maori want their former lands to be given back.

Antarctica is not settled. In 1959, a treaty set aside the continent for research. Eighteen countries have set up science stations there. Seven countries claim land in Antarctica.

2. How did New Zealand pass laws to help its citizens?

Economy: Meat, Wool, and Butter
(pages 721–722)

What *are the main sources of income for Australia and New Zealand?*

Australia and New Zealand both export farm products. New Zealand sells butter, cheese, meat, and wool to other countries. New Zealand is also the world's largest producer of kiwi fruit.

Australia exports more wool than any other country in the world. Much of Australia is dry. Only about ten percent of the land is used to grow crops.

Australia earns much money from mining. It is the world's top source of bauxite, diamonds, lead, zinc, and opals. Many minerals are in the outback.

Neither Australia nor New Zealand relies heavily on industry. In fact, Australia imports more manufactured goods than it exports. One big industry in both countries is the processing of farm products.

3. What are New Zealand's major exports?

Distinctive Cultures (page 722)

How *has New Zealand blended two cultures?*

Most Australians are of British descent. But the population of the country is changing. Many people move there from Greece, Italy, and Southeast Asia.

Australians speak English, but they have colorful terms of their own. For example, they call ranches "stations." They call wild horses "brumbies."

The Aboriginal people have an ancient art form of painting on cave walls. Australian painters and writers have portrayed the landscape in their works.

The majority of New Zealanders are of European descent. They are called **pakehas**, a Maori term for white people. New Zealand's culture blends British and Maori ways. Maori art includes woodcarving and poetic legends. Western art and writing also thrive.

4. How is Australia's population changing?

Modern Life (page 723)

How *does the climate affect lifestyles?*

About 75 percent of Australians and 70 percent of New Zealanders own their own homes. About 85 percent of the people in both countries live in cities and towns. This is one of the world's highest rates of city dwellers. Australia's large cities have pollution and traffic jams. New Zealand's cities are quiet and uncrowded.

In both countries, many ranchers live far from cities. In New Zealand, good roads make travel easy. Many ranchers in Australia own small airplanes to cross the vast distances.

5. What percentage of people in these two countries live in cities?

Name _____   Date _____

Glossary/After You Read

nationalism loyalty or devotion to nation

pension sum of money paid to a person after retirement

prehistoric time before a written history was kept

shantytown a town or section of town consisting mostly of small, crudely built dwellings

thatch plant material used as a sheltering cover for a house

Places & Terms

A. Write the letter of the place or term next to the description that explains it best.

a. subsistence activities   d. penal colony

b. Micronesia   e. mandala

c. Indochina

_____   1. a French colony made up of Cambodia, Laos, and Vietnam

_____   2. a state organized as rings of power around a central court

_____   3. region of Oceania, name means "tiny islands"

_____   4. activities that produces only the food, clothing, and shelter that a single family needs

_____   5. place to send prisoners

B. Circle the place or term that best completes each sentence.

1. The people of Oceania produce a product called _____, which is dried coconut meat.

    copra   mandala   pakehas

2. The _____ gave the British control of New Zealand.

    Khmer Empire   Vietnam War   Treaty of Waitangi

3. One region of Oceania is called _____, which means "many islands."

    Micronesia   Polynesia   Melanesia

4. Many Pacific Islanders grow _____, a plant with a starchy root.

    mandala   copra   taro

5. The earliest settlers of New Zealand where the _____.

    Maori   Aboriginal people   Khmer Empire

Main Ideas

1. Buddhism, Hinduism, Islam, and Catholicism are all found in Southeast Asia. From whom did the region get each of these religions?

   _____

   _____

2. For what reason was the Vietnam War fought?

   _____

   _____

3. If Pacific Islanders do not work for wages, what do they work for?

   _____

   _____

4. Who were the first European settlers of Australia?

   _____

   _____

5. How have humans interacted with the environment in Antarctica?

   _____

   _____

Thinking Critically

Answer the following questions on a separate sheet of paper.

1. Why do you think that there are so many different languages in Oceania, when the people originally started from the same place?

2. How did diseases from Europeans cause many of the original inhabitants of Australia and New Zealand to die?

Aboriginal Land Claims

BEFORE YOU READ

In the last section, you read about the culture and development of Australia, New Zealand, and Antarctica.

In this section, you will learn about issues surrounding Aboriginal land claims.

AS YOU READ

Use this chart to help you take notes about this section.

	Causes	Effects
Issue 1: Aboriginal Land Claims		

PLACES & TERMS

assimilation when a minority group gives up its culture and adopts the majority group's culture

Stolen Generation mixed Aboriginal/ European children who were given to white families to be raised, to promote assimilation

Land Rights Act of 1976 law that gave Aboriginal people the right to claim land in the Northern Territory

***Mabo* Case** court case that acknowledged Aboriginal ownership of land

pastoral leases land rented by ranchers from the Australian government

***Wik* Case** court case that ruled that Aboriginal people could claim land held under a pastoral lease

Aboriginal People Lose Land

(pages 727–728)

What was the traditional relationship between Aboriginal people and the land?

The Aboriginal people had a complex relationship with the land. They didn't farm or herd animals. They lived by hunting and gathering. Because of this, they depended totally on nature. And they saw many places as *sacred.*

Aboriginal people did not use land in the way that Europeans did. They did not farm it, mine it, or build on it. So British colonists believed that the Aboriginal people had no ties to the land. British authorities declared Australia to be *Terra Nullius,* This is a term that means empty land. The British government believed it could take land without making treaties with Aboriginal leaders.

Europeans began to settle Australia in 1788. They chose the most fertile regions. Aboriginal people tried to fight this invasion of their land. They were defeated because Europeans had better weapons.

Some Aboriginal people had to go live on reserves. These were tracts of less fertile land set aside for them. Others lived on the edges of settlements. Some of those went to work on ranches.

Between 1909 and 1969, the Australian government took about 100,000 mixed-race children. The government gave these children to white families to raise. This was meant to promote assimilation. **Assimilation** is when a minority group gives up its culture and adopts the culture of the majority group.

Today, Aboriginal people call those children the **Stolen Generation**. They are angry over the loss. Many Aboriginal people want to pass their culture on to their children. One reason they hope to regain land is to save their way of life.

1. What was the Stolen Generation?

_____

_____

Land Claims (page 728–729)

What *was the outcome of the* Mabo *Case?*

The Aboriginal people were not full citizens of Australia until 1967. In that year, a vote allowed the government to pass special laws about Aboriginal rights.

The **Land Rights Act of 1976** gave Aboriginal people the right to claim land in the Northern Territory. As a result, Aboriginal people began to own the reserves where they were living. They also gained some empty land that the government had owned.

In 1992, the High Court of Australia handed down a decision that affected land claims. The case involved Eddie Mabo. The law said Mabo's family did not own their traditional lands in the Murray Islands. Mabo sued to claim those lands. Because the Mabos had worked the land for ages, the High Court *upheld* Eddie Mabo's claim. This court case was called the ***Mabo* Case**. In this case, the High Court admitted that Aboriginal people had owned land before the British arrived. So the *Mabo* Case undid the idea of *Terra Nullius,* by which Britain took the land.

In 1996, the High Court decided another major case. The Wik people, an Aboriginal group, claimed land that some ranchers and mining companies were using. The case involved two issues that are unique to Australia.

- The government still owns huge chunks of Australia. Ranchers take out **pastoral leases**. That is like renting the land from the government.
- In earlier cases, Aboriginal people could claim land only if they could prove they had used it for a long time.

Aboriginal people could not use land that held farms or ranches. So it was hard to prove they had a tie to such land. And before 1996, whites assumed that pastoral leases wiped out any native land claims. But in the **_Wik_ Case**, the court ruled differently. Aboriginal people could claim land held under a pastoral lease.

As a result, many white Australians feared having to pay Aboriginal people for the land they were using. They also feared losing some land entirely. So the national government changed the *Wik* decision. It limited the number of land claims. In response, some Aboriginal groups said they would sue. No one knows how the issue will be resolved.

2. What is a pastoral lease?

_____

_____

Industrialization Sparks Change

BEFORE YOU READ

In the last section, you read about issues surrounding Aboriginal land claims.

In this section, you will learn about the benefits and problems of growing industry in Southeast Asia.

AS YOU READ

Use this chart to help you take notes about this section.

	Causes	Effects
Issue 2: Industrialization		

PLACES & TERMS

industrialization the growth of industry

push-pull factors forces that cause people to move: push factors drive them away from one place while pull factors draw them toward another

Moving to Find Jobs (pages 730–731)

What *impact is rapid growth having on the cities?*

Many people are trying hard to escape poverty. For example, Deth Chrib of Cambodia works in a factory that makes clothing. She works 16 hours a day, 7 days a week. Even so, she says the job is easier than working on a farm. All over Southeast Asia, people are moving from farms to cities to find work.

Because of this, the growth of cities is a major result of the growth of industry. (The growth of industry is called __industrialization__.) People move to cities because of **push-pull factors**. Push factors are forces that push people out of their homelands. Pull factors pull them to a new place.

Many forces drive people off their land. Push factors in Southeast Asia include:

- **Lost Resources** Rural areas are losing resources. They are losing fertile soil, forests, and water. For example, Thailand has a water shortage in farming areas. This is because people pump too much from wells.

- **Scarcity of Land** In the Philippines, 3 percent of the landowners hold 25 percent of the land. Sixty percent of families in the country cannot earn a living. They don't have enough land to farm on.

- **Population Growth** As the number of people grows, land shortages become worse. Farmers who do own land often divide it among many *heirs*. As a result, the plots become too small to support a family.

Strong forces draw people to cities. In Southeast Asia, pull factors include:

- **Industry** The chance to find a factory job is the biggest pull factor. Many people move to the city temporarily. They earn money to send home to their family. In 1993, workers in the Philippines sent $2.2 billion home.

- **Other Benefits** People move to cities for other reasons besides jobs. Many want to receive education and government services.

The cities of Southeast Asia are having trouble dealing with rapid growth. The number of places to live has not grown as fast as the population. As a result, many people who arrive in cities live in slums.

The growth of cities creates more pollution. Traffic has increased because more workers drive to jobs. Also, more trucks transport goods. This traffic causes more air pollution. High levels of *particulates* are the most serious concern. In Bangkok, Thailand, about 5,000 people a year die from breathing bad air.

Another problem is getting rid of human waste. Most cities in Southeast Asia do not have enough plants to treat all their sewage. Untreated sewage pollutes water supplies.

1. What "push factors" are driving people away from rural areas?

_____

_____

Other Results of Industrialization
(pages 731–732)

What have been the economic effects of industrialization?

The growth of industry in Southeast Asia has done more than make cities grow. It has also changed the economy and the environment.

Several Southeast Asian countries have had rapid industrial growth since the 1960s. One result of this has been an increase in trade and exports.

The region has seen higher incomes for some citizens. In many countries, the middle class is growing larger. But the income gap between rich and poor is still wide.

Industry can also hurt the environment. Factories can cause air pollution by burning fossil fuels. They can pollute the water and soil by dumping toxic waste.

The nature of industry in Southeast Asia makes it hard to control such pollution. A single city may contain thousands of factories and shops. Many of these are very small. But together, they create a great deal of waste. For example, 30,000 factories in Jakarta, Indonesia, release pollution into the waterways.

Industry has also used up resources such as water and trees. For instance, textile companies in Bandung, Indonesia, have built illegal wells that use up water supplies. As a result, some neighborhoods in that city have no water. In the future, Southeast Asia must reduce the negative effects of industrial growth.

2. How can small factories cause harm to the environment?

_____

_____

Chapter ◆32◆ **Case Study (pages 734–737)**   *Reading Study Guide*

Global Environmental Change

BEFORE YOU READ

In the last section, you read about the benefits and problems of industrialization in Southeast Asia.

In this case study, you will look at how global warming might affect Southeast Asia, Oceania, and Antarctica.

AS YOU READ

Use this chart to help you take notes about this case study.

	Causes	Effects
Case Study: Environmental Change		

PLACES & TERMS

fossil fuel fuels extracted from the earth, including coal, oil, and natural gas

CO₂ chemical symbol for carbon dioxide

ultraviolet rays the so-called "tanning" or "burning" rays of the sun; radiation outside the spectrum of visible light

Damage to the Environment
(page 734)

***What** is meant by "hole in the ozone"?*

Humans are changing the environment in ways that may harm the world. The burning of <u>fossil fuels</u> lets carbon dioxide (<u>CO$_2$</u>) gas into the atmosphere. Carbon dioxide is one of the greenhouse gases. Greenhouse gases stop all the sun's energy from escaping into space. Without them, the earth would be cold and lifeless.

Some scientists fear that the atmosphere now has too many greenhouse gases. Emissions of CO$_2$ have grown 50 percent since the 1970s. Scientists believe that the increase in CO$_2$ levels causes the atmosphere to trap too much heat. Temperatures have been slowly rising.

Many people do not believe the theory of global warming. Some say that natural processes may cause the temperature rise. Others say that the temperatures have not risen. Those people believe temperatures fall within a normal range.

Another change is damage to the ozone layer. This layer exists high in the atmosphere. It absorbs most of the sun's harmful <u>ultraviolet rays</u>. In the 1970s, scientists learned that the ozone layer over Antarctica was growing thinner. This thinning is often called a hole in the ozone. Chemicals such as the chlorine found in CFCs react with the ozone layer and destroy it. (CFCs are used in aerosol cans.) Many governments have limited the use of such chemicals. Others have delayed passing such laws because they are costly to industry.

1. What are "greenhouse gases"?

_____

_____

Looking Toward the Future
(pages 734–735)

***How** might environmental changes affect weather?*

Scientists fear that many problems may result from these changes. Many people and nations around the world are trying to stop the damage.

One fear about global warming is that even small temperature increases could melt the world's ice caps. This would cause sea levels to rise. Rising water could flood coastal cities and islands. The low islands of Oceania might disappear.

Some people predict that global warming might change weather patterns. This could make droughts and violent storms more common. The location of climate zones and agricultural regions might shift. Such change could upset the world's economy.

People worry about the ozone hole because more ultraviolet rays will reach the earth. Ultraviolet rays are linked to such problems as skin cancer, eye damage, and crop damage. Because it lies close to Antarctica, New Zealand may be at higher risk than other regions.

In 1992, the UN held the Earth Summit. This was a conference to discuss ways to pursue economic growth and protect the environment. Representatives of 178 nations attended.

In 1997, the UN held a convention in Kyoto, Japan, to discuss climate change. The conference wrote the Kyoto Protocol. This set up guidelines for countries to reduce greenhouse gas emissions. In time, 165 nations signed the treaty. The United States signed the treaty, but the Senate did not ratify it. The Senate feared that the guidelines might harm U.S. businesses.

2. Why might New Zealand be at risk?

_____

_____

Opinions Differ (page 736)

What *opinions exist about global warming?*

Educational Pamphlet: A United Nations pamphlet reports that results of tests are uncertain. But it is believed that humans are changing the global climate. The biggest change is in the earth's atmosphere. Human activity appears to be increasing greenhouse gases. This might result in "global warming."

Political Commentary: The American Policy Center states that there is no global warming. No scientists in the world will say that they are certain global warming exists. U.S. Government satellite and balloon measurements show that the temperature is cooling in some places.

3. Which document has the strongest arguments?

_____

_____

Data Fuels the Debate (page 737)

What *do satellites reveal?*

Data: A graph from the National Climatic Data Center shows changes from the average yearly temperature for a period of 120 years. Temperatures above the average occur most often in the late 1900s. This pattern may show global warming.

Satellite Images: These images are of the ozone over Antarctica. They were collected over an 18-year period. They show that the area with low amounts of ozone appears to be growing.

News Article: An article in the *New York Times* says that the "ozone hole" opens over Antarctica each spring. Satellite images show that it formed earlier than usual. It was also bigger than before.

The finding renewed debates over the hole. Some say that global warming could be helping to destroy ozone. Many still say the growth of the hole could be the result of natural changes in climate.

4. How do some people think global warming and the ozone hole are related?

_____

_____

Name _____   Date _____

Glossary/After You Read

heir one who inherits or is entitled to inherit property

particulates minute particles; in the case of pollution, particles of toxic elements suspended in the air

sacred holy; worthy of religious worship

upheld given support; supported against an opponent

Places & Terms

A. If the statement is true, write "true" on the line. If it is false, write the word or words that would replace the underlined words to make it true.

_____ 1. <u>Industrialization</u> is when a minority group gives up its culture and adopts the majority group's culture.

_____ 2. When land is rented by ranchers from the Australian government, it is called a <u>pastoral lease</u>.

_____ 3. The <u>Land Rights Act of 1976</u> refers to the raising of mixed Aboriginal-European children by white families.

_____ 4. The <u>*Wik* Case</u> was a court case that ruled that Aboriginal people could claim land held under a pastoral lease.

_____ 5. <u>Urbanization</u> is the growth of industry.

B. Write the letter of the place or term next to the description that explains it best.

a. *Mabo* Case   d. push-pull factors

b. Stolen Generation   e. pastoral leases

c. Land Rights Act of 1976

_____ 1. things that drive people away from one place and draw them toward another

_____ 2. court case that acknowledged Aboriginal ownership of land

_____ 3. about 100,000 mixed-race children given to white families to promote assimilation

_____ 4. law that gave Aboriginal people the right to claim land in the Northern Territory

_____ 5. agreements that allow ranchers to use land owned by the Australian government

Main Ideas

1. What was the outcome of the Land Rights Act of 1976?

_____

_____

_____

2. What are some "pull factors" that draw people to cities in Southeast Asia?

_____

_____

_____

3. What are two industrial activities that have caused problems in Indonesia?

_____

_____

_____

4. What negative effects has the rapid growth of cities had in Southeast Asia?

_____

_____

_____

Thinking Critically

Answer the following questions on a separate sheet of paper.

1. What effect did declaring Australia to be *Terra Nullius* have on land ownership there?

2. Why do you think that people in Southeast Asia seem willing at present to put up with difficult work conditions and bad pollution?